Twentieth-Century Engli

Standard English has over the past hundred years. From pronunciation to vocabulary to grammar, this concise survey clearly documents the recent history of standard English. Drawing on large amounts of authentic corpus data, it shows how we can track ongoing changes to the language, and demonstrates each of the major developments that have taken place. As well as taking insights from a vast body of literature, Christian Mair presents the results of his own cutting-edge research, revealing some important changes which have not been previously documented. He concludes by exploring how social and cultural factors, such as the American influence on British English, have affected standard English in recent times. Authoritative, informative, and engaging, this book will be essential reading for anyone interested in language change in progress - particularly those working on English, and will be welcomed by students, researchers, and language teachers alike.

CHRISTIAN MAIR is Chair in English Linguistics at the Universität Freiburg, Germany, with research interests in the corpus-based description of modern English grammar, and in the study of regional variation and ongoing changes in standard English worldwide. He is author of *Infinitival clauses in English: a study of syntax in discourse* (Cambridge University Press, 1990).

Twentieth-Century English

STUDIES IN ENGLISH LANGUAGE

The aim of this series is to provide a framework for original studies of English, both present-day and past. All books are based securely on empirical research, and represent theoretical and descriptive contributions to our knowledge of national varieties of English, both written and spoken. The series covers a broad range of topics and approaches, including syntax, phonology, grammar, vocabulary, discourse, pragmatics, and sociolinguistics, and is aimed at an international readership.

Already published in this series

Christian Mair *Infinitival complement clauses in English: a study of syntax in discourse*
Charles F. Meyer *Apposition on contemporary English*
Jan Firbas *Functional sentence perspective in written and spoken communication*
Izchak M. Schlesinger *Cognitive space and linguistic case*
Katie Wales *Personal pronouns in present-day English*
Laura Wright *The development of standard English, 1300–1800: theories, descriptions, conflicts*
Charles F. Meyer *English Corpus Linguistics: theory and practice*
Stephen J. Nagle and Sara L. Sanders (eds.) *English in the Southern United States*
Anne Curzan *Gender shifts in the history of English*
Kingsley Bolton *Chinese Englishes*
Irma Taavitsainen and Päivi Pahta (eds.) *Medical and scientific writing in Late Medieval English*
Elizabeth Gordon, Lyle Campbell, Jennifer Hay, Margaret Maclagan, Andrea Sudbury and Peter Trudgill *New Zealand English: its origins and evolution*
Raymond Hickey (ed.) *Legacies of colonial English*
Merja Kytö, Mats Rydén and Erik Smitterberg (eds.) *Nineteenth century English: stability and change*
John Algeo *British or American English? A handbook of word and grammar patterns*

Twentieth-Century English

History, Variation, and Standardization

CHRISTIAN MAIR

CAMBRIDGE
UNIVERSITY PRESS

CAMBRIDGE UNIVERSITY PRESS
Cambridge, New York, Melbourne, Madrid, Cape Town, Singapore, São Paulo, Delhi

Cambridge University Press
The Edinburgh Building, Cambridge CB2 8RU, UK

Published in the United States of America by Cambridge University Press, New York

www.cambridge.org
Information on this title: www.cambridge.org/9780521115834

First published 2006
Third printing 2008
This digitally printed version 2009

A catalogue record for this publication is available from the British Library

ISBN 978-0-521-83219-9 hardback
ISBN 978-0-521-11583-4 paperback

The following authors and publishers have given permission to use extended
quotations from their work:

© Tom Leonard, from *Intimate voices: poems 1965-1983*, Etruscan Books Devon
2003 (for "i've not got a light")
© India Knight/*The Sunday Times*, 11 November 2001 (for the extract from India
Knight, "Speak proper? Not likely")
© Little, Brown Book Group (for the passage reproduced from Sarah Waters, *The
night watch*, London: Virago Press, 2006)
© OUP (for Appendix 4, "Motswana–mussy")

Every effort has been made to secure necessary permissions to reproduce copyright
material in this work, though in some cases it has proved impossible to trace or
contact copyright holders. If any omissions are brought to our notice, we will be
happy to include appropriate acknowledgments on reprinting or in any subsequent
edition.

Contents

Figures

Tables

Acknowledgments

When I started working on the corpus-based investigation of change in progress in present-day English in the early 1990s, writing a book on this topic soon began to seem an attractive idea, though one which was bound to remain rather theoretical for a long time. Now that the book is about to be published, I would like to take the opportunity to thank a number of organizations and people without whose help it is unlikely that *Twentieth-Century English* would have seen the light of day a mere fifteen years after the idea for the book was first conceived.

To the *Deutsche Forschungsgemeinschaft* (DFG) I owe thanks for generously supporting two corpus-related research projects from 1994 to 1996 and from 2003 to 2006. Without their funding, F-LOB and Frown, two corpora providing important evidence for the present study, would have been completed much later (if at all), and various laborious but extremely useful annotation schemes and other enhancements would not even have been attempted. If the DFG gave the money, more members of my team at Freiburg than can be named here have given their expertise and dedication over the years. If I single out Marianne Hundt, Andrea Sand, Stefanie Rapp, Birgit Waibel, and Lars Hinrichs by name, I hope that many others involved in the projects for longer or shorter periods of time will not take this amiss.

At CUP, I would like to thank Kate Brett, who, after discussing the idea of a history of twentieth-century English with me at the Edinburgh Late Modern English conference in 1998, encouraged me to formalize it by submitting a proposal to the Press. Helen Barton, who eventually took over from Kate, was equally sympathetic and additionally showed welcome patience in the final stages of completing the manuscript. Valuable suggestions for improvements were made by Merja Kytö, one of the series editors, who carefully went through the first version of the completed manuscript. At the very end of the production process, working together with Nikky Twyman as a copy editor was a pleasant and humbling experience, pleasant because of her quiet and good-humored efficiency, and humbling because of the number of oversights she spotted in a manuscript which I thought I had proofread carefully.

I hope that the book will convey to its readers some of my own fascination with the "living history" of English, its recent past, its rich and diversified present, and its future, and that it will encourage others to keep researching the many questions which I have had to leave unanswered.

Freiburg, February 2006   CM

1   Setting the scene

... ask yourself whether our language is complete; – whether it was so before the symbolism of chemistry and the notation of the infinitesimal calculus were incorporated in it; for these are, so to speak, suburbs of our language. (And how many houses or streets does it take before a town begins to be a town?) Our language can be seen as an ancient city: a maze of little streets and squares, of old and new houses, and of houses with additions from various periods; and this surrounded by a multitude of new boroughs with straight regular streets and uniform houses.

(Ludwig Wittgenstein, *Philosophische Untersuchungen/Philosophical investigations*, translated by G. E. M. Anscombe. Oxford: Blackwell, 1967: 18)

Anyone proposing to write a history of the English language in the twentieth century begs a number of questions, which it is necessary to answer at the very outset of what might seem an excessively ambitious project.

Isn't the topic too vast and complex for a single author to tackle? If one bears in mind that in contrast to historians of Old and Middle English, who in general suffer from a poverty of evidence, the historian of recent and contemporary English is deluged with data and, in principle, needs to write separate histories of several richly documented standard and nonstandard varieties, and a history of contact and influence among them, the answer to this question is an obvious "yes." The only justification that the present writer is able to offer for undertaking the project against the odds is that he has narrowed the focus from the very start to one highly codified variety, namely the written standard which – in the twentieth century – was in use throughout the English-speaking world with minor local differences in spelling, lexicon, idiom, and grammar. The spoken usage of educated speakers in formal situations, which can be considered the oral correlate of this written standard, will be considered where relevant. While this restriction is problematical for many reasons, it is justifiable because of the social prominence of the standard in the present, and also because most histories of English covering developments from the late Middle English period onwards have – explicitly or implicitly – been histories of the standard, too.

What about the observer's paradox? In a history of contemporary English, this paradox takes two forms. First, it might be impossible for us to identify and document recent and ongoing linguistic changes against the background noise of synchronic regional, social, or stylistic variation that surrounds us and in which these diachronic developments are embedded. Second, assuming that we can identify ongoing language change, we will still have to ask the question whether we can free ourselves from the social prejudices which have normally caused ongoing changes to be viewed negatively – as instances of erroneous or illogical usage or even as signs of decay or degeneration. As for the first manifestation of the paradox (our ability or inability to even perceive ongoing change), there is a long tradition of skepticism – exemplified, for example, in a much-quoted statement in Bloomfield's *Language*.[1] The optimistic tradition, by contrast, is a much younger one, going back to William Labov's 1960s work on extrapolating diachronic trends from synchronic variation, and is still largely confined to sociolinguistic circles. As a descriptive contribution to the history of English from around 1900 to the present, the current study will not be able to settle the dispute between the optimists and the pessimists in a principled way; rather, it has opted for a practical compromise by not concentrating on all aspects of linguistic change to the same degree. Little emphasis will be placed on the often futile search for the first authentic and/or unambiguous recorded instance of an innovation, or on speculations about possible reanalyses, rule reorderings, or other adjustments in speaker competence or the abstract system underlying the recorded data. Rather, the focus will be on the spread of innovations through varieties, textual genres, and styles, or on provable shifts in frequency of use in a defined period. In other words, the present study aims to exploit the full potential of the corpus-linguistic working environment that has become available to the student of English in recent decades – an environment which, in addition to corpora in the narrow sense (that is, machine-readable collections of authentic texts or natural discourse which have been compiled expressly for the use of linguists), now includes important electronic dictionaries such as the continuously updated online version of the *Oxford English dictionary* (OED) and a vast mass of digitized textual material not originally compiled for the purposes of linguistic study.[2]

---

[1] "The process of linguistic change has never been directly observed; we shall see that such observation, with our present facilities, is inconceivable" (Bloomfield 1933: 347). In Chapter 2 we shall see that Bloomfield's position – categorically negative in this passage – is modified elsewhere in his work and, more importantly, that there has been considerable improvement in "our present facilities."

[2] The corpora consulted for the present study and the methods used for their analysis will be discussed in the appropriate places, with a summary of the relevant information in the Appendix. Readers interested in a more general introduction to the thriving field of English corpus-linguistics are referred to introductory handbooks such as Biber et al. (1998) or Meyer (2002).

As hinted at above, the second manifestation of the observer's paradox in the study of ongoing linguistic change is the possible distorting influence of the prescriptive tradition. This is a serious problem which needs to be acknowledged. Of course, it is unlikely that professional linguists will repeat the often exaggerated and irrational value judgments on linguistic usage propagated by this tradition. The effect the prescriptive tradition exerts on research on current change is more subtle and indirect; it introduces a hidden bias into the study of ongoing change by setting the agenda of topics worth the researcher's attention. In this way, relatively minor points of usage and variation receive an amount of attention completely out of proportion to their actual significance (even if the linguist's intention may merely be to refute prescriptive prejudice), while much more important and comprehensive changes go unnoticed. To give a few examples, the literature on grammatical change in present-day English is rife with comment on the allegedly imminent disappearance of *whom* (a development for which there is very little documentary evidence – see Chapter 4) or the use of *hopefully* as a sentence adverb (which at least is a genuine twentieth-century innovation on the basis of the OED evidence, with a first attestation for the year 1932). This is so because these two points of usage have a high profile as linguistic markers in the community and are much discussed by prescriptivists. Measured against the sum total of ongoing changes in present-day English, however, both are mere trivia. Comprehensive and far-reaching developments, on the other hand, which affect the very grammatical core of Modern English, such as the spread of gerunds into functions previously reserved for infinitives, tend to go unnoticed because these changes proceed below the level of conscious speaker awareness and hence do not arouse prescriptive concerns. Again, the remedy here is the use of corpora. Corpora make it possible to describe the spread of individual innovations against the background of the always far greater and more comprehensive continuity in usage, and corpus-based studies of linguistic change in progress are therefore likely to correct more alarmist perceptions based on the unsystematic collection of examples or impressionistic observation, which are inevitably biased towards the strange, bizarre, and unusual.

Is there sufficient previous work on the recent history of English to write a survey such as the present one?

A mere twenty years ago, the answer to this question would have been in the negative. Throughout the twentieth century there was never a dearth of "state of the language" books aimed at the general educated public. Brander Matthews, the American man of letters, published his *Essays on English* in 1921. J. Hubert Jagger's *English in the future*, which – in contrast to what the title suggests – is mostly about English in the present, appeared in 1940. More recently, two collections of essays on the *State of the language* were edited by Leonard Michaels and Christopher Ricks (Michaels and Ricks 1980, Ricks 1991). Most such works cover ongoing changes (whether perceived or real), but they tend to do so only very superficially. A more reliable source of in-depth information on current change would thus seem to be the major scholarly histories of the language. However, until recently these tended to peter out at some point around 1800, leaving the history of English in the nineteenth and twentieth centuries as largely uncharted territory.[3]

Over the last twenty years, however, the situation has definitely improved. There has been a surge of interest in research on the recent history of English, which has also resulted in several landmark publications offering at least partial surveys. The recent history of English, with a strong (and, in the first two cases, exclusive) emphasis on the nineteenth century, is dealt with in two book-length studies (Bailey 1996, Görlach 1999), and volume IV ("1776–1997") of the *Cambridge history of the English language*. In a broad sense, the present book is a chronological continuation of Bailey's and Görlach's monographs – albeit with slightly different priorities. In comparison to Bailey (1996), it will aim for a fuller coverage of the structural history of the language (particularly the grammar), whereas in comparison to Görlach the two major differences are that the treatment is not restricted to England exclusively and that, in compensation for the widening of the geographical scope, less emphasis will be placed on the didactic presentation and annotation of source texts. The most important point of reference for most chapters, though, will be volume IV ("1776–1997") of the *Cambridge history*. As will become clear, this work's treatment of nineteenth-century developments is admirable and provides a good foundation for the present study. Its coverage of the twentieth century, on the other hand, is less complete and will be expanded here.

More problematical sources than these scholarly linguistic works are the many popular works on the recent history of English and the state of the language. For one thing, the number of such publications is vast – from books written by non-linguists for lay audiences (e.g., Michaels and Ricks 1980, Ricks 1991, or Howard 1984) to works such as Barber (1964) or Potter (1969 [1975]), which are valuable as provisional surveys of the field by experts. Many of these "state of the language" books are informed by a spirit of traditional prescriptivism and/or cultural pessimism or more concerned with the ideological and political aspects of language standardization than the linguistic facts themselves. But even a work such as Barber's (1964) excellent survey of "linguistic change in present-day English" needs to be treated with some caution. The insights and claims it contains are generally based on the author's anecdotal observations and unsystematic collection of examples, which – as will be shown in Chapter 2 – is a notoriously unreliable methodology in the documentation of ongoing changes.

---

[3] This is partly a matter of author interest, which gave priority to earlier developments, and partly a result of publication date, as classic works such as Jespersen (1909–1949) have not really been challenged or even equaled in comprehensiveness of coverage and authoritativeness until recently.

Among all the relevant publications, the one closest in spirit to the present book probably is Bauer (1994), as this work emphasizes the use of corpora and empirical documentation in the study of ongoing change. It is not to deny the merit of Bauer's pioneering effort to point out that it is comprehensive neither in its coverage of the phenomena nor in its use of the available corpora and textual resources, thus leaving many important topics for the present study and others to explore.

Methodologically sound work on individual instances of change in progress is, of course, abundant in the sociolinguistic literature. Again, however, the overlap with the present study is minimal, as it will focus on the one variety of English which has been largely neglected in sociolinguistics, namely standard English, in its spoken and written forms. Furthermore, the study of phonetic change, which is usually the most prominent topic in sociolinguistic analyses of change in progress, is not the priority in the present book, whereas lexical and grammatical change, which are studied in detail here, play a lesser role in the sociolinguistic literature.

In sum, there is, thus, clearly room for a project such as the present one: a concise and comprehensive history of standard English in the twentieth century, written by one author in a single volume.

As we shall see, standard varieties of languages differ from others in that they combine spontaneous historical evolution with elements of conscious planning. As Milroy and Milroy (1991) have shown, standardization, the suppression of optional variability in language, is as much of an ideological as a linguistic phenomenon. This means that a history of standard English is, ultimately, part of the cultural and intellectual history of the English-speaking peoples. It is, of course, extremely risky to make generalizations about cultural and social developments over a whole century and a huge community of speakers, but there are some trends which are immediately relevant to the history of standard English. For the post-World War II United States, Baron has identified the following trends:

- reduced emphasis on social stratification and on overt attention to upward mobility
- notable disconnects between educational accomplishment and financial success
- strong emphasis on youth culture (Baron 2003: 90).

Similar trends have been in operation in most English-speaking societies in the industrialized world, and it is easy to see how all of them have worked against narrow and elitist definitions of the standard. Some of the ways in which these trends have affected the shape of standard English today will be studied in greater depth in Chapter 6.

In the introduction, it will be sufficient to sketch briefly the social and cultural context of standard English in 1900 (the point at which the present history opens) and compare it to the situation in 2000.

In many fundamental regards, there was no change at all. Standard English, in 1900 as well as in 2000, was a fully mature written standard, displaying all the pertinent metalinguistic infrastructure of dictionaries, usage books, grammars, and other linguistic reference materials. Pedagogical materials were available for those wishing to learn English as a foreign language at both points in time, and 1900 as well as 2000 saw a flourishing tradition of social commentary and debate on linguistic issues. It is, indeed, even surprising to see that – with the exception of language regulation in the spirit of "political correctness," of which there was very little in 1900 – even many of the topics and issues have remained the same. The use of *ain't* or double negatives was proscribed in formal writing and educated speech then as now; the word *booze* was a mildly offensive slang term hovering on the edge of respectability in 1900 and in 2000; and then as now the educated guardians of the language tended to argue about where to put the stress in polysyllabic words of Latin and French origin such as *controversy* or *comparable*.

There is continuity also in the geography of English. The hold of English on West Africa and the Asian subcontinent may have been more tenuous, restricted to small elites, in 1900 than it is now, despite the fact that these territories were under direct British rule in the days of the Empire. Purely in terms of geographical spread, however, English was a global language in 1900 as much as in 2000, with the language being the dominant one in the British Isles, North America, Australia, and New Zealand, and having established itself firmly in smaller communities throughout the rest of the globe.

However, important changes loom beneath this veneer of stability. The technologization of the spoken word was still in its beginnings in the nineteenth century. Radio, talking pictures, and television all profoundly changed the everyday life of the ordinary citizen in the twentieth century and had a profound impact on the norms of spoken usage. Sometimes, technology serves to support pre-existing trends towards an establishment and spread of a spoken standard – as was the case with the BBC championing "Received Pronunciation" in Britain and internationally in the 1920s and 1930s. More informal but no less successful standardization efforts were made by the national broadcasting networks in the United States (Bonfiglio 2002). At other times, technology subverted the authority of such standard norms by ensuring worldwide exposure to nonstandard speech – from the Beatles-inspired boom of northern English working-class accents in the 1960s to the global spread of stylized African-American vernacular English through rap and hip-hop music. The most recent technology-driven transformation of English has, of course, taken place in the course of the digital revolution and the rise of computer-mediated communication, which has infused into written English some of the spontaneity, informality, and immediacy of speech (Crystal 2001).

Progress was made in the course of the twentieth century also in the recognition of the pluricentricity of English. In 1900, London, or the English upper and upper middle classes, had already ceased to be the exclusive source of linguistic prestige in the English-speaking world, even though this fact tended to be acknowledged in the United States rather than Britain at the time. By the end of World War I, there was widespread consensus that standard English came in two distinct but equal varieties – British (or English) and North American. Decolonisation started slowly with the establishment of internal self-government in the European-dominated "settler" colonies at various points of time in the early twentieth century and speeded up dramatically after World War II. In 1910, the British Empire was at the peak of its power, with direct control over a quarter of the earth's land surface and more than a quarter of its population. In 2000, three years after the return of Hong Kong, the last economically and demographically significant colony, to China, what was left of the Empire comprised around twenty minute and often isolated territories mostly in the Caribbean and the Atlantic and Indian Oceans, namely – in alphabetical order – Anguilla, Ascension Island, Bermuda, the British Antarctic Territory, the British Indian Ocean Territory, the British Virgin Islands, the Caymans, the Falklands, Gibraltar, Montserrat, Pitcairn (with Ducie, Henderson and Oeno), South Georgia and the South Solomon Islands, the Turks and Caicos, Tristan da Cunha, and St. Helena.

Not surprisingly, such far-reaching political developments were bound to have linguistic consequences. With a time-lag of about a century after political self-government, a degree of autonomy similar to that accorded to American and British English has now been attained by the Southern Hemisphere settler Englishes which have developed in Australia, New Zealand, and among the English-speaking community in South Africa. Australian English has even become an internationally relevant norm in language teaching especially in the South Pacific. This path of development from colonial dependence to growing autonomy is likely to be followed eventually by the Creole-influenced Englishes of the Caribbean, a region where norms of educated usage are now emerging in a three-way competition among a still powerful traditional British model, the currently dominant American norm, and local usage.

In principle, there is no reason why official or second-language varieties with a long history of institutionalization such as those found in West Africa or India should not be placed alongside these natively spoken varieties as legitimate new standards of English. In practice, the full recognition of these varieties is hindered by a feeling of linguistic insecurity among their own speakers and negative attitudes held by native-speaking outsiders. Speakers of these post-colonial non-native Englishes are often caught in a double bind. A too-perfect approximation to the former colonial norm is socially undesirable, especially in pronunciation, but many of the stable phonetic and grammatical features that have emerged still tend to be seen as interference-caused errors rather than potential harbingers of a new and legitimate local norm of English usage. In such a situation, rather than try and determine how many standard varieties of English there are – a pointless exercise unless one is willing to take on the Herculean task of investigating speakers' evaluation of their own

Table 1.1. *Population of major urban centers in the English-using world*

City	Population 1900 (in millions)	Population 2000 (in millions)
London	4.5	7.1
New York	3.4	8.0
Chicago	1.7	2.9
Los Angeles	0.1	3.7
Dublin	0.3	1.0
Sydney [metropolitan area]	0.5	3.9
Toronto [metropolitan area]	0.2	4.9
Kingston, Jamaica [metropolitan area]	0.1	0.7
Johannesburg [metropolitan area]	0.1	5.5
Singapore [state]	0.2	3.5
Bombay	0.9	12.5

practice and untangling the web of mixed loyalties to old metropolitan and new local norms in each community – it is instructive to trace shifts in the linguistic centers of gravity of the English-speaking world, such as are reflected, for example, in the population statistics in Table 1.1.[4]

Obviously, these figures are mere approximations, often hiding administrative boundary changes or, a typical phenomenon of twentieth-century US life, the flight to the suburbs. Thus, the population of the New York–New Jersey–Long Island CMSA ("census metropolitan statistical area") is considerably greater than the "mere" 8 million given in the table, namely 21.2 million. An even more drastic example is provided by Los Angeles, where the population for the LA–Riverside–Orange County CMSA is 16.4 million. Another thing worth remembering is that modern megacities are among the most multilingual communities in the world today, and that the figures for, say, New York or Los Angeles include large numbers of bilinguals or even people incapable of speaking English fluently.[5]

However, such possible distortions notwithstanding, the general trend is clear: London, New York City, and Chicago maintained their dominant roles throughout the period under review here, whereas the figures for Sydney, Toronto, and Los Angeles show formerly marginal regions developing into

---

[4] The figures in this table have been compiled from various sources, in particular the US Census website (http://www.census.gov), the Demographia database (http://www.demographia.com), the *Encyclopedia britannica*, and the *Cambridge international encyclopedia*.

[5] For New York, the 2000 Census gives a figure of 405,522 school-aged (5–17) children who spoke Spanish at home, which is almost 30 percent of the total school-age population in the city. In fact, at 52 percent, the monolingual-English school-age population is just barely more than half of the total.

Languages of academic publication 1879–1980

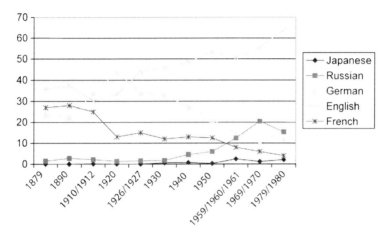

Figure 1.1 Languages of publication in five natural sciences (1879–1980) (Tsunoda 1983)

new demographic centers, both within their countries and regions (Australia, Canada, the western United States) and internationally. The figures for Kingston, Johannesburg, Singapore, and Bombay – all English-using, while definitely not monolingual English-speaking – would probably have been more difficult to predict by merely extrapolating 1900 trends, as would have been the fact that Creolized English emanating from Jamaica now has a speaker base in the Caribbean diaspora in Canada, Great Britain, and the US and, through reggae music and its derivatives, has become a formative influence on the language of global youth culture. What these figures also show is that English in 2000 is less "European" or "Eurocentric" and less "white" than it was in 1900.

A final noteworthy difference between the status of English in 1900 and 2000 is that, while English definitely was among the world's major languages in 1900, it was not the unrivaled world language that it is today. In international diplomacy it was second to French, and did not gain the lead until after World War I and the Treaty of Versailles, which was drafted in English and translated into French. As a language of publication in the natural sciences, it shared a prominent role with French and German in 1900, as is shown in Figure 1.1, whose figures were obtained from a representative sample of publications in five disciplines: biology, chemistry, physics, medicine, mathematics. It is interesting to note that English asserted its overwhelming role only in the third quarter of the century, at a time when – ironically – the political might of the British Empire was crumbling away and American power was at a temporary low ebb during the Cold War.

Table 1.2. *Percentage of languages in natural science publications, 1980 to 1996*

	1980	1984	1988	1992	1996
English	74.6	77.1	80.5	87.2	90.7
Russian	10.8	9.2	6.9	3.9	2.1
Japanese	2.3	2.5	2.1	2.3	1.7
French	3.1	2.4	2.4	1.6	1.3
German	3.5	3.3	2.9	1.6	1.2

Table 1.3. *Percentage of languages used in publications in the humanities, 1974 to 1995 (adapted from a graph in Ammon 1998a: 167)*

	1974	1978	1982	1986	1990	1995
English	66.6	69.1	69.9	70.6	71.7	82.5
French	6.8	6.6	5.9	5.9	5.9	5.9
German	8.0	5.2	6.0	5.4	5.7	4.1
Spanish	3.8	3.6	3.6	4.0	3.8	2.2

Building on Tsunoda's work, Ulrich Ammon (1998a: 152, 167) has followed developments to almost the end of the century (the year 1996, to be precise), when the proportion of English-language publications reached 90.7 percent and the four remaining languages were represented at levels between 2.1 percent (Russian) and 1.2 percent (German) – proportions which make a visual representation of the kind adopted in Figure 1.1 pointless. The figures for the sciences and humanities are given in Tables 1.2 and 1.3 respectively (compiled from a graph in Ammon [1998a: 152] by Mühleisen [2003: 113]).

At present, the position of English as the globally dominant language seems entrenched very firmly. It has a numerically strong and regionally diverse native-speaker base. It is an important second language in many former British colonies and American dependencies, and as an international lingua franca it is indispensable in prestigious domains such as business, trade, and technology, but in addition has a strong informal base in the global entertainment market and is associated with many civic and lifestyle issues – from "gender main-streaming," the "sexual revolution," "gay rights," and "political correctness," all the way to "jogging," "[Nordic] walking," "all-inclusive package tours," and "wellness resorts" (these words being used as borrowings from English in many languages[6]).

---

[6] Compare, for example, the comparative documentation of English lexical influence in sixteen European languages provided in Görlach (2001).

English is now the language which is routinely used to articulate human experience far beyond the boundaries of its native-speaking communities. Standard English comes with a rich historical heritage, and in its present use it represents a staggering variety of communicative concerns: from the politics of present-day Northern Ireland (as manifested, for example, in the recent vogue of the word "de-commissioning") to the politics of post-apartheid South Africa (as manifested in the neologism "de-racialization"), or from women's issues in Britain and the US (where "Miss" as a term of address is proscribed outside the classroom) to the Caribbean (where the word tends to be used as an honorific). Diversity of experience expressed in a language is not an index relevant to a technical linguistic description. On the other hand, for the present writer, who is not a native speaker, it is not the least among his motifs for undertaking the present work.

2 Ongoing language change: problems of detection and verification

2.1 "Visible" and "invisible" changes

The term "linguistic change" is ambiguous because it may refer to two fundamentally different aspects of the historical evolution of language. Our aim could be to describe changes that can be observed in the texts, and latterly also the sound recordings, which have come down to us – that is, in the documentary record or (to borrow the convenient term coined by Noam Chomsky) in historical *performance* data. On the other hand, we might want to go beyond these data and use them to make inferences about the changes that must have occurred in the underlying rule systems; that is, in native speakers' linguistic *competence*. It is clear that hypotheses about the second type of language change will be more difficult to arrive at and more controversial, because they are relatively more theory-dependent. The decision about which of the two perspectives on change to adopt will also crucially influence the chronology one is able to establish. For example, important changes in individual speakers' competence might not show up in the documentary record for centuries, because a traditional construction and its newer, reanalyzed variant may look identical in surface structure in the vast majority of cases.[1] This inevitable time-lag may explain why advocates of the second perspective have generally focused on the broad outlines of major changes in the remote past of the language, rather than on developments in the recent past and the present.

---

[1] Cases in point are provided by early instances of expanded infinitival clauses of the type *for* + NP + *to*-infinitive such as the biblical "It is good for a man not to touch a woman" discussed by Jespersen (1909–1949: V, 308–315), where it is impossible to decide whether *for* + NP serves as prepositional complement of the superordinate clause or as the notional subject of the subordinate infinitival one. Clearly diagnostic examples involving the passivization of the infinitive or the use of existential *there* after *for* (e.g., *it is good for this to be mentioned* or *it is good for there to be complete agreement on this issue*) are found only at a much later stage in the development of the construction. Similarly, whether a speaker of nonstandard English classifies contracted *gotta* (in *you gotta go*) as a realizational variant of the modal idiom *have got to* or as a contracted main verb like *wanna* will only become apparent in the choice of the corresponding negative form: *you ain't gotta go* in the former case, and *you don't gotta go* in the latter.

12

Of the two perspectives sketched out above, it is the first, performance-based one which has informed almost all traditional philological work and a fair amount of recent scholarship on the history of English. It will also be the dominant one in the present book. The approach taken here is best character-ized as empirical/inductive or utterance-based. The primary object of investi-gation is the extant textual record (which for the greatest part of the recorded history of English consists of written texts only), the linguist's chief task is the exhaustive description of this record, and any hypotheses about developments in the underlying system are framed as conservative generalizations on the basis of these data. Speculations about changes in the linguistic faculty of individuals belonging to successive generations (i.e., their *competence*) are largely beyond the reach of this approach. The "underlying system" which can be recon-structed, however, is a set of collective linguistic norms or conventions, perhaps best described as *langue* in the Saussurean sense.

The most compelling reason for adopting the performance-based approach in the present study is that it is probably the only one suited to the study of linguistic change at close range. Of course, it is naive to assume that all there is to be done is to hunt for the "earliest" attestation of a new form and then count how fast it spreads into which regional varieties, textual genres, or styles. Such a hunt will lead to the actual origin of a new form only in cases such as expert nomenclature, where a given term is coined by a known individual (or group of individuals) and immediately promulgated in writing.[2] As the earliest attestations of most other changes will occur in spontaneous speech, a short time-lag between actual origin and first attestation in writing or recorded speech is to be expected. Nor can proponents of an utterance-based approach entirely get around the problem of the "invisibility" of some changes. For example, centuries may pass between early signs of the possible grammatica-lization of a construction and the first diagnostic attestations whose structural or contextual properties show that grammaticalization must have occurred. Such problems, however, are in practice less severe in an utterance-based approach, which – owing to the more conservative and provisional nature of its generalizations and explanations – can take note of ambiguity and vagueness of examples without deciding for either one or the other analysis, or just record shifts in preferences and frequencies and note their possible significance.

---

[2] As an example, consider the word *Xerox*, coined as a proprietary term for the pioneering brand of electrophotographic copying machines in 1952 (cf. OED, s.v. *Xerox*, also *xerox* [noun], for the two crucial early attestations from the *Trade Marks Journal* of 19 August 1952 and the 12 May 1953 issue of the *Official gazette* of the US Patent Office). But of course it could be argued that the term became an ordinary word only with its generic use ("any photocopying machine") or in its extended meaning ("photocopy of a document"), which are both instances of a more gradual and difficult-to-pin-down development. So the only genuine instance of the phenomenon in question may be the coining of nonsense words such as *boojum* ("a particularly dangerous kind of 'snark'"), which in all likelihood was really invented by a named individual, C. L. Dodgson a.k.a. Lewis Carroll, writing the *Hunting of the Snark* (published in 1876).

The most obvious difference between the changes of the remote and the recent past, however, is that only in the former case do we have a clear idea about the goal of a development. Apart from some orientation gained from the study of comparable changes in earlier periods, we lack the benefits of hindsight in the study of ongoing diachronic developments. It is, thus, not surprising that even proponents of surface-oriented and utterance-based approaches to the study of linguistic change tend to be skeptical as to whether the direct observation of ongoing linguistic change is possible at all. Discussing several reasons which make it extremely difficult, for speakers and linguists alike, to identify recent and ongoing language change, a current standard textbook on historical linguistics claims that "there is an optimal time-lapse of say four or five centuries which is most favourable for the systematic study of change" (Bynon 1977: 6). The *locus classicus* of this skepticist position is the following remark in Bloomfield's *Language*, which was already mentioned briefly in Chapter 1:

> The process of linguistic change has never been directly observed; we shall see that such observation, with our present facilities, is inconceivable.
>
> (Bloomfield 1933: 347)

Although in a literal reading the statement is about linguistic change in general, the context in which it occurs is a long passage on phonetic change. Was Bloomfield, then, more optimistic about the study of ongoing change in morphology and syntax? Similarly pessimistic comments on the rise of new analogical plurals (1933: 408) suggest that this was not the case. It is only in the spread of already established morphological or lexical variants through the community that he sees some limited opportunities for the direct observation of ongoing linguistic change:

> *Fluctuation in the frequency of speech-forms* is a factor in all non-phonetic changes. This fluctuation can be observed, to some extent, both at first hand and in our written records. (1933: 393; emphasis in the original)

However, since the days of classical American structuralism there have been technological advances (probably unforeseen by Bloomfield) which have revolutionized descriptive linguistics. One of them is mobile and unobtrusive sound-recording technology, which, as Halliday has pointed out, was the precondition for discourse and conversation analysis:[3]

> Perhaps the greatest single event in the history of linguistics was the invention of the tape recorder, which for the first time has captured natural conversation and made it accessible to systematic study.
>
> (Halliday 1994: xxiii)

---

[3] The same point can obviously be made for all types of sociolinguistic inquiry on phonetic variation and change.

A comparable revolution in the study of the written language has been the digital storage of texts, which has stimulated the creation of increasingly sophisticated linguistic corpora, annotation schemes, and retrieval software in recent years. "Our present facilities" (to take up the formulation used by Bloomfield in the passage quoted) are thus rather different from his, and this is probably the main reason for the sharp contrast between Bloomfield's guarded views and the optimism expressed in the introduction to Bauer's *Watching English change*:

> This book will show that English is changing today and that you can watch the changes happening around you. (Bauer 1994: 1)[4]

All things considered, we are much better placed now than a century ago for the study of ongoing language change. Owing to the work of Labov (cf., e.g., his synthesis in Labov 1994) and other variationists, progress has been particularly impressive in the study of ongoing phonetic change – ironically, the area which Bloomfield was categorically pessimistic about. Less is known even today about ongoing changes in morphology and syntax (i.e., those areas in which Bloomfield saw some opportunities).

2.2   The pitfalls of anecdotal observation

It is unfortunate that, among all the methods available for the study of change in progress, the most commonly employed one – impressionistic comment based on anecdotal observation – is least reliable. Even at the hands of linguistically trained observers it distorts the facts in several ways.

As a first illustration, consider the following claim published in *Ozwords*, a popular magazine dealing with issues of language and usage from an Australian perspective:

> We used to say, "I hope to go to the football." Now I hear, "I hope I get to go . . ." In the past ten years our language has become cluttered with unnecessary words. "Up" is a favoured addition: winds "strengthen up" or "stiffen up" and rain "eases up." Managers "head up" a team or a company; actors "act up." . . . Sometimes there is a second addition as in: James "met up with" Ann. Is there a difference between meeting a woman and meeting up with her? (Wignell 2002: 7)

The errors and distortions in this entertaining little rant are so obvious that it is difficult to bear in mind that the author is dealing with a phenomenon potentially worth serious study. Before returning to the kernel of truth in the statement, let us clear away the misunderstandings.

---

[4] Readers troubled by the promotional tone of this brief statement are referred to Bauer's (2002) "Inferring variation and change from public corpora," which is probably the most comprehensive treatment of the potential (and limitations) of the corpus-based approach to the study of change in progress.

First of all, it is obvious that two unrelated developments are jumbled (up?) here:

1   the use of *get* as a catenative verb signaling the beginning of a verbal activity – a recent addition to the grammatical inventory of English but by no means a twentieth-century innovation (quite apart from the fact that *I hope to go* and *I hope I get to go* are clearly not synonymous);
2   the use of *up* as a post-verbal particle originally signaling terminative *Aktionsart* (*eat* vs. *eat up*) but now used more loosely, as well.

Apart from this confusion, there is a complete lack of independent evidence to back up the author's assertions. Indeed, the presence of the very example *meet up with*, a venerable bogey in this type of popular writing on language, is suspicious, suggesting that the author does not really derive his data from his own direct observation of usage, but rather from the rich store of linguistic folklore that has grown up around this phenomenon. With a first OED attestation in 1837 (OED, s.v. *meet* [verb] 13), the shock value of *meet up with* should by now have worn off. But, rather than any actual discourse frequency, the anger provoked by this form is due to its symbolic value – as a sign of an alleged modern tendency towards verbosity. From the British (and Australian?) purist point of view, the case against it is even stronger because of the word's probable origin in the United States.

Some of the other specimens in Wignell's list are almost as old as *meet up (with)* itself, and must be considered perfectly established in twentieth-century English, for example *ease up* (OED, s.v. *ease* [verb]). However, information that is publicly accessible in a major reference work such as the OED will usually not stand in the way of those who wish to predict imminent linguistic decay in a spirit of cultural pessimism.

A further dubious claim in Wignell's argument is that noticeable changes should have occurred in the ridiculously short time span of ten years – enough possibly for the creation and spread of a new word, but certainly insufficient for any phonetic or grammatical change to run its course. It requires a high measure of pre-established cultural pessimism and belief in linguistic decay to assume such speedy degeneration of the language.

What remains if we allow the alarmist fanfare to subside? Some of the verb forms illustrated – for example, *head up* – actually do seem to be fairly recent.[5] The history of this collocation in the twentieth century should thus be investigated, but of course what is more important than the story of any one word itself is the history of the pattern as a whole, which needs to be seen against the background of a large-scale reorganization of the English verbal

---

[5] There is no illustration either in the entry for *head* (v) in the OED or elsewhere in the quotation database of the dictionary. On the other hand, recent Web material contains several hundred relevant uses (Google, 8 May 2003).

morphology, in which prefixed forms such as *upset* or *overthrow* lost much of their productivity and made way for the prepositional-verb and phrasal-verb types (*set up*, *throw over*).

It would not be necessary to spend so much time discussing a short article from *Ozwords* if the "methodology" employed was confined to popular publications on language issues. Unfortunately, however, this is not so. Specialist academic publications on the topic of language change in progress will usually refrain from the type of emotional and combative rhetoric exemplified in Wignell's contribution, but unsystematic personal observation will lead to an incomplete picture of the facts even if observers happen to be acknowledged experts in the field.

Consider, for example, the following remark by Sidney Greenbaum, one of the twentieth century's leading experts on English grammar, who relates that "after spending fifteen years in the United States" he returned to his native Britain in 1983 and immediately noted a large number of neologisms which were unknown to him. He then goes on to ask:

> What about grammatical changes in those fifteen years? The only one that I have noticed affects an individual word: the word *nonsense*. I repeatedly heard it being used with the indefinite article: *That's a nonsense*, whereas I could only say *That's nonsense*. Many British speakers now treat *nonsense* in this respect like its near-synonym *absurdity*: *That's an absurdity/That's a nonsense*. My impressions of other differences from the British English I remembered involve differences in relative frequency. They all bring British English closer to the English I had grown used to in the States, and perhaps they reflect American influence.
>
> (Greenbaum 1986: 7)

Significantly, this is not really an example of far-reaching and systematic change in grammatical rules and patterns, but illustrates a minor lexical recategorization within a stable grammatical system. This seems to be the type of lexico-grammatical construction that we can "see" more easily than the more abstract and general core-grammatical patterns. To illustrate the frequency shifts, Greenbaum mentions phenomena such as the use of *shall* and *will* for the future in the first person, the use of auxiliary syntax or periphrastic *do* for the interrogative and negative forms of possessive *have*, variation between *should* + infinitive and the mandative subjunctive, and a few others. As will be seen in Chapter 4, Greenbaum's subjective impressions, namely that in each case the former variant is losing ground to the latter in British English, is correct. Again, however, he tends to exaggerate the speed of developments and is necessarily vague on the interesting question of whether the changes reported currently are in their fast and dynamic middle stages or in their slower incipient or terminal stages. More importantly, he has to remain silent on the differential speeds with which these developments are unfolding in speech and writing, or in different textual genres – areas in which the systematic analysis of corpus evidence will lead to important insights into the mechanics of change, as will be shown in Chapter 4. This chapter will also reveal that Greenbaum errs on one important detail of his analysis, probably because of a preconceived belief he holds about the globally dominant role of American English today. Contrary to his claim, Chapter 4 will prove that there are developments going on in British English grammar at present which will **not** bring it closer to American English. While Greenbaum minimizes the short-term manifestations of grammatical changes, other commentators seem to be taking the very opposite view, painting a somewhat apocalyptic picture of massive restructuring in the grammar. At the end of a longish list of grammatical changes alleged to be in progress in present-day English, Charles Barber ventures the following prophecy:

> We may well be on the eve of a change in which the large-scale formal structures of the language, now largely preserved in writing, will be broken down and replaced by smaller syntactic units loosely connected.
>
> (1964: 144)

How are we to reconcile the two positions: (1) syntactic change in standard English has largely come to a halt, and (2) the whole grammar is on the brink of collapse and, one hopes, subsequent recombination?

A "returning traveler" slightly different from Sidney Greenbaum is Kenneth G. Wilson, who spent the first sixteen years of his working life teaching American undergraduates, then went into college administration as dean and vice president and eventually returned to the classroom. College administration must have been worse than a mere stay abroad, for on his return he finds that, language-wise, "while much looks the same, even more seems strange" (1987: 1). Much of his comment on the language battles fought in American campuses is witty and instructive, but his remarks on developments in grammar (1987: 132–150) are comparatively stale – confining themselves to the standard catalogue of prescriptively salient items (*they were calling her and I*, *less* for *fewer*, etc.) or even misleading – in that they suggest that there were drastic statistical shifts in the use of *whom* or the subjunctive in the course of the mere twenty years (1966–1986) under review.

Sometimes anecdotal observations of this kind are repeated again and again, gaining a life of their own and solidifying into a body of folk-linguistic knowledge whose truth is taken for granted and no longer challenged even in scholarly publications. This can be illustrated with a well-known case of variable prepositional usage: the use of *from*, *to*, and *than* after the adjective *different*. From almost the beginning of the twentieth century, there has been a tradition of comment which, as will be shown, has little basis in actual usage as documented in reference works and corpora. While the use of *from* is accepted universally, the other two options are stigmatized, with the added complication that the legitimacy of *different than* has become a bone of contention in the British–American folk-linguistic wars. In *The American language*, H. L. Mencken quotes a letter to the editor of the *New York Herald* written by novelist Meredith Nicholson in September 1922:

> Within a few years the abominable phrase *different than* has spread through the country like a pestilence. In my own Indiana, where the wells of English undefiled are jealously guarded, the infection has awakened general alarm. (Nicholson, quoted in Mencken 1963: 570)

A few years later, the same claim, that *different than* is a widely used American English innovation about to replace British *different from* (or *to*), appears in a scholarly publication:

> Now that English people show they have pretty definitely decided we were right after all and they wrong about the proper preposition to put after "different," it seems we are beginning to have misgivings ourselves and to wonder whether we cannot do better. In this we are far from well advised. We have all the right on our side, as our apparent victory goes to show, in maintaining that one star must be different *from* another star and not different *to* it but how shall we ever have the rashness to defend "different *than*"? (Claudius 1925/1926: 446)

By the end of the twentieth century, if we are to trust the comments in the literature, the traditional *different from* is under threat in all parts of the English-speaking world. Commenting on Australian teachers' ingrained conservatism in matters of English usage, Eagleson says:

> Teachers can be remarkably outmoded in their knowledge of the current state of the language. In tests of acceptability conducted in the past five years I have found them to lag behind the rest of the community time and again. Of all informants they will be the ones to hold to *different from* while the majority of the community has moved to *different to*, and is possibly going on to *different than*. (Eagleson 1989: 155)

According to Trudgill and Hannah's widely used standard reference work *International English*, *different than* is now the normal form in American English: "The comparative adjective *different* is usually followed by *from* (or sometimes *to*) in EngEng, while in USEng it is more usually followed by *than*" (2002: 74). In Jenkins' textbook *World Englishes*, *different from* has disappeared from American English altogether: "The comparative adjective 'different' is followed by 'than' in USEng and by 'from' (or more recently, 'to') in EngEng" (2003: 75).

Both the claims and the occasional emotional intensity in this debate are surprising in view of the relevant OED entry – available to all contributors –

which takes note of the debate but at the same time makes clear that there is no historical basis for it:[6]

> The usual construction is now with *from*; that with *to* (after *unlike*, *dissimilar to*) is found in writers of all ages, and is frequent colloquially, but is by many considered incorrect. The construction with *than* (after *other than*), is found in Fuller, Addison, Steele, De Foe, Richardson, Goldsmith, Miss Burney, Coleridge, Southey, De Quincey, Carlyle, Thackeray, Newman, Trench, and Dasent, among others.
>
> (OED, s.v. different [a.], 1b)

It is appropriate at this point to quote *Webster's Dictionary of English Usage* (Webster 1989), enlightened modern-day successor to the usage guides much derided in the linguistic literature, because its assessment of the issue is fully in line with the corpus results that will be reported in section 2.3.1 below:

> We have about 80 commentators in our files who discourse on the propriety of *different than* or *different to*. The amount of comment – thousands and thousands of words – might lead you to believe that there is a very complicated or subtle problem here, but there is not. These three phrases can be very simply explained: *different from* is the most common and is standard in both British and American usage; *different than* is standard in American and British usage, especially when a clause follows *than*, but is more frequent in American; *different to* is standard in British usage but rare in American usage. (1989: 341)

Faced with such a statement, which presents the factual truth in moderate and reasonable formulations, one cannot help wondering why there has been a century of emotional and impressionistic comment on usage, during which, coming from opposite directions, conservative and progressive language mavens hovered on the verge of an interesting discovery about ongoing change, but were unable to identify the central facts correctly.

In sum, we can say that anecdotal observation and the unsystematic collection of examples of usage are not entirely without use in the study of ongoing change. They may provide first hints about what might be worth investigating, but the pitfalls of the method when used on its own tend to outweigh its advantages by far (as has been shown). First, it leads to an emphasis on the perceived novelty and on unusual and bizarre usages, while ordinary usage and the strong continuities with the past remain invisible. Secondly, too much attention is focused on the study of specific isolated or trivial usages, chiefly because it is these which arouse prescriptivists' concern, and not enough emphasis is placed on important and comprehensive developments that are

---

[6] The quotations show that both *different from* and *different to* go back to the sixteenth century, so that neither form can be regarded as historically prior to the other.

going on below the level of conscious awareness. Thirdly, the upper time limit for a change in this perspective is the human lifetime, and the many changes which are taking longer will be perceived as going on at a much faster rate than is the case.

2.3   Documenting change

2.3.1 Documentation in real time

Language change can be studied in "real time;" that is, by comparing the state of the language at at least two different points in time, or in "apparent time," by extrapolating diachronic developments from synchronic variation. Other things being equal, the real-time approach would seem to be preferable as the more direct one, which is why it will be treated first. Unfortunately, however, the direct approach meets with a number of difficulties in the study of change in progress which will force us to make some concessions.

The ideal type of a real-time study is a sociolinguistic community survey repeated after a decent interval. Writing on phonetic change, Labov suggests that confirmation of a suspected linguistic change in real time is obtained:

> if it is demonstrated in the near future that the trend detected has moved further in the same direction. "Recent past" and "near future" must mean a span of time large enough to allow for significant changes but small enough to rule out the possibility of reversals and retrograde movements: we might say from a minimum of a half generation to a maximum of two. (1981: 177)

For lexical change, the minimum span of observation may be shorter, whereas for grammatical change it will almost certainly be longer. The obvious imprac-ticality posed by this method in the study of ongoing change is that if one documents the current state of development of a variable, one will have to wait for an unreasonably long time to carry out the follow-up study. The reverse method, looking back and comparing the current state with the recent past, will generally not work for spoken data, which in their vast majority are not recorded for posterity.

The massive logistical and organizational difficulties of real-time studies explain why hardly any major sociolinguistic study has ever had a follow-up. In a recent survey, William Labov (1994: 85–98) lists only four projects which qualify for the status of a genuine follow-up, two of them concerned with English-speaking communities. Fowler (1986) restages Labov's own 1966 New York City department store survey, and Trudgill (1988) follows up his own 1974 study of language use in Norwich. Since Labov surveyed the field, there has been one more follow-up study, revisiting Martha's Vineyard, the site of one of Labov's own pioneering studies of change in progress (Josey 2004). It is interesting to note that only the follow-up to the New York City study shows developments which fully corroborate assessments arrived at through apparent-time extrapolation from synchronic variation (the alternative method of study which will be discussed in section 2.3.2 below). Trudgill's second study presents a mixed picture, showing some of the expected developments but also important unexpected ones, while Josey's replication of the original Martha's Vineyard study shows a reversal of the 1960s trends. Josey's and, to some extent also Trudgill's, results must thus be seen as a warning against exclusive dependence on the apparent-time methodology in the study of ongoing change.

One concession to the practical difficulties of organizing real-time studies is to move from the community study to the longitudinal observation of one single informant. A recent example of this approach is provided by Harrington et al. (2000), who chart developments in the Queen's English as evident in her annual Christmas broadcasts. The authors conclude that:

> the Queen no longer speaks the Queen's English of the 1950s, although the vowels of the 1980s Christmas message are still clearly set apart from those of an SSB [= Standard Southern British] accent. The extent of such community influences is probably more marked for most adult speakers, who are not in a position of having to defend a particular form of English (the Queen's English in this case). The chances of societies and academies successfully preserving a particular form of pronunciation against the influence of community and social changes are as unlikely as King Canute's attempts to defeat the tides. (Harrington et al. 2000: 927)

The three researchers were fortunate in that their informant had such a high public profile and they had data representing her speech at several successive times, but in an otherwise identical setting – the Christmas broadcast. Their disadvantage was that they captured their informant's speech in a formal and perhaps artificial situation, and that, as they acknowledge themselves, the Queen may not have been the best speaker to investigate in a study of recent developments in the Queen's English.

As the focus of the present study is on standard, especially written, English, it is fortunately not necessary to restrict the investigation to the production of a single informant. The variant of the real-time approach adopted for the present study is the use of matching corpora representing the state of "the language" or some specified variety at different times. Other available digital text resources for the study of English, such as the OED Online, will be used as complements as and when appropriate. Corpora and databases which are publicly available will be referred to by their standard names, e.g., the "Brown Corpus" for the "Standard Corpus of Present-Day Edited American English, for use with Digital Computers" completed in 1964 by W. Nelson Francis and Henry Kučera at Brown University in Providence, Rhode Island. The reader is expected to have a basic knowledge of corpus-linguistic resources and procedures, or (if this is not so) to consult Appendix 1, which provides documentation about these sources to the extent necessary here.

The use of parallel or matching corpora has a long and distinguished tradition going back to the pre-computational era in English historical linguistics. It was the method used by all those traditional philologists who based their observations on analyses of successive translations of the Bible into English – as Otto Jespersen did, for example, when he illustrated the increase in the frequency of the progressive since the Middle English period in this way (see Jespersen 1909–1949: IV, 177). What the advent of digital language processing has brought about is thus not so much an entirely new method as a widening of the scope of an existing one. It is now no longer just a small number of sacred or otherwise privileged texts which are translated at successive points of time or concordanced, but an increasingly broad range of registers and styles. In addition, the computationally assisted retrieval of forms from digitized corpora makes it possible to access the data faster and, in many cases, to tackle problems which the great philologists such as Visser and Jespersen shied away from because they were unable to spare the time required. Writing about the variation of gerundial and infinitival complements after the verb *begin* a little more than thirty years ago, Visser deplored the following apparent dilemma:

> Today *begin* + form in *-ing* is used with striking frequency alongside of *begin* + infinitive. Which of the two alternatives predominates cannot be ascertained because of the lack of statistical data.
>
> (Visser 1970–73: III, 1888)

Today, at least for a language such as English, with its rich panchronic corpus-linguistic working environment, it is easy to fill in this gap in our language-historical knowledge. The extent to which the gerund has gained ground as a complement of the verb *begin* in the course of the past century will be documented in Chapter 4 of the present study.

The early phase of corpus-based computer-assisted research on the history of English was inaugurated by the publication of the Helsinki Corpus and centered on Old, Middle, and Early Modern English. Diachronic coverage was extended to the present in the subsequent ARCHER (= "A Representative Corpus of Historical English Registers") project, which offers coverage of British and American English, sampled according to genre, at fifty-year intervals from c. 1650 to the present (1990). The chief limitation of ARCHER for the study of very recent and ongoing changes is the small size of its twentieth-century components. In a research project conducted by the present writer, the Brown and LOB corpora – one million-word corpora which document fifteen different genres of written texts in American and British English in 1961 – were complemented with matching databases representing the state of the two varieties in 1992 and 1991 respectively. These corpora are generally known under the abbreviations "Frown" (for "Freiburg update of

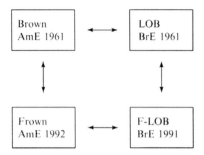

Figure 2.1 Four matching one-million-word corpora of written English

the Brown corpus") and "F-LOB" ("Freiburg update of the LOB corpus"). A visual representation of the relations among the four corpora is provided in Figure 2.1.

The arrows show that this quartet of corpora makes it possible not only to study developments in each of the two varieties in real time, but also to investigate the question of how these short-term diachronic developments are related to synchronic (i.e., regional or stylistic) variation at any one time. The corpus-based real-time approach has recently been extended to cover spoken English by researchers based at the Survey of English Usage (University College London), who are in the process of creating a diachronic corpus of spoken British English by matching fitting samples of the London-Lund Corpus (1959–1988) and the British component of the International Corpus of English (ICE) (1990–1993).[7]

A drawback that is shared by all of these customized historical corpora is that they are too small to allow research on medium- and low-frequency phenomena. This is why in the present study they have frequently been complemented by further digitized text collections which are neither historical corpora in the narrow meaning of the term (i.e., in the sense of having been explicitly designed for the purposes of linguistic analysis) nor easy matches or parallels for existing corpora. To give some examples, there are digital newspaper archives, which constitute annually updating records of usage in one textual domain,[8] and the huge quotation base of the OED, which since the publication of the second edition in 1989 has been available for increasingly sophisticated digital searches.

---

[7] For information on the "parsed and searchable diachronic corpus of present-day spoken English," see http://www.ucl.ac.uk/english-usage/diachronic.index.htm.

[8] Most major British and American newspapers started electronic archives in the late 1980s, which is a suitable time-depth for the study of recent neologisms. Lexis-Nexis, a commercial digital archive assembling a vast array of media sources even has a time-depth of three decades. A convenient portal to electronic newspapers from all parts of the English-speaking world and beyond is offered at http://www.refdesk.com/paper.html.

Most of the present study's corpus-based findings on language change in progress in present-day English will be discussed in the appropriate places in Chapters 3 and 4. Here I will confine myself to two illustrative examples intended to show: (1) that the corpus-based real-time approach works; and (2) how it works. For this purpose, let us return to the case of *different*, for which, as was pointed out in section 2.1, impressionistic observations suggest rapid diachronic change and considerable regional divergence between varieties of English. Table 2.1 has the figures from the four one-million-word twentieth-century reference corpora mentioned above, which suggest that the impressionistic analysis needs to be qualified.

Note that only instances were counted in which the adjective *different* occurred next to the preposition. This led to some under-collection, because forms such as "a different theory from/to/than my own," with the adjective separated from the preposition, are possible. On the other hand, the results of two previous studies on the use of *different* in Brown and LOB, which apparently attempted to capture all relevant instances (Hundt 1998a: 106; Kennedy 1998: 195), are not necessarily encouraging: the two authors agree on the results of just a single one out of six counts.[9]

Whichever set of figures one chooses to adopt, though, one thing is obvious: they all show that, contrary to claims, American and British English are rather similar, and little seems to be happening diachronically. Impressionistic observation is supported to the extent that *to* is restricted to British English. A closer look at the three instances of *different than* reveals the influence of syntactic environment on the choice of the preposition. Only the Frown example has *than* interchangeable with the other two ("the second Olympics is different than Seoul" – A 19, 1);[10] the LOB case has *than* in front of another preposition ("different than in the first part" – D 4, 88), while in Brown it introduces a clause ("no evidence that anything was different than it had been" – L 10, 670). As regards long-term developments, the stable and overwhelming dominance of *different from* can easily be established from an analysis of the OED quotation

[9] Neither author makes completely explicit the criteria that a form had to meet for inclusion, so that it is difficult to account for the following disparities: Hundt reports 34, 7, and 1 cases of *different from*, *different to* and *different than* respectively for LOB (as against Kennedy's 38, 4, and 2), and there is similar disagreement on the corresponding figures for Brown (39, 0, and 6 in Hundt vs. 40, 0, and 12 in Kennedy). Apart from error, differences may be due to the uncertain status of examples such as the following: "a different and less radical solution than that proposed by the Commission" (LOB H 11, 40; see note 10 for an explanation of the notation). Here it is not easy to decide whether *than* merely refers back to *less radical* or also to *different*.

[10] When quoting examples from standard corpora or digital databases, the usual conventions are followed. In this particular example, which is from the LOB (Lancaster-Oslo/Bergen) Corpus of written British English, "A" refers to the textual category, in this case "Press/ Reportage," "19" is the number of the 2,000-word text sample the quote is from, and "1" the line number of the quote itself. Readers unfamiliar with corpus-linguistic conventions and/or the corpora used for the present study are referred to Appendix 1 for further information.

Table 2.1. *Prepositions following* different *in four corpora*

	Brown (US 1961)	LOB (Britain 1961)	Frown (US 1992)	F-LOB (Britain 1991)
different from	29	20	32	39
different to	—	1	—	3
different than	1	1	1	—

base:[11] it contains 650 cases of *different from*, 40 of *different to*, and a mere 9 of *different than*. While the impressionistic observers may have had some point about regional diversity in English, historical change seems to have been all in the eye of the beholder.

A particular, but by no means uncommon, complication in work based on small corpora has become evident in the above analysis. The regionally and diachronically interesting variants, namely *to* and *than*, are too infrequent to allow a conclusive judgment on their spread. An easy way of obtaining more data would be to turn to English-language material from the World Wide Web. The Web is a "corpus" unrivaled in size but potentially too messy for most types of linguistic analysis. For the present purpose, though, returns from regionally stratified searches of the Web are surprisingly robust and show that the picture suggested by the four corpora analyzed above – dominance of *different from* in all varieties of English, and a minor contrast in the preference for *than* and *to* in American- and British-influenced varieties respectively – is correct.

The robustness of these findings has come about against all odds. For example, it is not guaranteed that material supplied on a Canadian server was produced by a native speaker of Canadian English (or a native speaker of any other variety of English, for that matter). Also, it is particularly difficult to identify American content on the Web. The ".us" domain is not much used. The ".edu" domain, which contains enough material, is used mainly by US institutions of higher learning but includes some others. The ".gov" domain (US government) is biased for text type and register, and so on. On the "micro"-level of analyzing the returns of the search, cases of *different from* and *different than* are identified fairly reliably (> 95 percent), whereas there is significant over-collection in the case of *different to*.[12] It seems, however, that all the many potential sources of error seem to cancel each other out, for we get the same "North American" profile in the Canadian material (".ca") and, in the US domains, from the vast ".edu" down to the very small ".nasa.gov". Other

---

[11] Again, the search was restricted to occurrences of *different* and *from/to/than* in direct contact, in full awareness that this meant some under-collection of relevant examples.

[12] Many cases, for example, exemplify the two words in accidental contiguity, as in "it is one thing to say such a thing but it is different to write it" or "that's no different to me" (in the sense of "makes no difference to me"). In American samples, such spurious returns usually accounted for more than half of all instances of *different to*.

Table 2.2. *Prepositions following* different *in regionally stratified Web material (Google, 30 May 2004)*

Total	from 8,160,000	than 2,500,000	to 825,000
.us	194,000	85,200	6,060
.edu	1,450,000	343,000	33,100
.gov	787,000	152,000	6,050
.nasa.gov	11,000	3,180	235
.ca	253,000	68,700	11,200
.uk	469,000	33,000	157,000
.au	171,000	14,800	98,800
.nz	45,400	4,290	17,700
.za	28,700	2,910	11,600
.ie	25,600	2,330	11,600
.cn	18,700	921	729
.de	94,500	16,000	13,500

interesting findings contained in Table 2.2 are that – at least on the present criterion – Irish English (".ie") patterns with British English and that the Southern Hemisphere ex-colonial Englishes (".au," ".nz," and ".za" for Australia, New Zealand, and South Africa) have not gone American yet. (The two final lines illustrating English-language text presented in the China and Germany national domains were included to show that in non-native-speaker communities the influence of both the British and the American norms can be felt and obscures a clear result.)

Strictly speaking, the above results do not disprove the anecdotal observations reported in section 2.1, for after all these might be based on informal speech rather than the usually more conservative written standard. And indeed *different than* and *different to* turn out to be more frequent in spoken corpora. The direct conversations from the British component of the International Corpus of English (ICE) (c. 185,000 words) show an even spread of *different from* (4 instances) and *different to* (5), with *than* being absent. In the much larger "spoken-demographic" texts of the British National Corpus (BNC) (more than 4 million words), there are 21 instances of *different from*, 46 of *different to*,[13] and 4 of *different than* (of which 3 show *than* being used to

---

[13] In contrast to American samples, the vast majority of them are genuine. There is only one clear instance of accidental contiguity of *different* and *to*, and several examples which are difficult to interpret because of unclear transcriptions or contexts.

Table 2.3. *Proportion of* on/upon *in four corpora*

	1961	1991/1992
British English (LOB/F-LOB)	6,913/407	7,123/243
American English (Brown/Frown)	6,719/493	6,900/196

Significances: LOB: F-LOB $p < 0.001$, Brown: Frown $p < 0.001$; LOB: Brown $p < 0.01$, F-LOB: Frown $p > 0.05$

introduce clauses). The Santa Barbara Corpus of Spoken American English, which contains spontaneous dialogue, is too small to yield results (1 instance of *different from*), while the Corpus of Spoken Professional American English, which covers press briefings and faculty meetings, has 91 instances of *different from* slightly outnumbering the 82 cases of *different than* (and none of *different to*).[14] The Longman Corpus of Spoken American English (LCSAE) (around 5 million words) has 97 instances of *from*, 64 of *than*, and 15 of *to* (of which only 6 are genuine). Note, however, that if these figures lend some support to impressionistic assessments, they also make clear that the commentators underestimate the persistence of *different from*. It is the biggest drawback of impressionistic observation that stylistically and regionally neutral and traditional usage is not noticed, and the new and unusual is focused on to an extent far in excess of its statistical weight.

A second example to show that a diachronic development does show up even in four relatively small reference corpora is the gradual obsolescence of archaic *upon*. The figures in Table 2.3 happen to be big enough for statistical significance testing.

The major significant development is a parallel decline in the frequency of *upon* in both varieties, which has proceeded somewhat more rapidly in American English (from a frequency slightly higher than the British in 1961 to one lower in 1992). Regional contrasts, by comparison, were less significant statistically (and probably not salient psychologically) in 1961, and have weakened further since. In terms of choice between the variants, *upon* had a share of around 7 percent of all relevant forms in Brown, which decreased to less than 3 percent in Frown.

The short-term late twentieth-century trend reflected in the four corpora smoothly continues a long-term development, which can be documented on the basis of data from the OED quotation base. For comparative purposes, three "Baseline" corpora were compiled from the OED quotation base which

---

[14] These figures differ slightly from those given in Iyeiri et al. (2004: 30–31), who apparently also counted discontinuous and borderline uses of *different* + preposition and, at least for *different to*, discuss cases such as *there are two different connotations to what* easy *means*, which do not represent instances of the construction under study.

Table 2.4. *Proportion of* on/upon *in three samples from the OED quotation base*

Baseline1700	1,824/1,000
Baseline1800	2,525/744
Baseline1900	5,999/902

represent the state of the language c. 1700, c. 1800, and c. 1900 (see Appendix 2 for a discussion of the compilation procedures). Table 2.4 shows a linear increase in the proportion of *upon*, as one goes back in time – from c. 13 percent in 1900, to c. 22 percent in 1800, and c. 28 percent in 1700.

2.3.2 Documentation in apparent time

In view of the organizational obstacles involved in many types of real-time studies, extrapolation of diachronic trends in "apparent time" has become a favored method in the study of change in progress. The basis of this method is the fact that most linguistic changes start with younger speakers, lower-class speakers, and in spoken and informal language, and then spread into formal and written registers and educated middle-class usage. If in a synchronic sample a form is favored by the younger informants or more frequent in speech or informal writing, it is plausible to regard it as an innovation in the early stages of its spread through the community.

The method is convenient, but certainly not without its pitfalls. It assumes that older speakers add little to their grammar and phonology after adolescence. This is a plausible working hypothesis which has never been proved conclusively. For the study of lexical change, the method is unsuitable from the start, as speakers modify their vocabularies throughout most of their lives and neologisms can be coined by young and old members of the community. Two additional problems need to be solved. One is to find a way to identify "prestige" innovations, which do not follow the usual trend of spreading from "below" but diffuse from educated into general use, from formal into informal language, from writing into speech, and – presumably – from old to young. This is not very difficult in most cases, as such usages are in the category of what Labov calls "linguistic markers," which the community is aware of and uses consciously (unlike the "linguistic indicators," which tend to operate below the level of conscious awareness). A much trickier problem is the phenomenon of age-grading, which usually manifests itself in a temporary adolescent affinity to nonstandard usages which disappears in an individual's later life. This means that in such cases generations of teenage linguistic rebellion will not lead to a lasting change in community norms.

Apparent-time analyses of ongoing change are usually very easy to undertake on the basis of corpora. The only condition is that the corpus texts have been

Table 2.5. *Lexical items most characteristic of four groups of speakers in a corpus of spoken British English (compiled from Rayson et al. 1997)*

10 words most characteristic of	Over-35s	Under-35s	Middle-class speakers	Working-class speakers
1	yes	mum	yes	he
2	well	fucking	really	says
3	mm	my	okay	said
4	er	mummy	are	fucking
5	they	like	actually	ain't
6	said	na*	just	yeah
7	says	goes	good	its
8	were	shit	you	them
9	the	dad	erm	aye
10	of	daddy	right	she

* As in *gonna* or *wanna*, which for the purposes of the CLAWS tagger are counted as two words

produced at roughly the same time and that the corpus contains texts from more than one speaker, text type, or genre. Apparent-time studies in a wider sense can also be based on other digitized textual sources – for example, electronic newspaper archives from the same year but different regions – or even on regionally stratified selections of web texts. As for the interpretation of the results, the general cautions on the use of the method apply.

For a practical illustration of the potential and limitations of corpus-based apparent-time analyses of ongoing change, consider the following findings from the spoken-demographic component of the British National Corpus, more than 4 million words of transcribed spontaneous speech produced by a sociologically representative sample of British speakers. Table 2.5 shows the ten most typical words in the speech of the over-35s and under-35s, and middle-class and working-class speakers, with typicality being defined not in terms of absolute frequency but as statistical over-representation in the sample in question.

In the speech of the under-35s, four out of ten words are obvious and trivial cases of age-grading: *mum*, *mummy*, *dad*, and *daddy*. The words are not non-standard but they are clearly of the type which children and adolescents living with their families have special occasion to use. The over-representation of two common swear words, *fucking* and *shit*, is most likely due to age-grading, too. It certainly does not show "new" words spreading in the community. If anything, the change involved is not lexical but one of community norms governing what is acceptable speech. The presence in the list of *like* and *goes* might be due to their uses as discourse particle and speech-reporting verb respectively ("he's like fifteen years old like" or "and then she goes: no way"). Sources claim that both usages are spreading in Britain, but to verify this on the basis of BNC data would involve an extremely time-consuming qualitative analysis of tens of thousands of attestations. The most typical features in the language of the older speakers all point to phenomena which are unlikely to be part of diachronic change. The over-representation of *the* and *of* suggests the presence of more complex noun phrases; discourse markers such as *well, mm*, and the hesitation phenomenon *er* indicate a different conversational atmosphere. Even the question of whether the over-representation of *yes* should be interpreted as a sign of the obsolescence of this form and its impending replacement by *yeah* cannot be answered straightforwardly. So what we are left with as a plausible genuine reflection of ongoing change in apparent time is the morpheme **na*, the second element in the contracted forms *gonna* and *wanna*. The BNC codes speakers for six age groups, and the frequency of *wanna* (measured in occurrences per million) gives a near-perfect gradient in apparent time (Table 2.6).

It is not precisely clear which of the three age classifications targets the phenomenon most precisely. Measuring by "age of respondent"[15] (columns 2 and 5) captures hits produced by the respondents as well as those he or she interacts with, and could thus be seen as a good representation of the linguistic habitat of the person in question. Also, this analysis covers all 1,985 instances of *wanna* in the spoken-demographic material. "Age of speaker in the spoken-demographic dialogues" (columns 3 and 6) is based on the evaluation of those 1710 instances of *wanna* for which speaker age was known. It is probably the most precise measure in this case because it documents active usage in informal situations by individuals belonging to the relevant age groups. "Speaker age in all spoken texts" (columns 4 and 7) extends the database (to 2,383 cases) while diluting the informal quality of the data somewhat. No matter which parameter is chosen, however, the figures always provide clear evidence for the spread of *wanna* in contemporary British English. The apparent-time distribution is perfect for speaker age and near perfect for respondent age. In the other half of the table, covering the use of *want to*, the situation is more complex. There is no opposing trend towards the disappearance of the uncontracted form, which shows that the overall discourse frequency of the verb *want* is increasing. This finding is in line with long-term developments since Early Modern English, and is to be expected in this instance, and similar others, of incipient grammaticalization. In active usage (see columns 6 and 7) *want to* is considerably more frequent in the youngest age group than in all the others, which suggests an element of age-grading. It is also interesting to compare usage in the three older age groups, for whom the contraction *wanna* is an infrequent option, with that of the under-35s, and particularly the under-24s, for whom the contraction is one of two normal choices.

---

[15] In BNC terminology, "respondents" are the 153 individuals equipped with recording apparatus and charged with collecting the spoken-demographic data "in the field."

Table 2.6. *Frequency of wanna in the BNC per age group (×1,000,000 words)*

	wanna			want to		
Age	By age of respondent (spoken–demographic)	By age of speaker (spoken–demographic)	By age of speaker (all spoken texts)	By age of respondent (spoken–demographic)	By age of speaker (spoken–demographic)	By age of speaker (all spoken texts)
0–14	1,127	1,178	1,096	633	1,210	1,161
15–24	641	700	605	662	605	632
25–34	505	496	363	854	669	715
35–44	375	368	241	813	780	871
45–59	428	330	201	659	684	852
60+	173	159	99	676	679	548

Apparent-time interpretations aren't any easier to deduce from lexical differences based on speaker's class (columns 4 and 5 in Table 2.5). Middle-class speech is characterized by a large number of discourse features such as *actually*, *okay*, or *right*, none of which is old-fashioned or obsolescent. In the spoken BNC, for example, the use of *actually* peaks at a frequency of 1,309 instances per million words in the 15–24 age group and hovers inconclusively between the values of 538 and 838 in the five others (0–14, 25–34, 35–44, 45–59, 60+).[16] The working-class sample indicates that *yeah* might be spreading at the expense of *yes*, which – as will be remembered – has its strongest base among the over-35s, but more research is needed for a conclusive answer.

In sum, such exploratory studies show that it is possible to construct apparent-time analyses of ongoing change on the basis of generically stratified corpora such as the BNC. However, the greatest part of age-based and social variation that can be observed involves stable stylistic and social contrasts or is affected by age-grading, so that "apparent time" is not a suitable methodology to be used on its own. Its main use is to serve as a complement to corpus-based real-time studies, and to provide clarification in those cases in which there are strong independent grounds to assume that a change is underway.

2.4   Outlook: a plea for methodological pluralism

The subject of the present study is change in progress in present-day English or, more specifically, in written standard English and its oral analogue, formal spoken English. What is the best way to identify, describe, and analyze ongoing changes in these two varieties?

No method, not even the notoriously unreliable unsystematic collection of examples, should be ruled out. All methods serve a purpose, however limited it

---

[16] It is interesting to note in this connection that *actually* (spelled *akchully*) figures prominently in the fictional representation of London teenage speech in Zadie Smith's recent best-selling novel *White Teeth*, where – unsurprisingly in view of the corpus data cited above – it is associated with female characters such as Irie, who show some social aspiration. Consider, for example, the following conversation (on appropriate food items to include in a charity food parcel for old-age pensioner J. P. Hamilton):

> "Well, I got some *more* and *better* apples, *akchully*, and some Kendal mint cake and some ackee and saltfish." . . .
> "Well, *akchully*, don't worry 'cos you're not going to get it –"
> "Oooh, feel the heat, *feel the heat!*" squealed Magid, rubbing his little palm in. "You been shamed, man!"
> "*Akchully*, I'm not shamed, *you're* shamed 'cos it's for Mr. J. P. Hamilton –"
> "Our stop!" cried Magid, shooting to his feet and pulling the bell cord too many times.
> "*If you ask me*," said one disgruntled OAP to another, "*they should all go back to their own* . . ." (Penguin paperback edition, p. 163)

Here, '*akchully*' is quite appropriately used to characterize the speech of a youngster in the group who, as turns out in the course of the novel, is not without her social aspirations.

may be, and very often they complement each other in their strengths and weaknesses. Impressionistic observation, for example, despite its obvious shortcomings, may provide valuable hints as to phenomena worth investigating systematically – even if the results of such systematic investigation usually force considerable modification of the initial assumptions about change. Typically, impressionistic observation tends to overestimate the speed of a change, underestimate the persistence of traditional usage and overlook those changes which are not the subject of conscious discussion in the community. It is precisely in regard to these three aspects of ongoing change that the systematic analysis of corpora can serve as a complement and corrective, by showing that – outside the lexical sphere – innovations spread slowly, and at differential speeds in different genres and regional or social varieties. Students of the history of English are fortunate in being able to draw on a uniquely rich corpus-linguistic working environment, which makes it possible to chart the spread of innovations (and the disappearance of old forms) with a degree of delicacy impossible for most other languages. Apart from adding to our factual knowledge of the history of English, such investigations will also contribute to the development of usage- and utterance-based models of linguistic change in theoretical and general linguistics.

The ordinary use of corpus data is to correct or refine current assumptions on ongoing change. In some cases, however, corpus analysis will turn out to be a genuine discovery procedure, making it possible – through a systematic comparison of frequencies in matching corpora – to identify changes which have gone unnoticed – either because they have proceeded below the threshold of speakers' conscious awareness and/or have escaped prescriptive censure.

Sociolinguistic work on change in progress in English, with its focus on spoken and nonstandard usage, will be an additional point of reference for the present study, both empirically and methodologically. Its chief limitation, however, is that it has little to offer for the study of change in written English. Thus, while acknowledging the usefulness of all frameworks (including impressionistic observation), the present study, with its focus on standard usage and written English in the twentieth century, will generally proceed from comparisons of (ideally) well-matched corpora and complement these with analyses of larger but usually messier digitized text databases of various types.

Corpus-based empiricism, however, will lead to nothing more than the accumulation of under-analyzed and frequently pointless statistics unless the interpretation of the results is carried out in an appropriate theoretical framework. To illustrate this point with an example from the preceding section of the chapter, for the proper understanding of the spread of *wanna* in contemporary British English it is not enough to record increases of frequency in corpora. This is a necessary first step, but the full interpretation requires a theory of grammaticalization to handle the formal and structural changes involved,[17] and a proper sociolinguistic model to assess the extent to which the spread of the innovation is speeded up or slowed down by prestige and stigma.

The interdisciplinary and open spirit in which the study of ongoing change should be approached is well put by Rickford and his co-authors, who recommend "exploration on the boundaries of sociolinguistic variation, corpus linguistics, historical linguistics, and syntax" (Rickford et al. 1995: 129) as the appropriate method for getting a grip on change in progress.[18]

---

[17] Broadly, these add up to an auxiliation process in which a formerly independent lexical verb undergoes semantic extension and functional specialization in the grammar – in this case, as an expression of volition and, increasingly, weak obligation.

[18] The quotation is from a paper about a particular instance of change in progress in late twentieth-century American English; namely, the creation of an idiomatic topic-introducing formula *as far as* through regular ellipsis from an *as far as X is concerned* clausal base.

3 Lexical change in twentieth-century English

3.1 Introduction

Lexical innovation is where linguistic change in progress is most obvious to the lay observer. It is also an area in which corpora have long been used systematically, both as resources for the regular updates of dictionaries and in academic linguistic work on new words.[1] And not least, vocabulary is "the part of the language probably most affected by change" in the recent history of English (Romaine 1998: 2). Lexical obsolescence, the converse of innovation, is somewhat less spectacular but in principle equally accessible.

If there is one feature of the rich literature on neologisms in English which occasionally leaves the reader dissatisfied, it is that too often the focus is on individual words rather than general trends in the vocabulary, on the compilation of lists of disconnected items rather than the evolution of the underlying word-formation mechanisms. Scanning collections of new words in English, one usually cannot help being impressed by the ingenuity that goes into the coining of some words. On other occasions one will be shocked or amused by the more colorful importations into standard English from various subcultural slangs. But even as one savors the lists, there is a feeling that some of the forms

---

[1] One pioneer in computer-assisted corpus-based new-word lexicography is Clarence L. Barnhart, who started covering lexical innovations from the 1960s in a dictionary which has now gone into the third edition (Barnhart et al. 1990). Selected groups of new words have been discussed in regular columns ("Among the new words") in the journal *American Speech* for more than half a century, and the most important material from 1941 to 1991 is available as a book (Algeo 1991). Ayto's *Twentieth-century words* (1999) is a good example of the many dictionaries of neologisms aimed at a wider audience. As for the major English-language dictionaries, four massive supplements were published after the first edition of the OED. These were incorporated into the 2nd edition (1989). The OED Online publishes quarterly updates, combining systematic revision of the entries in specified portions of the alphabet with "out-of-sequence" additions documenting important new words. A 12,000-word supplement is available for *Webster's third new international dictionary* (Mish 1986). For corpus-based studies of neologisms with a more theoretical orientation, including an interest in patterns of productivity of various morphological processes, compare Baayen and Renouf (1996), Plag et al. (1998), and Plag (1999).

recorded are curiosities, coined tongue in cheek and propagated as passing fads, especially in the media. In academic work on new words the collection and documentation of individual items is, thus, but a first step. The more important task is to uncover shifts in the relative importance of the underlying word-formation processes.

Accordingly, the present chapter will proceed in two steps. Section 3.2, "Case studies," will discuss selected illustrative examples to give an idea of the range and diversity of neologisms in twentieth-century English. In the analysis of individual neologisms corpus data are very helpful in the purely quantitative-statistical documentation of the spread of a form, but also in research on problems which require additional qualitative-philological analysis, such as, for example, the degree of institutionalization and lexicalization of a word. Institutionalization is here defined as the reasonably frequent occurrence of a word in non-specialist registers, combined with "time stability" (i.e. the regular recurrence of the word independent of the trigger event causing its creation). Lexicalization refers to the emergence of word-specific additional semantic content beyond what can be predicted from productive word-formation processes.[2]

Section 3.3, "Major trends," will turn to the question of whether beneath the confusing variety of individual new words there is stability in the underlying inventory of productive word-formation mechanisms. With very rare exceptions, new words exemplify existing productive patterns of word formation. Some of these, such as compounding, have been mainstays of lexical creativity all through the recorded history of English. Others, such as zero-derivation or conversion, moved from a marginal to a central position among word-formation mechanisms in late Middle English/Early Modern English. In a very few instances, the last century saw the emergence of entirely new word-formation patterns which have by now become impressively productive, such as acronyms or endocentric verb–verb compounds of the type *crash-land*, *freeze-dry*, *slam-dunk*, *stir-fry*, or *strip-search* (on which, see Wald and Besserman 2002).[3] Above and beyond the listing of many individual new words, a study of the changing lexicon of English in the twentieth century must therefore also cover the adjustments which have taken place in the underlying system, for example with regard to the relative importance of competing word-formation strategies through time.

There is partial systematicity also in the extralinguistic, social, cultural, or psychological factors determining lexical creativity. Some of these, such as the

---

[2] For an example, consider the noun *goer*, whose meaning "active, enterprising person" is clearly based on specific idiomatic uses of *go* (e.g., "give it a go," etc.) and thus much narrower than the "somebody who goes" suggested by the productive agent–noun formation pattern associated with the suffix *-er*.

[3] It may be a sign of the novelty of this latter type that most such forms are recorded inconveniently in the OED – not as verbal entries in their own right but hidden away as difficult-to-categorize combinations in the noun entries corresponding to their first element.

need to replace intensifiers whose meaning has been depleted through inflationary use, are virtual linguistic universals, whose effects will be seen in any language at any time. Others, such as the instability of the terminology of race in twentieth-century English, are due to factors that are temporally and geographically more narrowly circumscribed. Aspects of the fascinating language–culture interface in lexical productivity will be discussed in Section 3.4, "Neologizing in its social context."

While it is useful to separate the linguistic (Section 3.3) and extralinguistic (Section 3.4) constraints on word formation in the presentation here, they obviously interact in practice. For example, the massive twentieth-century increase in acronyms (itself a twentieth-century neologism, with a first OED attestation from 1943), which today represent the most important[4] word-formation process based on shortening (the others being clippings and blends), presupposes widespread literacy in the community. After all, the forms are created and understood on the basis of the written, "visual" word. We thus would not expect acronyms to be a very productive word-formation process in Old and Middle English times, when only a small segment of the population was literate. However, literacy rates in English-speaking communities have been high enough for several centuries to allow the creation of acronyms in principle, and in order to answer the question of why speakers and writers made so little use of this option we need to move from the question of medium – speech or writing – to the sociocultural context. Acronyms are so productive now because they are a direct response to the communicative habitat of the twentieth century. They are a coping strategy helping us to make manageable in everyday communication the vast amount of scientific and scholarly terminology that we seem to need in a world that has grown technologically complex.

3.2   Case studies

The most salient type of neologism is a word which is new in its form (typically because it was borrowed from another language or created with the help of a productive word-formation process of Modern English) and which refers to a concept which is new (either because it denotes a new object/referent in the outer world or a notion not previously lexicalized in the language). The terms *information superhighway* (plus some of its less successful variants), *Google/to google*, and *maquiladora* will be used as illustrations for this category of neologism below.

More often than one would expect, innovation affects the form of a word only, while the associated meaning is carried over practically unchanged from

---

[4] For example, *NTC's dictionary of acronyms and abbreviations*, edited by Richard A. Spears (1993), which concentrates on acronyms current in present-day American English, runs to more than 300 pages. More comprehensive dictionaries of acronyms also include international and technical forms and usually are several times the size of this work.

an old word. From a purely utilitarian perspective, such neologisms are unnecessary because they do not extend the range of concepts which can be expressed lexically in a language. Semantic domains marked by rapid lexical turnover of this kind are colloquial and emotive terms of approval or disapproval. For example, s.v. *awesome*, 3b, the OED records a "trivial use, as an enthusiastic term of commendation: 'marvellous', 'great'; stunning, mind-boggling," of US origin and documented from 1980, which is created by extending more narrow and established meanings of this adjective, thus repeating a similar previous development undergone by *terrific*, which on OED evidence underwent a similar development around 1930 (s.v. *terrific*, 2b). *Over the top*, *wicked*, and *massive*, some further current examples of the phenomenon, will be discussed in greater depth below.[5]

The converse constellation, meaning change without form–change, is also very common. Striking illustration is provided by the recent history of the English verbs of communication, many of which have assumed additional senses in the context of computer-mediated communication. Thus, the extension of a word like *mail* to electronic messages or the verb *chat* to certain institutionalized forms of computer-mediated "talk" will strike a native speaker of English as natural and undeserving of comment. That polysemy is involved becomes apparent only on reflection, or if one looks at other European languages, many of which have borrowed their computer vocabulary from English. In German, for example, *Mail* refers to electronic mail, whereas the traditional term *Post* continues to serve for the traditional referent. Similarly, face-to-face chatting will be *sich unterhalten* (or some more colloquial synonym), but chatting via computer will usually be *chatten*.[6]

The one instance in which the extension of a word's meaning through polysemy tends to be noted – and criticized – by educated members of the community is some cases involving the Latin- and Greek-based formal vocabulary of English. Speakers familiar with the "original" meanings of such words respect the long shadow of etymology and tend to view any independent development of the meanings in English as illegitimate. The call for the use of *depend from* rather than *depend on* (because only the former preposition is compatible with the Latin sense of *de-pendere*, "hang from") is usually quoted in present-day linguistics classes as proof of the benighted and irrational views of eighteenth-century language purists. Obviously, this particular issue was

---

[5] Lest it be thought that words with such a high turnover rate are exclusive to slang or informal English, consider the case of *interdisciplinary*, a buzzword in contemporary academic and funding politics. Its first recorded use in the OED dates from 1937 (see Frank [1988] for ante-datings to 1926), to be followed by *multidisciplinary* (from 1944), and *transdisciplinary* (from 1972). Note that each new form instantiates a highly productive contemporary word-formation pattern, i.e., the use of combining forms derived from classical and neoclassical coinages.

[6] Surveying words for "email" in sixteen European languages, Görlach has noted that "mainly Germanic languages have adopted the loanword whereas others have preferred to calque" (2001: 104).

settled in favor of prevailing community usage long ago, but the twentieth century saw similar battles being fought over the use of *anticipate* in the meaning of "expect," or more recently *cohort* in the sense of "companion" (see Webster [1989: 99–100, 255–256] for a comprehensive documentation and discussion).

An important and productive word-formation strategy in contemporary English is the creation of multi-word lexical units, whose importance has grown in the history of English as a result of the increasingly analytical and isolating typological profile of the language. *In your face* (sometimes spelled *in-yer-face*), for example, has clearly traveled the full course from free syntactic unit ("But surely they can't say that in your face") to multi-word adjective ("an aggressive in-your-face atmosphere that made me want to leave the pub") and is recorded as such in most recent dictionaries of English.[7] By contrast, the status of a lexicalized phrase such as "over the top" (in the sense of "unreasonable, exaggerated") is less secure and will be investigated in more detail below. The concluding case study, on the origin of the lexicalized phrase *nine eleven*, presents an example of linguistic response to an unexpected historic disaster or calamity.

In conclusion to these introductory remarks, it must be pointed out that the documentation for the following case studies is derived from large corpora of spoken English, such as the spoken-demographic BNC or the Longman Corpus of Spoken American English[8] and further digitized databases, from the OED on CD-ROM to the Internet/World-Wide Web, none of which would have been available to the linguist a mere fifteen years ago. The study of lexical innovation thus obviously profits from the digital revolution as much as from any advances in linguistic theorizing, and this reminds us of the fact that "our present facilities" (cf. Bloomfield's statement discussed in Chapter 2) to investigate change in progress have indeed improved tremendously since the days of his classic *Language*.

3.2.1 Information superhighway

In its current dominant sense, this word refers to a network for the high-speed transfer of digitized information. Unlike the personal computer, the monitor, the keyboard, the disk drives, or the mouse, this is a referent which the ordinary PC user has only vague ideas about. Naming it is a task which can be expected to stimulate considerable linguistic creativity, and choosing the familiar highway metaphor is an obvious coping strategy to reduce the complexity of the unknown.

---

[7] The OED (s.v. *face*, 5f) claims an American origin of the expression and documents it from 1976.

[8] I am grateful to Sebastian Hoffmann, Zurich, for assisting with the queries in the Longman Corpus, which is not publicly accessible.

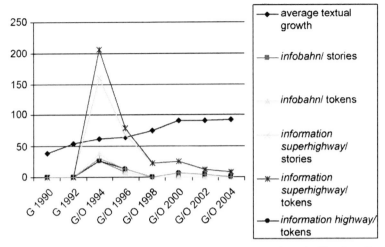

Figure 3.1 Frequency of use of selected computer neologisms in *The Guardian* *(and Observer) on CD-ROM*

The word has a sub-entry in the OED Online (s.v. *information*), which gives a 1983 reference to fiber-optic cable networks as the first citation. The first metaphorical use of *highway* in information technology is recorded for 1949 (s.v. *highway*): "A number of source gates . . . on the right, and a number of destination-gates on the left, are connected by a single bus labelled 'Highway'." *Data highway* and *information highway* are also attested before *information superhighway* emerged.

The time, place, and circumstances of its creation, however, are not the only things about this word which are worth studying. It is even more interesting to investigate when it moved from the technical language of IT experts into general usage, and here neither the OED entries nor the full quotation base are of much help. Frequency shifts in the use of the word show up in newspaper archives, though. Consider, for example, Figure 3.1, which represents uses in the *Guardian* (and, from 1994, the *Observer*) on CD-ROM plotted in two-year intervals from 1990 to 2002.

What can we see from these graphs? The gradually rising line plots the averages calculated from the frequency of ten common collocations (*deep breath, early age, biggest problem, coming year, bad luck, heavy rain, greatly exaggerated, wildly exaggerated, badly damaged, severely damaged*), for which there is no indication whatsoever to indicate that they are currently undergoing change of any kind. As clearly there is no guarantee that the annual CD-ROMs with the *Guardian's* text contain a comparable amount of data, these frequencies serve as a convenient indication of the textual growth of the database over the years. Developments which are drastically out of step with this general trend can be interpreted as signs of a spread or obsolescence of a particular form. A further use of these averages is to assess the amount of text contained on a particular annual compact disc by comparing them to the corresponding values for the BNC, whose size is known to be around 100 million words (see Appendix 3 for details).

How can we interpret the far from normal distribution that we find for the neologisms investigated? The graphs certainly do not tell us who coined the terms, or when they were first used: in the year 1992, almost ten years after the first citations are recorded in the OED, none of the terms in question happens to be attested in the sizable amount of material surveyed here. What shows up in the *Guardian*, a quality paper with a mission to mediate between current developments in various technical fields of expertise and a general educated readership, is the spread of the word into general usage, and – in a subsequent qualitative analysis of the examples – the semantic bleaching an originally technical term is bound to undergo in the process. In this connection, it is also very instructive to compare the number of stories in which a term is used with the number of tokens, as a very systematic pattern emerges. At first, the number of tokens is far greater than the number of stories, because the new phenomenon to be named is the topic of articles which explicitly introduce the subject to the readers, repeating, describing, and defining essential terms in the process. As the new words are institutionalized, the number of stories tends to approach the number of tokens, showing that the new word is used unself-consciously and probably also in articles which are not necessarily devoted to information-technology topics.

As regards the competition among rival terms around 1994,[9] the diagram makes clear that *information superhighway* carried the day, with the less boosterish *information highway* persisting as a minor variant. The emotively/masculinely charged *infobahn*[10] ceased to be used after enjoying a few years of vogue.

The fact that the frequency of successful and unsuccessful coinages alike peaked so obviously around 1994 shows the force of extralinguistic topicality as a determinant and motivator of lexical change. The development of a national fiber-optic network was high on the agenda of the first US Clinton administration (1993–1996), and the word used for promoting it was *information superhighway*. As priorities changed in later years, this particular project was talked and written about less and less. Still, the information superhighway, both as a phenomenon and as a word, has carried on in use. What has disappeared is the fairly precise meaning originally attaching to the word. In

---

[9] In addition to the terms covered in Figure 3.1, the pair *data highway* and *data superhighway* and the variant *bitbahn* (for *infobahn*) played some role. The last-named one was always a bit of a non-starter, and in the 2004 *Guardian*, the most recent database available at the time of writing, none of them are used.

[10] A blend of *information* and the German *autobahn* (highway), probably intended as an allusion to the notorious absence of speed limits on German freeways. The word now lives on mainly in names for various IT companies around the globe.

none of the 2002 citations from the *Guardian* is there any particular connection to fiber-optic cables, and only one has a clear reference to the high-speed exchange of data in general. Typically, *information superhighway* is used in vague metaphorical contexts or as just another way of saying Internet or World Wide Web.[11] As such, it may be losing some of its currency and follow the course of *infobahn*.

It is instructive to compare the distribution of these popular IT terms with recent neologisms from the military domain, another prominent source of lexical renewal throughout the twentieth century. Figure 3.2 shows occurrences of *smokescreen*, *friendly fire*, and *collateral damage* in the *Guardian/Observer*. These three expressions were introduced at different points of time in the twentieth century. The oldest one, *smokescreen*, is attested in the OED as a noun from 1915 and as a verb from 1922. Like the better-known *blitz*, it has gone through the full circle of institutionalization and lexicalization, adding numerous "civilian" meanings which by now have probably become the dominant ones (cf., e.g., "advertising blitzes" and "smokescreen rhetoric"). Next in line is the technical-military use of *friendly*. As an antonym of *enemy* it is attested in the OED from 1925 (in a sub-entry added in 1993). From c. 1976, collocations such as "friendly artillery fire," which suggest accidental damage inflicted on one's own forces, are attested alongside established ones such as "friendly boats" or "friendly Radar station." Widespread use of the collocation *friendly fire* outside military circles dates back to the First Gulf War of the early 1990s. *Collateral damage* is so recent that it is not yet recorded as an institutionalized expression in the OED, though the quotation base contains one 2003 instance of metaphorical use in the entry for *red-top*, a British synonym for popular tabloid newspapers such as the *Sun* or *Daily Mirror* (which are, of course, notorious for their circulation "wars").

The distribution of *friendly fire* is tied most closely to current affairs. When the US or Britain are at war the frequency of the phrase rises in the *Guardian*. *Smokescreen* becomes more frequent in proportion to general textual growth in the database, which is to be expected, as the word is established and now dominantly used metaphorically beyond its military domain of origin. The most interesting case is presented by *collateral damage*, whose emergence in newspaper discourse is clearly due to current affairs but which seems to have captured the popular imagination in a way that *friendly fire* has not. *The Guardian on CD-ROM* for the months of January to March 2004, the most recent material available for comparison at the time of writing, has 8 instances

---

[11] Compare, for example, the following citation from 20 August 2002: "This month, apart from being very hot, has been characterised by a fair amount of hysteria concerning the information superhighway (which is another term for the internet). The upset has come mainly from the two major political parties, and from a spectator's point of view, it's been a lot like watching your grandparents play Grand Theft Auto (which is a game for the Playstation 2 console): they don't understand it, they're pressing the controls too hard, and they're going to break it if they're not careful."

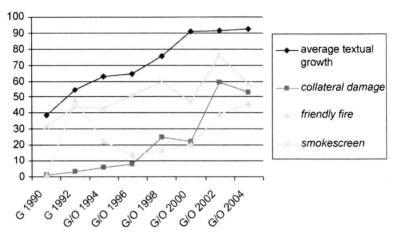

Figure 3.2 Frequency of use of selected military neologisms in *The Guardian*
(and Observer) on CD-ROM

of the expression, 5 of which are used in reference to civilian events, such as,
for example, the following:

> Even assuming that a more aggressive tightening of monetary policy
> would end the house price boom painlessly, the collateral damage to
> manufacturing would be enormous. (*Guardian*, 8 March 2004)

Friendly fire, by contrast, though more frequent in absolute terms (17
occurrences), continues to be almost exclusively used in its original military
meaning.[12] Arguably, therefore, the "successful" neologisms are those whose
statistical distribution closely follows the trend for general textual growth after
the irregular first years of institutionalization with its externally determined
wild ups and downs.

3.2.2 Google *(noun)* and google *(verb)*

These two IT-inspired additions to the English vocabulary are so recent that the
relevant senses are not covered in the OED Online at the time of writing (March
2004). Googling for the word *google*, however, shows that it is firmly established
in all major varieties of English: a search for the form *googled* (chosen to identify
clearly verbal rather than nominal generic or proper-name uses) yielded 1950
examples from ".uk" sites, 1630 from ".edu," 721 from ".ca," 717 from ".au,"
191 from ".nz," 406 from ".za," and 160 from ".ie" (9 March 2004).

---

[12] The one exception being "'Blair ducks bullets on Iraq, but cops friendly fire,' the paper
reported – a reference to the Government's narrow victory over tuition fees" (*Observer*,
1 February 2004).

Google is best known as the name for the popular Web search engine created in 1998 by former Stanford students Larry Page and Sergey Brin. In the span of a few years, the word developed an additional verbal use through conversion or zero-derivation, the highly productive modern English word-formation process effecting change of part-of-speech class without corresponding form change on the base, and a generic use. As is shown by pairs such as *Hoover/to hoover* and *Xerox/to Xerox*, this twofold extension – from proper name to common noun and from noun to verb (which need not necessarily have occurred in this order) – is not without precedent in the recent history of English.

At first sight, the word *Google* seems to meet the definition of a spontaneous creation; that is, a neologism not resulting from borrowing or the use of productive word-formation processes but created "ex nihilo," directly from the raw material of sounds. Closer inspection, however, reveals that its origins are embedded in an etymological haze of some complexity.

The OED lists *google* as an obsolete variant of *goggle*, a form which is preserved in the modern expression *googly eyes*. In addition, there is *goog*, Australian slang for *egg*, which in turn is probably not unrelated to *google*, back-formed from *googly*, which in cricket jargon denotes a ball breaking "from the off, though bowled with apparent leg-break action" (OED, s.v. *googly*). It seems safe to assume that none of these uses provided the motivation for those who named the search engine. They may have been inspired by what the OED lists as *googol*, an informal term for ten raised to the one-hundredth power (10^{100}). The entry has a 1940 citation, which credits the coining of the term to one "Dr. Kasner's nine-year-old nephew . . . who was asked to think up a name for a very big number." We may thus have an example of spontaneous lexical creation, but it is creation at a remove, because for the computer science students developing the search engine *google* was a conventionalized, if technical, word. Whether the millions of users who popularized the Google search engine in a very short time were aware of the established use in the mathematical community may, however, be doubted. After its successful launch, Google (with a capital G) underwent the fate of many similarly successful trade names and went into generic use, also as a verb. The popular site 'Wordspy' (http://www.wordspy.com/words/google.asp – accessed on 14 July 2003) proposes the following definition:

> **google** (GOO.gul) *v.* To search for information on the Web, particularly by using the Google search engine; to search the Web for information related to a new or potential girlfriend or boyfriend. (Note that Google[TM] is a trademark identifying the search technology and services of Google Technologies Inc.)

As is to be expected, the verb *google* when used in this sense is not necessarily restricted to the use of the *Google* engine, but acquires the more general sense of "searching the web through any engine," much as hoovering today can describe the use of any brand of vacuum cleaner. The Wordspy site gives the following relevant citation:[13]

> These days, date-readiness requires roughly the same amount of time, during which the investigative dater, suited up in her regulation black shift and clumpless mascara, gives the boyfriend-applicant a once-over. This process reflects none of the cuddliness implicit in the term "**Googling.**"
> With the assistance of her high-speed Internet connection, she scans and fact-checks her suitor's resume. Her short, buffed nails pull up his credit history, mortgage schedule, publications record, professional reprimands, genealogy and horoscope.
>
> (Leah Eskin, "Getting to know ALL about you,"
> *Chicago Tribune*, 9 February 2003)

3.2.3 Maquiladora

The OED defines this word as "a factory or workshop owned by a U.S. or other foreign company, which employs low-cost local labour to assemble goods (esp. electronic equipment or clothing) from imported components, and then exports the completed products to the company's country of origin" and gives citations from the year 1978. The word was borrowed from Mexican Spanish, and – on the basis of results from the Corpus de Referencia del Español Actual (CREA) of the Spanish Academy (http://corpus.rae.es/creanet.html) – it is still largely restricted to Mexican Spanish (59 of 75 instances, with 15 coming from other Latin American sources and only one mention in a document from Spain). Nor has the word become established in varieties other than American English. The British National Corpus contains nine instances of *maquiladora(s)*, all referring to US–Mexican economic cooperation. A web search retrieved 173, 44, and 29 instances from the Australian (".au"), New Zealand (".nz"), and South African (".za") domains respectively, which is in stark contrast to the 6,540 instances from the dominantly American ".edu" domain (access date 8 March 2004).

This restriction is interesting, as the type of economic cooperation in question is certainly not unknown in parts of the world other than the US–Mexican border. There is no widely used existing synonym, and American coinages generally tend to spread fast into other varieties of English. However, there is little sign that *maquiladora* is about to replace the technical term *export-processing zone* (frequently abbreviated as *EPZ*)[14] in the near future.

---

[13] It is uses such as these which prompted an – apparently unsuccessful – intervention by Google's lawyers to have the entry removed from this online glossary (cf. Jonathan Duffy, "Google calls in the 'language police'," BBC News Online, 20 June 2003, http://news.bbc.co.uk/2/low/uk_news/3006486.stm).

[14] Ironically, unlike *maquiladora*, neither the full form nor the acronym is as yet entered in the OED.

3.2.4 Over the top, wicked, massive

The three cases of change studied in this section all show how existing and long-established words and expressions may acquire additional senses and uses through extending polysemy.

In addition to its literal meaning and two established idiomatic uses,[15] *over the top* has recently acquired an idiomatic meaning which the OED (s.v. *top*, 22c) defines as "beyond reasonable limits, too far, into exaggeration." Two good illustrations from the spoken BNC are:

> But I still think Tesco's is the cheapest supermarket, I do, Waitrose is way over the top. (KBF 10131)

– and the laconic but typical:

> Bit over the top innit? (KD3 5413)

In some examples from the written BNC texts, *over the top* is used in attributive function, modifying nouns and displaying typically adjectival features such as premodification by adverbs:

> And it all meant another marvellous morning of wonderfully over the top tabloid headlines. Bliss! (K3P 90–91)

The two earliest OED citations are from 1968 and 1974. By the early 1990s, when the recordings for the spoken-demographic component of the BNC were made, the usage was well established in all age groups, with the idiomatic sense being the only or most likely interpretation in at least 26 out of 90 examples. By contrast, there is only one clear case in the contemporary and similarly sized Longman Corpus of Spoken American English, which provides convincing apparent-time support for the British origin of the construction suspected by Heacock and Cassidy (1998: 97–98). In addition to being new, this usage is thus interesting also because it is among the few recent lexical innovations which have traveled from British English into American English, rather than (as is usual) the other way round.

Wicked is one of those all-purpose positive evaluators exemplified by *terrific* and *awesome* in the introductory discussion to this section. The history of the term in the twentieth century is somewhat convoluted, as the OED attests the first relevant use in a 1920 US source (s.v. *wicked* 3b, glossed as "excellent, splendid; remarkable"). While the use seems to have remained marginal in American English, there was a surge of popularity in recent British English from around 1989 (Tulloch 1991: 309). This makes it a perfect candidate for an apparent-time analysis in the spoken-demographic texts of the BNC, which were sampled in the early 1990s (Table 3.1).

---

[15] "Be in excess of a quota or goal" and, in military slang, "leave the trenches for attack."

Table 3.1. Wicked – *frequency in the spoken-demographic BNC per million words by age group*

Age group	Frequency (n/ 1,000,000)
0–14	178.05
15–24	38.21
25–34	14.58
35–44	15.69
45–59	6.86
60+	10.50

Literal uses are rare outside the two oldest age groups. It is often difficult to distinguish between ironic uses of *wicked* in its literal senses and the routinized evaluator use, but the statistical trend is so clear that there cannot be any doubt about the rapid spread of the usage among young people in Britain. Unfortunately, a second search aimed at identifying uses of *wicked* followed by an adjective – that is, clear instances of the evaluator use – yielded only five examples, of which just one was an unambiguous instance. Expectedly, it came from a 13-year-old: "they look like wicked nice girls" (KSN 1433). Not surprisingly in view of the salience of such features of teen language for adults, the usage was commented on by older informants.[16]

A comparative analysis of the Longman Corpus of Spoken American English (at around 5 million words, 25 percent or so greater than the spoken-demographic sample of the BNC) yielded a far smaller number of instances of *wicked*. Interestingly enough, however, true evaluator syntax was attested regularly in collocations such as *wicked long*, *wicked thirsty*, *wicked bad* (twice), *wicked expensive*, *wicked dangerous*, *wicked nice*, *wicked late*, *wicked fast* and *wicked pissed*. These figures show that the US slang use pinpointed as the origin of the expression in the OED still persists, but that *wicked* is not a teenage vogue word in American English.[17]

---

[16] The following extract is from KBH 5ff., the participants in the conversation both being in their thirties.

Carole: This will get modern usage of words. Of, one of the words that she was talking about, people have started using wicked for <unclear> a normal phrase. I mean, it doesn't mean what it says in the dictionary any more.

Pauline: That's a really wicked thing to say, he went, no it's not it's bad, it's not wicked. He thinks of wicked as being good, he doesn't, cause Mandy says wicked.

Carole: Yeah.
          <pause> Well, that's the idea anyway.

Pauline: He goes round saying wicked, it's his favourite word. <pause>

[17] This market at the time seems to have been cornered by *awesome* (133 instances in LCSAE against 0 in the spoken-demographic BNC).

Table 3.2. Massive – *frequency in the spoken-demographic BNC per million words by age group*

Age group	Frequency (n/1,000,000)
0–14	76.31
15–24	108.60
25–34	26.24
35–44	22.82
45–49	24.71
60+	12.00

Time has not stood still since the 1990s, and *wicked* is being complemented with a potential successor in British English, the word *massive*. The use of *massive* as an evaluator is not yet recorded in the OED, but already well attested in the BNC, with the expected age-grading (Table 3.2).

The following extract from a conversation between Andy (18 years), Joanne (13) and Helena (16) is typical (KCE 2693 ff.):[18]

Andy: Did I see the rainbow? I was in it.
Joanne: It was abs– shut up, it was absolutely <pause> <--> massive. <-->
Helena: <--> What, in the <--> rain?
Andy: In the rain, yes.
Joanne: <--> Absolutely massive. <-->
Helena: <--> So was I. <-->
Joanne: Absolutely massive it was.
Helena: Cos I had to walk home <--> from school today. <-->
Joanne: <--> By Tesco's it was <--> it was coming out the field.

Unlike the corresponding use of *wicked*, which is probably American in origin and subsequently spread to Britain, figures from the Longman Corpus suggest a reverse development here. At 27 instances, *massive* is comparatively rare in spoken American English, and traditional collocations such as "a massive coronary attack," etc. far outnumber generalized uses such as "a massive party." While, as has been mentioned above, the OED does not yet recognize the use of *massive* under discussion, its entry for *massive* (noun) refers to an originally Black British use of this word in the sense of "a group or gang of young people from a particular place; the people who follow a particular type of music, esp. a

---

[18] That *massive* in this use is still in fashion in British English is shown by current British Web material. For example, the BBC homepage's "Quick Fix" for linguistically challenged holidaymakers suggests "really massive" and "that's massive" as translations of "das ist ja krass" und "konkret krass" in its "Cool-German" section (http://www.bbc.co.uk/languages/german/quickfi/coolgerman.shtml – accessed on 1 August 2004).

form of dance music, regarded as such a group." This may well have provided a motivation for the development in the adjective.

3.2.5 Nine eleven

Nine eleven, or *September eleven*, have become the most common conventional expressions used to refer to the terrorist attacks on the World Trade Center in New York City and the Pentagon in Washington[19] on 11 September 2001. Depending on one's perspective, it is consoling or disconcerting to see that, as with other historical calamities before, what was horror beyond words was conveniently reduced to a fixed expression within a few weeks. As one of the doyens of British history writing remarked bitterly:

> For an old and sceptical historian born in the year of the Russian Revolution, it [11 September] had everything that was bad about the twentieth century: massacres, high but unreliable technology, the announcements that a global struggle to the death was now taking place once again as real life imitated Hollywood spectaculars. Public mouths flooded the western world with froth as hacks searched for words about the unsayable and unfortunately found them.   (Hobsbawm 2003: 411)

In recent US history these events are rivaled only by the Japanese attack on Pearl Harbor on 7 December 1941 in their unexpectedness and the number of casualties. In both instances, contemporary usage fluctuated for a short time before consensus was reached on a name for the national disaster: the "Pearl Harbor Raid" or "Attack" in the first case, and "September 11" or "9–11" in the second. Aitchison (2003), the first systematic study of the linguistic consequences of the attacks, quotes a contemporary witness on the apparent inability of people to settle on a name in the wake of the disaster:

> Oddly, for all the media coverage . . . the events in New York, Washington and Pennsylvania have not yet found a name. Atrocity, outrage, terrorist attack: nothing quite conveys the enormity of it all, and "apocalypse" is overdoing it a little in the absence of four horsemen. The French vision of "megacatastrophe" comes close.
> (Douglas Fraser, *Sunday Herald*, 30 September 2002,
> quoted in Aitchison 2003: 195)

However, in a more detailed analysis of US newspaper coverage of the events Meyer (2003) finds evidence that *nine eleven/September eleven*, the expression eventually prevailing and replacing alternatives such as "Bloody Tuesday" or "Twin Towers Disaster," caught on very early. He supplies the

---

[19]   And a further planned attack which failed to reach its target and ended in a plane crash in Pennsylvania.

following citations, which make explicit some of the sometimes rather fortuitous motivating factors in the naming process – such as the accidental parallel[20] between the date of the attack and the American emergency phone number:

> You want a defining national moment for your lifetime? No? You don't have a choice in the matter. If Dec. 7, 1941, lives in infamy, then Tuesday is going to endure as the day that evil ambushed America. Sept. 11, 2001. The ninth month and 11th day. 9–11. 9-1-1. Apocalypse. Now.   (*Times Union*, 12 September 2001)

> Shoreline resident Michael Rush carries a personal memorial to the victims of Tuesday's terrorist attacks on his walk yesterday from Shoreline to Seattle Center along Highway 99. On his flag, the twin towers of the World Trade Center stand in for the "11" in "9–11," the date of the tragedy and the call for emergency help.   (*Seattle Times*, 15 September 2001)

After a few more days the expression seems to have been accepted by the general public and is being used entirely unselfconsciously, and without explanatory glosses:

> We are beyond celebrity gossip and frivolity now; beyond media-created sideshows. That's a recurring theme of these post-9–11 days.
>   (*Boston Herald*, 20 September 2001)

> If 9–11 was a wake-up call, we can choose its lessons.
>   (*Washington Post*, 5 October 2001)

> "But it's not just the laid-off worker," she said. "It's also the individual who may have just bought the new car or got the house, then gets laid off. Everybody's vulnerable right now. That's one of the truths of 9–11."   (*Boston Globe*, 15 November 2001)

In March 2002, the New York-based writer Siri Hustvedt looked back on the institutionalization of this expression as completed:

> 9/11 has become international shorthand for a catastrophic morning in the United States. . . . The two numbers have entered the vocabulary of horror.   (quoted in Aitchison 2003: 199)

At the time of writing the expression still awaits inclusion in the OED Online. The OED may also have to modify its entry for *Ground Zero* (s.v. *ground* [n.] 18a), which it defines as "that part of the ground situated immediately under an exploding bomb, esp. an atomic one" and attests from 1946.

---

[20] The parallel rests on the American convention of giving the month first, and the day second, which is the converse of the British and European model.

3.2.6 A note on lexical obsolescence

Lexical innovation is, of course, paralleled by lexical obsolescence. This is more difficult to document for two reasons. First, the fact that a word stops being used, or a meaning stops being current, is less striking than the appearance of new word forms or meanings. Second, loss of currency of vocabulary is a complicated notion to define in a literate culture. English dictionaries are full of words which are extremely unlikely to turn up in contemporary corpora. This does not automatically make them archaisms. Even if a word can no longer be attested in contemporary general-purpose writing, it may persist in specialist discourses. Thus, the word *recusant* – denoting a Catholic refusing to attend Anglican services (cf. the OED definition) – is not now part of the politico-religious discourse in contemporary Britain but continues to be encountered in historical works on the seventeenth century. Similarly, most contemporary speakers will have little occasion to use words such as *brougham, landau,* and the many other terms for types of horse-drawn carriages current in the nineteenth century, but all these words will retain a marginal presence for as long as the general public reads nineteenth-century fiction or historians consult nineteenth-century sources. Even more interesting is a case such as *township* – a word which has largely become obsolete in British English but continues in vital, if highly differentiated, use in several ex-colonial varieties (see OED, s.v. *township,* 5, 6a, 6b for current US/Canadian, Australian/New Zealand, and South African usage respectively).

For a morphologically interesting example of an early twentieth-century vogue word which has largely gone out of use, consider the verb *to maffick.* The OED glosses it as "to celebrate uproariously . . ., esp. on an occasion of national celebration." Formally, it is a back-formation on the place name *Mafeking,* where during the South African wars of 1899–1902 a British garrison was relieved after a fierce siege. Interestingly enough, the word did not pass into memory along with the war that created it but outlived it, albeit with increasingly derogatory connotations. The last OED quotation is from 1990, and from a South African source. Contemporary Web evidence is extremely sparse, and mostly metalinguistic, in the sense that it discusses rather than uses the verb.

The examples discussed above show lexical losses brought about by changes in the physical and social environment. But, just as there is lexical innovation not prompted by such external stimuli, some cases of obsolescence are not determined by changes in the extralinguistic referent. The gradual decline of *wireless* against *radio* in British English in the second half of the twentieth century is an obvious and much-commented-on example, and so are informal terms of approval/disapproval, whose life-cycle is notoriously short. Denison, for example, has commented on the "peculiarly old-fashioned (and upper/middle-class British)" (1998: 126) connotations of the premodifying adverb *frightfully* and goes on to say that:

I expect that native-speaking readers of this chapter will find particular times or places suggested to them by some of the intensifiers in *awfully kind*, *dreadfully nice*, *jolly difficult*, *main happy*, *dead friendly*, *real smart*, *clean wrong*, *right fed up*, *sure pretty*, *wicked funny*, *pure brilliant*.   (1998: 127)

In the short time since the publication of this contribution, *massive* has been added to *wicked* and *pure* as an all-purpose positive evaluator (see above).

3.3   Major trends

New word forms can arise in three ways – by borrowing from other languages, by drawing on the language's own productive word-formation processes, and (in a very small number of cases) by creating words directly from the raw material of sounds. The three strategies have been illustrated above with the words *maquiladora*, a borrowing from Mexican Spanish; *information superhighway*, a compound whose second element has a complex internal structure; and the verb *google*, which combines spontaneous creation involved in the creation of its original nominal base with a very productive modern English word-formation process, namely conversion.

From tracing the history of individual new word forms (or new meanings of existing forms), we will now turn to the investigation of general trends in contemporary lexical creativity. Questions that could be asked, for example, concern the overall statistical growth of the vocabulary of standard English, or the growth or decline of the productivity of individual word-formation patterns.

3.3.1 Measuring the overall growth of the vocabulary

A good first approach to measuring vocabulary size would seem to be to analyze dictionaries, especially works which go through regular and systematic updatings. Linguists who have tried it, however, generally report unsatisfactory results. John Algeo (1998), for example, who has tested the method in great depth, and with some results, nevertheless cautions against the use of the method as a means of estimating comprehensive trends in lexical change and expansion. The most damaging drawback in his view is that often fairly drastic and short-term changes in lexicographical practice obliterate the underlying "real" trends in word formation and borrowing:

> The neat and impressive-looking graphs that have been drawn to show the peaking of word-making in the vigorous, language-intoxicated high Renaissance, its deep valley of decline in the eighteenth century, and its subsequent rise to a new, if lesser, high in the mid-nineteenth century show nothing about the language. What they show is the extent and assiduousness with which the OED volunteers read and excerpted books.   (1998: 64)

Another problem pointed out by Algeo is that lexicographers' assessments of lexical creativity are sometimes distorted by cultural stereotypes. Thus, there is a tendency to celebrate the lexical inventiveness of speakers of new Englishes and nonstandard varieties, which will result in a fuller documentation of new words or slang terms, whereas standard British English is considered comparatively stodgy and sterile in this regard. As he (1998: 73) convincingly argues, such claims usually evaporate when formal written British English is compared to comparable stylistic ranges elsewhere (or when more colloquial data from Britain are admitted to the comparison).

If estimates based on dictionaries are unreliable, one alternative is to go straight to the corpora or, in the case of the OED, the quotation base, and find ways of measuring morphological productivity there, as has been done by Plag (1999) or Baayen and Renouf (1996). This method may work very well for the study of individual word-formation patterns, but unfortunately it is extremely difficult to integrate the case studies into a comprehensive survey of the major trends in recent vocabulary development.

The one finding which is supported by practically all studies of recent lexical change in English is that borrowing from other languages, which was an extremely important source of lexical enrichment from the Norman Conquest to around 1750, is much reduced in importance today – especially if one does not include instances of neoclassical word manufacturing in the counts. This is demonstrated by, among others, Algeo (1998: 97) and Bauer (1994: 34), and is also evident from the typical list of quarterly updates from the OED Online discussed below (Figures 3.3 and 3.4).

One resource which was not available to Bauer and Algeo for their calculations of vocabulary growth is the online version of the OED. An obvious advantage of the continuous updating of this online dictionary is that the gap between the origin of a new word and its being recorded in the dictionary will be narrowed considerably, which is, of course, particularly important in the study of recent and ongoing lexical change. The OED Online offers quarterly updates, which combine routine revisions of entries in a span of the alphabet with high-priority "out-of-sequence" additions over the whole alphabetical range. For example, 13 March 2003 saw the publication of entries from *Motswana* to *mussy* for the New Edition. In this stretch of the alphabet there were 398 completely new entries, an additional 320 sub-entries added to existing ones, and 104 out-of-sequence entries from all over the alphabet (see Appendix 4 for details).

As can easily be seen from the lists in Appendix 4, the vast majority of these new words are very uncommon and of specialist interest only. Some are not even new, but merely reflect the OED's current policy of extending its coverage beyond British and American sources (Price 2003). But several features of the list are characteristic. For example, the astounding productivity of the combining form *multi-*, which – like *poly-*, *super-*, *hyper-*, *cyber-*, and many others – was first introduced into English in a small number of

multi-address, *a.*
multi-addressing, *n.*
multi-angle, *a.*
multi-angled, *a.*
multibarrel, *n.* and *a.*
multibit, *a.*[1]
multibit, *a.*[2]
multibuy, *n.* and *a.*
multicalibre, *a.* and *n.*
multicast, *a.* and *n.*
multicast, *v.*
multicasting, *n.*
multicell, *a.*
multicentrically, *adv.*
multi-channelled, *a.*
multi-choke, *n.* and *a.*
multicoat, *v.*
multi-coat, *a.*
multi-coated, *a.*
multi-coating, *n.*
multicopy, *n.* and *a.*
multicopying, *n.*
multicult, *n.* and *a.*
multiculti, *a.* and *n.*
multiculturalist, *n.* and *a.*
multiculturism, *n.*
multicursal, *a.*
multi-cylindered, *a.*
multidrug, *a.*
multiexposure, *n.* and *a.*
multiflex, *a.*
multifocally, *adv.*
multifork, *a.*
multiforked, *a.*
multiformly, *adv.*
multifractal, *a.* and *n.*
multi-fuelled, *a.*
multifunctionality, *n.*
multigene, *n.* and *a.*

multigenic, *a.*
multigravid, *a.*
multi-gym, *n.*
multihole, *a.*
multilamellated, *a.*
multilayeredness, *n.*
multilayering, *n.*
multiline, *a.* and *n.*
multilocularity, *n.*
multi-male, *a.*
multi-member, *a.*
multi-membered, *a.*
multi-mike, *a.* and *n.*
multimiked, *a.*
multimiking, *n.*
multimineral, *a.* and *n.*
multimodally, *adv.*
multi-mode, *a.* and *n.*
multimorph, *n.* and *a.*
multinuclearity, *n.*
multipack, *n.*
multipass, *a.*
multipathing, *n.*
multi-pattern, *a.*
multipedal, *a.*
multiphonic, *a.*
multiphonics, *n.*
multiplatform, *a.*
multi-play, *a.*
multiplayer, *a.* and *n.*
multiplicate, *v.*
multiplicated, *a.*[2]
multiplicating, *n.*
multiport, *n.* and *a.*[2]
multi-port, *a.*[1]
multipotency, *n.*
multipotentiality, *n.*
multiprogrammability, *n.*
multiprogrammable, *a.*

multiregional, *a.*
multiregionalism, *n.*
multiregionalist, *n.*
multiring, *a.*
multiroom, *a.*
multiroomed, *a.*
multiserver, *a.*
multiservice, *a.*
multisession, *a.*
multi-skill, *a.*
multi-skilled, *a.*
multi-skilling, *n.*
multi-speciality, *a.*
multi-specialty, *a.*
multistandard, *a.*
multistate, *a.*
multi-station, *a.*
multistrand, *a.* and *n.*
multistratal, *a.*
multistratified, *a.*
Multisync, *n.* and *a.*
multitask, *v.*
multitasker, *n.*
multithread, *v.*
multithreading, *n.*
multitone, *a.*
multitrack, *v.*
multitracked, *a.*
multitracker, *n.*
multitracking, *n.*
multi-utility, *a.* and *n.*
multivalver, *n.*
multivariable, *a.*
multivesicular, *a.*
multivocality, *n.*
multiwell, *a.*
multiwindow, *a.*
multiwindowed, *a.*
multi-year, *a.*

Figure 3.3 March 2003 OED updates for words containing the combining form
multi-

Latin borrowings (*multiply, multifarious,* etc.), then spread into new technical
and scientific terms such as *multi-dimensional* and finally generalized to forms
such as *multiwindowed,* one of several comparable formations in the list in
Figure 3.3.[21]

Multiwindow(ed) is not different from *many-windowed,* and *multi-problem* is
essentially the same as "with many problems." Such correspondences point

---

[21] Just to illustrate the immense productivity of the combining form, an almost equal
number of additional words is listed in the entry for *multi-* itself, and some further cases
are added to existing entries for words beginning with *multi-.*

apotemnophilia, *n.*
arsehole, *n.*
arseholed, *a.*
arse-lick, *v.*
arse-licker, *n.*
ass-backward, *adv.* and *a.*
ass-backwards, *adv.* and *a.*
backassward, *a.*
backasswards, *adv.*
bagsy, *v.*
bass-ackward, *a.*
bass-ackwards, *adv.* and *a.*
Batswana, *n.* and *a.*
bed-space, *n.*
bigorexia, *n.*
bigorexic, *a.* and *n.*
blog, *n.*
blog, *v.*
blogger, *n.*
blogging, *n.*
bruschetta, *n.*
bumbershoot, *n.*
chronon, *n.*
Cineplex, *n.*
Claddagh, *n.*
clapometer, *n.*
clear water, *n.*
clientelism, *n.*
clientelistic, *a.*
clientism, *n.*
clocked, *a.*[2]
clocker, *n.*[3]
clocking, *n.*[2]
dead-leg, *v.*
dead leg, *n.*
deaf-blind, *a.* and *n.*
deaf-blindness, *a.* and *n.*
deal breaker, *n.*
disabled list, *n.*
disappeared, *a.* and *n.*
dischuffed, *a.*
disintermediate, *v.*
disintermediated, *a.*
disintermediator, *n.*
dolee, *n.*
doley, *n.*
Down, *n.*[4]
dragon boat, *n.*
dragon lady, *n.*

Dungeons and Dragons, *n.*
dysmorphia, *n.*
dysmorphic, *a.*
dysmorphism, *n.*
dysmorphophobia, *n.*
dysmorphophobic, *a.* and *n.*
early doors, *n.* and *adv.*
emotional intelligence, *n.*
extranet, *n.*
felch, *v.*
First World, *n.* and *a.*
First Worlder, *n.*
flat-pack, *n.* and *a.*
fly-through, *n.* and a.
Fortean, *a.* and *n.*
Forteana, *n.*
frittata, *n.*
funkadelia, *n.*
funkadelic, *a.* (and *n.*)
Furby, *n.*
FX, *n.*
geek, *n.*
geek, *v.*
geekdom, *n.*
geeked, *a.*
geekfest, *n.*
geekhood, *n.*
geekiness, *n.*
geekish, *a.*
geekishness, *n.*
geeksville, *n.*
geeky, *a.*
gomer, *n.*[3]
intranet, *n.*
leaderless resistance, *n.*
lollo biondo, *n.*
lollo rosso, *n.*
lone parent, *n.* and *a.*
lookism, *n.*
lookist, *a.* and *n.*
novela, *n.*
pear-shaped, *a.*
pepper-spray, *v.*
pepper spray, *n.*
Polle syndrome, *n.*
rageaholic, *n.* and *a.*
rellie, *n.*
rello, *n.*
rent-a-quote, *a.* and *n.*

reoffender, *n.*
right on, *int.* (*n.*) and *a.*
rugger bugger, *n.*
rumpo, *n.*
rumpy-pumpy, *n.*
scenester, *n.*
schemie, *n.*
screenager, *n.*
SFX, *n.*[1]
SFX, *n.*[2]
Shake 'n Bake, *n.*
Shake 'n Bake, *v.*
sizeism, *n.*
sizeist, *a.* and *n.*
slaphead, *n.*
slap-headed, *a.*
spread bet, *n.*
spread betting, *n.*
stude, *n.*
studenty, *a.*
studmuffin, *n.*
Sturgeon's Law, *n.*
surf and turf, *n.*
sussed, *a.*
taqueria, *n.*
telenovela, *n.*
three-peat, *n.*
three-peat, *v.*
tobaccy, *n.*
transgender, *a.* and *n.*
transgendered, *a.* and *n.*
transgenderism, *n.*
transgenderist, *n.*
tween, *n.*[2]
tween-age, *n.* and *a.*
tweenager, *n.*
tweenie, *n.*
twelve-step, *v.*
twelve step, *v.*
twelve-stepper, *n.*
unplugged, *a.*
UNSCOM, *n.*
wakeboard, *n.*
wakeboard, *v.*
wakeboarder, *n.*
wakeboarding, *n.*
weblog, *n.*
weblogger, *n.*
weblogging, *n.*

Figure 3.4 OED updates – out-of-sequence entries

towards one possible reason for the popularity of the combining form. It increases options for nominal premodification and therefore works as a textual compression strategy: "multi-problem families" or "multi-problem violent youths" – to borrow two typical contemporary uses of the word – are shorter than "families with many problems" or "violent youths with many problems." The *multi*-forms also sound more technical than the *many*-variants and, in an age which thrives on the trivialization of expert terminologies in everyday speech (on which see section 3.4 below), this may be a further reason for the popularity of the combining form.

The most interesting part of the list is certainly the out-of-sequence entries (Figure 3.4). These were published because they are current in contemporary general English and the OED lexicographers considered their inclusion urgent.

In general, this list, like most other quarterly updates, bears out the assessment of contemporary lexical developments in Bauer (1994) and Algeo (1998). Borrowings from other languages, such as *lollo biondo*, *lollo rosso*, *taqueria* or *telenovela* are relatively rare, and a large number of word forms are based on shortening processes of various kinds. For example, *blog* is clipped from "weblog." *SFX*, pronounced /ɛsɛfɛks/, is a playful initialism representing "sound effects") through punning on the identity between the pronunciation of the final two letters and one colloquial pronunciation of the word *effects*. That the list affords an interesting glimpse into the social and cultural contexts of the use of English in the late twentieth century is a point which will be returned to in section 3.4 below.

Even with the quarterly updates, however, we still look at individual new words rather than general trends in lexical expansion. In addition to monitoring the quarterly updates, I have therefore used several of the advanced search strategies provided by the OED Online in order to get an idea of the relative productivity of the paths of lexical enrichment in nineteenth- and twentieth-century English.

In a first attempt at measuring vocabulary growth globally, a search was carried out for any new entry first attested between 1901 and 2000. It yielded a total of 28,317 (22,646 from the Second Edition [1989] and a further 5,671 from the New [Online] Edition), while the corresponding search for the period 1801 to 1900 produced 68,073 (61,047 from the Second Edition and a further 7,026 from the New Edition). That these frequencies should reflect an actual dramatic decrease in lexical creativity in the twentieth century is unlikely. Much rather, the explanation is that much work still remains to do for lexicographers of present-day English.

This also explains why there is an apparent decrease in lexical creativity as one moves through the twentieth century. New entries attested first (second and new edition combined) number as follows:

- 2,485 for the period 1901–1905
- 2,056 for the period 1921–1925.

Table 3.3. *OED Online – new words first attested in the twentieth century*

Period	Second Edition	New Edition
1901–1905	abiotrophy, abstentionism, accelerometer, acetoacetic, achieving [as participial adj.], acholuria, achondrite, acron, actinobacillosis, actinotherapy	approximant [noun], clocker, creative [noun], Everywoman, mac [noun], MacConkey, machinofacture, Maconochie, macrergate, macrogametocyte
1921–1925	abmigration, Abo/abo, acallosal, ace [verb], acidophilus, Acridid, adamantinoma, adamsite, Adlerian, adnex	360-degree [adjective], boff, botch-up, Claddagh, Coleman, comfort zone, genetic modification, gimp, headcount, internal auditor
1941–1945	abortee, absent [quasi-preposition], acrocentric, acronym, actin, actinide, actomyosin, adage, Adamesque, add-on	America Firster, Bharatanatyam, boff [noun], boffo, callback, card-carrying, changeup, con [noun], dog-and-pony, doh [interjection]
1961–1965	ablator, abscisin, Acapulco, access [verb], aceramic, achiasmate, achiasmatic, acidy, acritarch, acrolect	all-you-can-eat, amphitelic, arse-licker, A-team, auteur, bait and switch, benchmark [verb], bitstream, blag, blagger
1981–1985	ableism, acetogenic, acumentin, adaptationalism, adaptationism, add-in, Aerobie, AIDS, aliteracy, amnio	24–7, abortuary, A-lister, am-dram, app, arseholed, asteroseismology, balti, barista, B-boy

- 1,402 for the period 1941–1945
- 1,708 for the period 1961–1965
- 475 for the period 1981–1985.[22]

Numbers are not all, though. It is also interesting to look at the kind of material one discovers in this way. Table 3.3 gives the first ten words returned for each of the above searches, separated according to whether they are from the Second Edition or the New Edition.

As in most of the lists of OED neologisms discussed so far, the one hundred words assembled here are unlikely to be used by, or even known to, ordinary speakers of English. This, however, is not the point here. What the list shows is that the collecting priorities for the New Edition must have been completely different from those employed for the first and the second. While the Second-Edition entries are dominantly technical terms, the priority of the New Edition seems to have been slang, multi-word lexical items, and idiomatic phrases. In

---

[22] These figures were obtained on 22 July 2003. Later re-counts will give slightly different ones, without, however, altering the fundamental tendency.

other words, each edition constructs its own picture of lexical trends in twentieth-century English.

In the digital OED, searches can be conducted for words borrowed from specific languages first attested at various periods of time. To get an idea of the reliability of results thus obtained, I decided to undertake a comparative study of recent Yiddish and Spanish borrowings,[23] as these two languages stand for contrasting types of language contact in the history of English. Yiddish was not a significant contributor to the vocabulary of English before the second half of the nineteenth century, when mass immigration of Eastern European Jews started to the United States, and – to a lesser extent – to Britain. The OED lists one single Yiddish word as an addition to the English vocabulary for the entire eighteenth century: *minyan* – a technical term in the context of orthodox religious practice ("quorum of ten males over the age of thirteen").[24] Stratified searches for the nineteenth and twentieth centuries reveal the distribution shown in Table 3.4.

Given the search strategy used – a twin requirement for "Yiddish" to be the etymological source and for the entry to be "first cited" in the period in question – some under-collection was inevitable. For example, a word such as *mohel* ("circumcizer," attested in English since 1613 from Hebrew and later re-borrowed as *moel* from Yiddish) would not be returned. The impact of this factor, however, is minimal, and it is clear that the peak of borrowing showing up in Table 3.4 coincides with the period of mass immigration and subsequent language shift of most immigrants to English. With Yiddish ceasing to be an important spoken language in the Jewish communities of Britain and the US in the second half of the twentieth century, the decline in the number of borrowings towards the end of the century is to be expected.

Not unexpectedly, early and late borrowings are not merely different in quantity but also in quality. In the forty-year period from 1801 to 1840 the following five words are attested: *mamaliga*, a Romanian food term which may have entered English indirectly through Yiddish, and four slang terms (*cocum, kibosh, shoful, finnip*) for which the citations suggest an origin in language contact between lower-class speakers of Yiddish and English for example in the East End of London, but certainly a contact situation still outside the social

---

[23] Yiddish borrowings are usually identified directly as such in the etymologies. For Spanish borrowings, the search was conducted conservatively, using the presence of the abbreviation "Sp." in the text of the etymology as a criterion, which means that some words of Spanish origin may have been missed. Searching for "Spanish" as well, on the other hand, would have led to considerable over-collection.

[24] A survey of the period 1300–1799 revealed a few more possible cases, which, however, most likely are not borrowings through face-to-face language contact between speakers of Yiddish and English. For example, *mamzer* (first attested in 1562) entered the English language via Hebrew and the post-classical Latin of the Vulgate translation of the Bible. As such, the term remains confined to theological discourse. On the basis of more colloquial twentieth-century citations, the OED assumes recent re-borrowing from Yiddish.

Table 3.4. *Nineteenth- and twentieth-century borrowings from Yiddish in the OED*

Entries first attested in	Second Edition	New Edition	Total
1801–1820	—	1	1
1821–1840	4	—	4
1841–1860	7	1	8
1861–1880	3	2	5
1881–1900	38	11	49
1901–1920	19	3	22
1921–1940	31	—	31
1941–1960	18	4	22
1961–1980	18	4	22
1981–2000	1	—	1

mainstream. Unsurprisingly in the case of such slang terms, some of the etymologies given are rather dubious (e.g., *kibosh*).

For the period from 1881 to 1920, the statistical peak of the borrowing (61 entries), we get a broad variety of terms covering:

- food, garments, etc.: *blintze, gefüllte fish, kreplach, kittel, koppel, yarmulke*
- (typically Jewish) social institutions: *rav, reb, rebbe, rebitzim, shadchan* (marriage broker), *shegetz* (gentile, or assimilated Jew), *Sedra*
- slang terms, from the mildly taboo to the generally informal: *putz, chutzpah, schnorrer, schlock, luftmensch*
- interjections: *nu, nebbich* (also in nominal use: "non-entity")
- abstract/ideological concepts: *Yiddishist, Yiddishkeit.*

The variety of terms and even more so the variety of citations suggest massive language contact during mass immigration, with speakers of Yiddish being part of the social mainstream in British and American centers of immigration, interacting with the English-speaking population and, ultimately, shifting to English in the process.

The two lists covering the years from 1961 to 2000 are largely made up of informal and slang terms which seem to function as linguistic markers of ethnic identity in informal registers of present-day American English. While most of them have straightforward Yiddish sources (e.g., *glitzy, heimisch, klutz, kvell, schlepp, schmatte*), some more specific meanings and uses have arisen in response to the social context of Jewish life in the US (for example, *Hymie* and *schvartze(r)*). A noteworthy item in the list is *meister*, which has developed into a very productive combining form (*schlockmeister, spinmeister* etc.).

In this particular investigation, the results from the OED are valuable because they flesh out what we know about English–Yiddish language contact. However, the reason that the method works well in this case may be that we are studying the nineteenth century and not the more recent past. A study of twentieth-century borrowings from Spanish undertaken on the same principles produced results which are difficult to credit (see Table 3.5). Given immigration demographics especially in the United States, one would predict a steady increase in borrowing throughout the century. The figures, however, do not conform to this expectation.

It is unlikely that the decline setting in at mid-century reflects a genuine decrease in the intensity of the language contact. Rather, it shows – once again – that for the very recent history of the English vocabulary the documentation work has not been completed, even in the OED.[25]

3.3.2 Changing productivity of specific word-formation processes: the case of acronyms and prefixed verbs

Bauer (1994: 37–39) offers tentative evidence pointing towards an "increase in the numbers in the abbreviations category and the blends category, and [a] decrease in the numbers in the suffixation category and the category of neo-classical compounds" in a small sample of OED supplement entries published in the course of the twentieth century.[26] As for the first-named phenomenon, increase in the number of abbreviations, it is possible to cite supporting corpus-based evidence from a comparison of the tagged LOB and F-LOB corpora, because most of the relevant forms are spelled as capital letters and therefore easy to retrieve automatically. Table 3.6 lists all forms tagged as proper nouns consisting entirely of capital letters (in practice, given tagging conventions, the category of acronyms and initialisms).[27]

Unlike the dictionary updates, which record **new** acronyms and initialisms, the corpora show changes in the discourse frequency of **all** such forms, whether old-established or not. What they also show is that the impressive

---

[25] Similarly counter-intuitive results are obtained if one investigates the contribution made to the vocabulary from the various scientific disciplines which have so profoundly transformed present-day life. A notable decrease in the course of the twentieth century in the frequency of terms from biology, for example, is most likely due to sampling delays rather than any genuine linguistic development.

[26] This analysis is based on the OED supplements and three sampling periods, and assumes that lexicographical practice in the OED has remained constant.

[27] These figures differ considerably from the results of an earlier count published in Mair et al. (2002: 253) – partly because the current figures are based on the fully post-edited F-LOB, but mainly because a new search algorithm was adopted. The older count made a distinction between acronyms (pronounced as words) and initialisms (pronounced as sequences of letters) and assumed that this distinction was fairly systematically reflected by the use of punctuation in spelling; for example, *NATO* for acronyms and *B.B.C.* for initialisms. However, spelling is not a very reliable guide in these matters, with initialisms variously appearing with or without stops (*BBC* or *B.B.C.*). As the textual functions of acronyms and initialisms are identical, the distinction was abolished for the present count. The present count also removes a minor flaw in the original one in that it no longer includes single-letter words (such as the X in "Malcolm X").

Table 3.5. *Twentieth-century borrowings from Spanish first attested in the OED*

Entries first attested in	Second Edition	New Edition	Total
1901–1920	66	—	66
1921–1940	103	—	103
1941–1960	57	—	57
1961–1980	38	1	39
1981–2000	5	—	5

Table 3.6. *Proper nouns consisting entirely of capital letters: comparison of frequency in LOB and F-LOB*

Sub-corpus	LOB corpus		F-LOB corpus		Difference	
	Raw frequency	Per million	Raw frequency	Per million	% of LOB	Log likelihood
Press	244	1,372	905	5,078	+270.0 %	403.0
General prose	257	620	1,335	3,244	+423.4 %	807.6
Learned	74	460	645	4,028	+775.3 %	522.5
Fiction	35	136	183	712	+421.6 %	109.8
Total	610	604	3,068	3,043	+403.8 %	1,798.2

overall increase (more than 400 percent) hides considerable differences in individual textual genres. Least change is evident in the press, whose language has long constituted a favorable domain for the use of acronyms and initialisms. The increase noted here is probably smaller because it started from very high 1960s levels already. The most massive diachronic shift, on the other hand, can be noticed for academic (learned) writing, where acronyms and initialisms might be superseding the "neoclassical" scientific terminologies prevailing earlier. The drastic increases in the "general prose" and "fiction" categories are more difficult to account for by pointing to a specific individual factor. The increase in the textual frequency of acronyms and initialisms in these two genres probably reflects the wider currency of such forms in contemporary language in general. The domestication of the new word-formation type in everyday English may also be signaled by a tendency to create irregular acronyms of the type *quango* (from *quasi non-government (al) organization*), *footsie* (from *Financial Times Stock Exchange 100 Share Index*), or *Humvee* (from *high-mobility multi-purpose wheeled vehicle*), which sacrifice some derivational rigor to achieve forms which are pronounceable and have a hypocoristic ring to them.

Large corpora such as the BNC or databases such as *The Guardian/Observer on CD-ROM* were used above to trace the development of individual lexical items, such as *information superhighway*. I shall now investigate whether these resources can also be used to study changes in an entire morphological pattern, namely word formation by prefixation of verbal stems.

This pattern was extremely common in Old English and has left Modern English with a large number of verbs such as *upset* and *overthrow*. Its productivity since Middle English times has been limited, its functions largely being taken over by the modern "phrasal verb" type (e.g., *set up, throw over*). Verbal prefixation, though increasingly marginalized, was never quite dead, however. The OED, for instance, contains pre-twentieth-century entries for (with the years for the first and last quotations in brackets): *uparch* (1877, 1979), *upbear* (a1300, 1891), *upbind* (1590, 1746), *upboil* (1435, a1902), *upbreak* (c1205, 1894), and 77 further cases spanning the entire range from the perfectly current *uproot* to the extinct *upnim* ("take up," c1250, 1340) (see Scheible 2005 for a complete list).[28] To these we can add numerous twentieth-century additions, such as the common *upload* or *upgrade*, which suggests that this particular word-formation process might even be making a comeback after centuries of decline. In the study just referred to, Scheible has pointed out an interesting asymmetry: while there are 82 pre-twentieth-century instances of *up*+V, there are only four of *down*+V – *downbear* (c1330, 1834), *downcast* (a1300, 1839), *down-lie* (1526, a1628), and *downweigh* (1600, a1851). In the twentieth century itself, though, such forms are by no means rarer than the *up*- ones. Table 3.7 gives the relevant forms obtained in searches of the OED (twentieth-century neologisms only) and the BNC.

On the face of it, the recent surge in the productivity of *down*+V seems to be a genuine twentieth-century development.

What does one notice when moving from the dictionary-based assessment of morphological productivity to a corpus-based analysis of changes in discourse frequency? A first indication that the productivity of the pattern is currently increasing is provided even in the four small matching corpora used in the present study. Table 3.8 gives the relevant type and token frequencies for Brown, LOB, Frown, and F-LOB.

The trend is as expected, though the figures are too small to warrant any far-reaching conclusions. A more differentiated picture is provided by Figure 3.5, which charts the occurrences of seven relevant forms in *The Guardian on CD-ROM* over a fourteen-year period.

The past/past participle forms were searched for to exclude nominal uses of the forms in question. The most impressive growth is, of course, registered by

---

[28] Among the more curious twentieth-century attestations from the OED quotation base are *upblown* and *unupblown*, both from a text by Evelyn Waugh, who seems to be mocking certain features of the "telegraphese" register: "Cables were soon arriving . . ..'Require earliest name life story photograph American nurse upblown [sc. bombed] Adowa.' We replied 'Nurse unupblown,' and after a few days she disappeared from the news" (s.v. *un*-, 16).

Table 3.7. *Prefixed verbs in* up- *and* down- *in the OED (twentieth century) and the BNC (compiled from information in Scheible 2005)*

up+-V	*down+-V*
upchat, update, upend, upgrade, uphaul, upheave, uphold, upkeep, uplift, upload, upraise, uprate, upregulate, upright, uprise, upseat, upsize, upthrust, upturn, upvalue, upwarp	downclimb, downface, downgrade, downhurl, downlink, download, downplay, down-point, downrate, downregulate, downscale, downshift, downsize, downthrow, downturn, downwarp, downwash, downwaste, downweight, downwell, downzone

Table 3.8. Up/down + *V in four corpora – types (tokens)*

	1961	1991/92
British English (LOB/F-LOB)	2 (2)	6 (24)
American English (Brown/Frown)	3 (13)	6 (17)

the word *download,* which reflects the emergence and spectacular growth of the Internet/World Wide Web during the 1990s. *Upgrade* and *downgrade* also grow faster than expected (cf. the flatter line indicating textual growth), with the frequency increase proceeding from an already established plateau, as is to be expected for forms first attested in the OED in 1920 and 1930 respectively. Such common instances of the prefix + verb pattern probably function as familiar models enabling further, more restricted creativity through analogy. *Downplayed* and *downsized* seem to be firmly established but do not record above average growth rates; that is, they are not spreading. *Downscaled* and *downturned,* though attested occasionally, remain marginal throughout the period of observation.

The theoretical challenge posed by such creativity is the question of what has made the revival of an apparently moribund morphological process possible. It seems that we are not dealing with a straightforward revival of verbal prefix-ation as a productive process. Rather, some limited productivity which this process has apparently always retained is activated in the presence of ancillary factors. For example, an existing form in *up-* may encourage the creation of an antonym in *down-* or, more rarely, vice versa.[29] Also, established high-frequency forms make it possible to coin low-frequency analogues, sometimes as facetious

---

[29] Thus *upplay* – as yet marginal – might eventually be established as a complement to the common and familiar *downplay* (OED citations from 1968). In the pair *download/upload* current frequency distributions reflect a trivial fact, namely, that it is more common for people to download files than upload them.

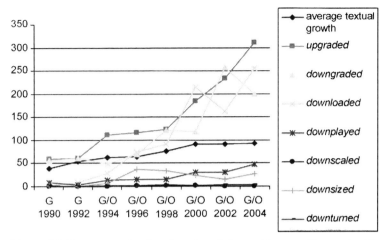

Figure 3.5 Frequency of selected verbs of the *up/down* + V type in *The Guardian (and Observer) on CD-ROM*

or nonce-formations. This is illustrated by the form *upchat*. It exists as the title of the popular TV sitcom *Upchat Line*, with its eponymous hero Mike Upchat. A presumable verb *to upchat* (for *chat up*) would then instantiate conversion from the noun rather than derivation through adding the prefix *up-* to the verbal stem *chat*. Another, unrelated line of development is presented by the following advertisement for a computer program:

> upchatter v4 gold: at first, this (v1) was quickly made in about 5 min for a friend of mine, sara, but i have taken it and took it a step further. in v4 the upchat feature is a lot better, it will also keep you from getting logged off due to in-activity.
>
> (*most features AOL3, all features AOL4 and AOL5 Compatible*)
>
> what upchatting is: it will allow you to chat while you are uploading. this is very useful for those of you who do a lot of uploading.
>
> (http://www.cdxdvd.com/magikweb/magikproggs.htm,
> access date 1 July 2004)

The nouns and verbal noun are coined first here, as well, and on the basis of these data the verb *to upchat* would probably have to be analyzed as a back-formation from one of the nouns (on the *babysitter* → *to babysit* model).

Similarly, an established instance of the pattern, the verb *to outsource* (OED 1979) has encouraged the neologism *to offshore* (not yet recorded in the OED), again via an intermediate verbal noun (*offshoring*, related *to outsourcing*), which tends to be far more common in texts.

A related minor development in the present connection is the creation of adjectives of the type prefix + V-*ing*, such as *ongoing* or *incoming*, which clearly

Table 3.9. Ongoing *in four corpora**

	1961	1991/1992
British English (LOB/F-LOB)	0	12 (2)
American English (Brown/Frown)	0	21 (2)

* First figure gives totals; bracketed figure indicates number of hyphenated spellings included in totals

fill a functional need in practical terms because the corresponding phrasal-verb participles are ruled out in attributive position (**a going on change*, **a coming in president*). A look at relevant forms in the four one-million-word corpora hints at relatively rapid ongoing developments. First consider the spread of one such form, *ongoing*, in British and American English within a very short period (see Table 3.9).

The oldest OED citation for this adjective is from 1851, but its wider currency seems to date back no earlier than the middle of the twentieth century:

> Written evidence of adjective use was scanty until the 1940s, when we collected 13 citations for it from . . . diverse sources . . . It was in the 1950s, however, that *ongoing* really became a common word: . . . The popularity of *ongoing* has continued unabated – and may even have grown somewhat – in the years since.   (Webster 1989: 690)

In Britain, the word was widely perceived to be an Americanism – and denounced as such in the House of Lords (Webster 1989: 691). By 1961, the sampling date for the LOB and Brown corpora, the word was apparently not frequent enough to make it into either of the two corpora, a situation which had clearly changed by the early 1990s, both in American English and, prescriptive and purist sentiment notwithstanding, also in British English. It is interesting to survey other forms of the same type. Tables 3.10 and 3.11 list all relevant forms starting in *on-*, *off-*, *in-*, *out-*, *up-*, and *down-*:[30]

---

[30] Tables 3.10 and 3.11 do not list forms such as *upsetting*, which are not related to corresponding phrasal verbs (in this case *set up*) but to prefixed verbs (in this case *upset*). Numerous borderline cases are encountered, the most prominent being the adjective *outstanding*, which occurs both in a literal meaning ("outstanding debts") and a transferred one (roughly synonymous with "excellent"). Note that, in contrast to core examples of the constructional type studied, *outstanding* in the latter meaning is stressed on the second syllable (*out'standing*) rather than the first (*'upcoming*). Similarly, the meaning of *outgoing* ranges from a literal one in close relation to the corresponding phrasal verb *go out* (e.g., "outgoing president") to lexicalized idiomatic ones ("extrovert"). For forms included in the counts, no differentiation of senses was undertaken.

Table 3.10. On/off/in/out/up/down + *V+ing in four corpora – survey*

	1961	1991/92
British English (LOB/F-LOB)	onrushing (1), incoming (2), outrushing (1), outlying (4), outstanding (46), uplifting (1), upshooting (1)	ongoing (12), offlying (1), offputting (1), incoming (5), outlying (3), outgoing (3), outstanding (23), upcoming (1), uplifting (2)
American English (Brown/Frown)	oncoming (2), onrushing (1), incoming (5), indwelling (1), outstanding (37), outgoing (8), outlying (2), outreaching (1), upjutting (1), upcoming (1), upstanding (1), downtalking (1)	ongoing (21), oncoming (3), onsetting (1), offputting (2), incoming (9), outgoing (6), outlying (2), outstanding (23), upcoming (19), uplifting (2)

Hyphenated spellings are included in totals

Table 3.11. On/off/in/out/up/down + *V+ing in four corpora – type/token ratios**

	1961	1991/92
British English (LOB/F-LOB)	6/10	8/28
American English (Brown/Frown)	11/24	9/65

* *Outstanding* is not considered

As can be seen, especially from the high number of types attested in the Brown Corpus, it is not so much the word-formation process itself which is new. What is new, however, is the readiness with which writers make use of the available option, propelling words like *ongoing* and *incoming* into the middle range of lexical frequency for adjectives. Current British and American frequencies differ most strikingly for the adjective *upcoming*, which may have taken over from *ongoing* as the prescriptivists' favorite target of criticism. The latest edition of the (British) usage manual *Fowler's modern English usage* has this to say:

> American use of the word (first recorded in the *OED* in this [i.e., the current] sense in 1959) is gradually making its way into English-speaking countries outside the US.   (Burchfield 1996: 813f., s.v. *upcoming*)

The (American) *Webster's dictionary of English usage*, on the other hand, claims that the word:

> was coined in the early 1940s and did not come into frequent use until after World War II. By the 1950s it had establised itself as a common word, and it continues to be one today. . . *Upcoming* is a standard and reputable word, recognized as such by current dictionaries. Disapproval of it has never been especially widespread, and recent evidence suggests that it is becoming less so. You have little to worry about if you choose to use *upcoming*.   (Webster 1989: 932, s.v. *upcoming*)

Recent data from *The Guardian on CD-ROM* suggest that *upcoming* has been spreading continuously in British English – faster than *incoming* and more slowly than *ongoing*, as Figure 3.6 shows.

3.3.3 Dictionary-based and corpus-based methods of studying lexical growth: concluding remarks

Our efforts to document current trends in word formation and vocabulary enrichment on the basis of the OED Online and selected corpora and full-text databases have not been without success, but a final note of caution is in order. Previous work by Algeo (1998) and Bauer (1994), which had to rely on the printed OED and the CD-ROM version of the second edition, was frequently unable to document very recent developments, because of the time-gap between the emergence of a new word or meaning and its inclusion in the dictionary. With the continuously updated online edition of the OED and the use of self-renewing textual databases such as *The Guardian on CD-ROM* this weakness is now largely remedied. As for Algeo's and Bauer's second major problem, shifts in lexicographical fashion obscuring "real" developments in language history, working with these new and constantly updating resources remains as much of a risk as it was for them. When it comes to documenting and quantifying lexical change, the digitized OED quotation base presents a paradox. On the one hand, it is a source of unsurpassed quality for the study of individual new words – in particular, those which already have an entry. On the other, analysis of the quotation base in the search for changes in word-formation patterns tends to produce plausible results for the past, but unreliable ones as one approaches the present. It is an additional paradox that the very material which needs to be used with caution when assessing trends in

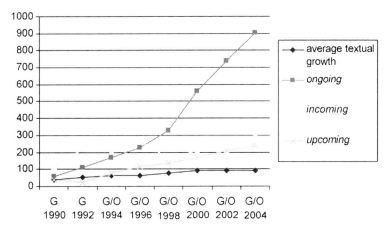

Figure 3.6 Spread of three deverbal adjectives in *The Guardian (and Observer) on CD-ROM*

lexical innovation should allow such striking insights into recent grammatical trends, as will be shown in Chapter 4.

As for the newspaper databases, they allow interesting insights into the interplay of topicality in current affairs and lexical creativity. Newspapers are a genre that displays some stylistic differentiation, both between different newspapers and (within one and the same paper) between more formal sub-genres such as foreign news and more colloquial ones such as sports reportage. As media whose chief function is to report news of all kinds, newspapers are very likely to cover a wide range of neologisms and are, therefore, an ideal text type to study lexical innovation. Nevertheless, as a written genre, newspapers also introduce some bias, as they will under-document developments arising and spreading chiefly in the spoken language.

3.4 Neologizing in its social context

It has not escaped linguists' notice that neologisms open an interesting window on contemporary life. Robert Burchfield, who as the editor of the OED Supplements from 1957 to 1986 had to devise lexicographically sound ways of coming to terms with the protean growth of the vocabulary of English in the twentieth century, produced the following list which, as it was devised at the beginning of his labors, is largely intuitive but nevertheless telling:

action painting	meson	self-service
automation	morpheme	skiffle
chain-reaction	mixomatosis	sound-barrier
cybernetics	nylon	trafficator

disinflation	paratroop	Welfare State
ionosphere	penicillin	
jet (-engine)	plutonium	
megaton	radar	

These seemed to me to be the words of the age. If we could prepare satisfactory entries for them, all would be well with the rest. Or so, misguidedly, I thought at the time.   (Burchfield 1989: 7)

The priority here is on science and technological innovation in warfare. A homely and trivial innovation such as *crossword puzzle* (attested in the OED from 1914) does not make it into the list. Somewhat unexpectedly in view of its orientation, the list does not contain a single acronym, in spite of the fact that it was the military and science which – from *ANZAC* to *ZIFT*[31] – contributed masses of such forms to the general-purpose vocabulary of twentieth-century English.

When almost three decades later Burchfield returned to the same topic, commenting on the lexical innovations of the second half of the twentieth century, the emphasis has shifted – to the lexical reflections of the decay of the established social order:

The period since 1950 was marked at its beginning by the *beatniks* (1955) of the *beat generation* (1952), by *hippies* (1953), and by the lawless, leather-jacketed motor-cyclists called *Hell's Angels* (1957). It has ended with the spectre of *Aids* (first noted in 1982). *Amphetamines* (1938) like *benzedrine* (1933) and *cannabis* (1798) ceased to be drugs prescribed only under medical supervision and passed into the hands of the rebellious young, to be joined at a later stage by *heroin* (1898) and *crack* (1985). New vocabulary poured in from the wars (Korea and Vietnam), dissenting movements of various kinds, and from the world of computers. This is not a history lesson but just a reminder that great global events inevitably produce bucketsful of new vocabulary. A small list of new words since 1950 gives something of the flavour of the period:

ayatollah (1950, *fig.* 1979)	Ms. (1952)
baby boom (1967)	the pill (1957)
bananas, to go (1968)	Sloane Ranger (1975)
bar code (1963)	sputnik (1957)
beta-blocker (1970)	user-friendly (1977)

---

[31] *ANZAC* derives from "Australian and New Zealand Army Corps" and is attested in the OED from 1915. *ZIFT* is short for "zygote intra-fallopian transfer," attested from 1986, when this new technique in reproductive medicine was first published in the medical journal *Lancet*.

black economy (1969)   yomp (verb) (1982)
hi-fi (1950)   yuppie (1984)
monetarism (1969)

(Burchfield 1989: 77–78)

Such lexically based diagnosis of the age is often instructive but always highly subjective. This is shown, for example, by the following chronological survey given in Bauer (1994: 31), which illustrates additions to the vocabulary of twentieth-century English decade by decade and whose priorities only partly overlap with Burchfield's:

1900s: goo, smog
1910s: cartoon (film), cellophane
1920s: finalize, montage
1930s: burp, documentary (n.)
1940s: bikini, car-pool
1950s: chopper [= helicopter], do-it-yourself
1960s: biodegradable, brain-drain
1970s: creative accounting, miniseries
1980s: daterape, jetway (*or* airbridge)

In spite of their different priorities, however, Burchfield and Bauer – and the many others who have compiled similar lists – agree that war has been one of the most potent lexical innovators in twentieth-century English. In addition to the words listed above, the lexical heritage of one of the most violent centuries in human history includes the following words inspired by two world wars: *air-raid, anti-aircraft, bomber* (in the sense of bomber aircraft, first attested in the OED in 1917), *camouflage, chemical warfare, depth charge, dogfight, gas mask, incendiary bomb, mustard gas, U-boat* (World War I); *air-lift, blitz, bomb-site, doodlebug, flying bomb, heliport, jeep, paratroops, radar, Sten gun, strafe* (Aitchison 2003: 200, based on Ayto 1999; see also Zandvoort 1957). *Genocide* (OED 1944) and *ethnic cleansing* (1991) were words unknown to the nineteenth century. *Biocide* (1947), *overkill* (verb, 1946; noun, 1958), and the falsely endearing abbreviation *nuke* for "nuclear weapon" (noun, 1959; verb, 1967) are among the lexical responses to the nuclear arms race during the Cold War.[32]

The study of systematic correlations between lexical change and social and cultural change has a long and controversial tradition – both within linguistics and outside the discipline, in literary and cultural studies. A classic study of this type is C. S. Lewis' *Studies in words* (1932/1960), in which the author proposes to reconstruct the origin of the modern consciousness from observable changes in the meanings of individual English words. Ultimately, what we

---

[32] In a similar vein, Algeo concludes his survey of recent lexical innovation in English (1998: 89–91) with exemplary analyses of words containing the elements *communist* and *welfare*. The productivity of such forms is shown to have peaked at different periods, closely mirroring the dominant political preoccupations of the times.

are dealing with here is a specific manifestation of the Sapir–Whorf Hypothesis of linguistic determinism. Language is seen as closely reflecting the culture of its speakers, and – in the strongest form of the model – as determining their world-view. Whorfianism has been an inspiration to many people outside linguistics – from language rights activists, writers, and critics, to feminist language reformers. Within linguistics, the idea has been received more critically and is considered controversial. In full awareness of how tempting it is to short-circuit linguistic and cultural history, I have attempted to err on the side of caution in the following remarks.

As a modest starting point, let us return to the list of quarterly updates to the OED Online which was discussed with regard to its formal features above. What does it tell us about the cultural preoccupations of the present? Not unexpectedly, it contains a large number of computer neologisms. These are not usually technical terms in the narrow sense but show ordinary users trying to cope with the new technology in their everyday lives. As Barry (1991) has shown in his study *Technobabble*, this is to be expected: while in the early days of its development information technology was important for a small number of specialists only, who not unexpectedly created a hermetic specialist terminology, there is now a colloquial register of computer talk which is characterized not so much by a technical precision but shows users grappling with the effects of the digital revolution in their everyday environment. Their requirements are fulfilled by vivid metaphors and slangy terms rather than lengthy Latinate compounds or impenetrable acronyms. The terms (e.g., *weblogger*) are catchy, often informal and based on vivid metaphors. For *client* the list shows so many new uses that a restructuring of the meaning of this word is likely in the mid-term (see Appendix 4).

Very informal and slangy terms, some of them taboo (cf. the copious list of terms based on *arse*) are well represented not only in the popular IT vocabulary but in the list in general. To some extent this is no doubt due to the OED's changing editorial policy on such matters. After all, the taboo vocabulary of English was not covered too well until the 1989 edition. But there is nevertheless a genuine element of linguistic and cultural change involved here. Since the beginning of the twentieth century, but especially since the 1960s, Western European and North American societies have come to value informal and spontaneous modes of expression also in public and previously formal modes of discourse. Standard English has, accordingly, become more informal, and the norms of the written language have moved closer to spoken usage, with one symptom of this development being the large number of slang terms recently added to the OED.

The extensive update of the entry for *sex*, a word which has lost its taboo connotations for some time, is part of the same trend but also reveals a more specific phenomenon. Particularly interesting are the new compounds containing *sex* as their first element: *sex industry*, *sex worker*, *sex work*. Prostitution, obviously not a new social phenomenon, but certainly a subject likely to inspire lexical creativity through a never-ending stream of euphemisms, is verbally recast as an industry. This is a plausible development in the last quarter of the twentieth century for two reasons. Sex has become a commodity outside the narrow sphere of prostitution – in advertising, in popular journalism, and in many trendy urban lifestyles, and making the "sex workers" part of this scene is a verbal strategy intended to take away some of the seediness of the trade.[33]

The use of business and trade vocabulary for prostitution is just one instance of a far more general development in which an increasing number of communicative domains have been "colonized"[34] by the discourse of business and economics. Fairclough (1992), for example, has drawn attention to the fact that in institutions of higher learning the traditional student is increasingly referred to as customer and client, and the teacher as a provider of marketable packages of knowledge. Similarly, there has been a tendency for complicated human interaction such as counseling or therapy to be broken up into simpler and marketable communicative routines. It is probably not too far-fetched to point to this social trend as the motivating force behind several neologisms in the list – for example, the *emotional quotient* or the construct *emotional intelligence*.[35]

Outside professional linguistics, where moderate "Whorfianism" is the mainstream in discussions of the relationship between developments in society, culture and the vocabulary, people seem to be quite willing to believe that a particular era's social and cultural concerns, and especially its perceived flaws, are directly reflected in its vocabulary. The philosopher Leo Strauss has famously remarked on the social causes of a development which has turned the word *virtuous* from an epithet denoting male prowess to one denoting female chastity – a particularly drastic instance of semantic change because a meaning has practically been turned into its opposite.[36] In a similar vein, Gertrude Himmelfarb, author of *The de-moralization of society*, a neo-conservative critique of the liberal welfare state, subtitles her work (1995) *From Victorian virtues to modern values*, implying that a "Victorian" ethical discourse, based on an absolute and ultimately constructive code of virtues, was replaced by a modern relativistic network of values, which was corrosive because they could be defined in context-dependent and arbitrary terms.

[33] In this connection, it is interesting to note that the lexical phrase *sex and shopping* should have become common enough to merit inclusion in the list, as well.

[34] The metaphor is from the work of German sociologist and social theorist Jürgen Habermas (1988).

[35] For a similar late twentieth-century lexical innovation, compare the phrasal neologism *tender loving care*, defined in the OED as "especially solicitous care such as is given by nurses" (s.v. *tender* 8a), originally a colloquialism which is now also in ironic use. In view of the quantifiable and routinized caregiving that it implies, it is not surprising to see it abbreviated as an acronym, *TLC*, with the attendant technical and scientific connotations.

[36] Incidentally, this is not the only example of such a drastic semantic change in the history of English. Others include *nervous*, *affected*, and *sententious* (see Stark 1999: 6). From 1400 to around 1700, *sententious*, for example, meant "full of meaning; also, of persons, full of intelligence or wisdom" (OED, s.v. *sententious* 1). Now, its dominant meaning is "pompous."

An obvious problem in such argumentation from a linguistic point of view is that the diagnosis – decay of the social fabric – is taken for granted even before the linguistic symptoms are being investigated. However, it is certainly worthwhile to put Himmelfarb's claims to the "usage" test on corpora, because in this way we might be able to correct for a possible bias in her unsystematic selection of examples.

The relevant OED entries do seem to lend some initial support to her argument. No interesting formal or semantic developments are recorded for the word *virtue* for the twentieth century, which could be a sign that it is becoming obsolescent in contemporary moral discourse.[37] The entry for *value*, by contrast, shows a continuous expansion during the past century, particularly in the many plural uses. The most important portion of the directly relevant sense 6a is quoted in full below:

> 6. a. The relative status of a thing, or the estimate in which it is held, according to its real or supposed worth, usefulness, or importance. In *Philos.* and *Social Sciences*, regarded esp. in relation to an individual or group; *gen.* in *pl.*, the principles or standards of a person or society, the personal or societal judgement of what is valuable and important in life.
>
> *c*1380 WYCLIF *Sel. Wks.* I. 195 Oure bileve techiþ us þ at God kepiþ þingis after her valu, for if ony þing be betere, God makiþ it to be betere. *c*1385 CHAUCER *L.G.W.* 602 *Cleopatra*, Loue hadde brought this man in swich a rage..That al the world he sette at no value. 1470–85 MALORY *Arthur* II. ii. 78 Your bounte..may no man preyse half to the valewe. 1584 B. R. tr. *Herodotus* I. 68 These words with Cyrus came in at one eare and went out at the other, lighter in value then the wynd in waight. 1651 HOBBES *Leviath.* I. x. 42 [Let men] rate themselves at the highest Value they can; yet their true Value is no more than it is esteemed by others. 1779 *Mirror* No. 5. 33 It unfortunately happens, that we are very inadequate judges of the value of our own discourse. 1828 DUPPA *Trav. Italy*, etc. 21 These landscapes have no value but as being the earliest attempts to represent scenes from nature. 1844 H. H. WILSON *Brit. India* I. 217 Attaching to its commerce and alliance more value than belonged to either. 1884 J. GILMOUR *Mongols* xvii. 205 Buddhism..tells him that each prayer repeated has a certain value in cleansing away sin. 1902 J. M. BALDWIN *Dict. Philos. & Psychol.* II. 823/2 Since value is a function of desire or judgment, expressing a relation between subject and object. 1918 THOMAS & ZNANIECKI *Polish Peasant* I. 21 By a social value we understand any

---

[37] The 1986 printed *Supplement IV (Se–Z)*, which followed up twentieth-century developments for the words, contains one trivial addition to the entry for *virtue*, a later example from 1980 for one of the nominal senses (OED I.4.a).

datum having an empirical content accessible to the members of some social group and a meaning with regard to which it is or may be an object of activity. 1933 *Economica* XIII. 30 Like all human action social behaviour is determined..in accordance with standards of value or through conscious belief in standards assigning intrinsic value to certain types of behaviour.

pl. 1918 THOMAS & ZNANIECKI *Polish Peasant* I. 33 Sociology..has this in common with social psychology: that the values which it studies draw all their reality, all their power to influence human life, from the social attitudes which are expressed or supposedly expressed in them. 1921 *Times Lit. Suppl.* 3 Nov. 705/4 In the effort, again, to give his characters and scenes the vivid impression of reality, the novelist, whether voluntarily or not, cannot avoid revealing not merely his powers of mind and imagination, but his spiritual and philosophical bias, his views of society, of religion, his "values". 1938 E. BOWEN *Death of Heart* III. iv. 394 You've got a completely lunatic set of values. 1950 I. BERLIN in *Foreign Affairs* XXVIII. 382 Crumbling values and the dissolution of the fixed standards and landmarks of our civilization. 1955 *Times* 10 May 8/3 Restoring to Germany the basic values of democratic civilization. 1958 *Listener* 9 Oct. 548/1 The reason..lies, I believe, in the structure of Arab society..and in its economic values. 1964 GOULD & KOLB *Dict. Soc. Sci.* 744/1 Social scientists for the most part..have confined their attention to values..as empirical variables in social life whose *scientific* importance is not so much dependent on their validity and correctness as..upon the fact that they are believed..by those who hold them. 1970 N. CHOMSKY *At War with Asia* vi. 299 By their willingness to die, the Asian hordes..exploit our basic weakness–our Christian values which make us reluctant to bear the burden of genocide, the final conclusion of our strategic logic.

There is also a large number of institutionalized and lexicalized combinations with *value* as the first element, almost all of which are of twentieth-century origin. The list is reproduced in full below, whereas the quotations are given only for those forms which play a role in ethical discourse:

8. Special Combs.: **value analysis**, the systematic and critical assessment by an organization of design and costs in relation to realized value; also *transf.*; **value analyst**, one who undertakes a value analysis; **value calling** *Bridge*, a system of estimating bids which takes into account the scoring values of the suits; **value engineering**, the modification of designs and systems according to value analysis; **value-free** *a.*, free from criteria imposed by subjective values or standards; purely objective; = *value-neutral*; hence *value-freedom*; **value-judgement** [cf. G. *werturteil*], a judgement predicating merit or demerit of its

subject; **value-laden** *ppl. a.* = *value-loaded* ppl. adj.; hence *value-ladenness*; **value-loaded** *ppl. a.*, weighted or biased in favour of certain values; **value-neutral** *a.*, involving no value judgements, neutral with respect to (personal or group) values; **value-orientation**, the direction given to a person's attitudes and thinking by their beliefs or standards; so *value-oriented ppl. a.; value-system*, any set of connected or interdependent values; **value theory**, (*a*) *Pol. Econ.*, the (Marxist) labour theory of value; (*b*) *Philos.*, axiology.

1949 J. A. PASSMORE in Feigl & Brodbeck *Readings in Philos. of Sci.* (1953) 674 (*heading*) Can the social sciences be value-free? **1979** *Nature* 19 July 185/1 Science and technology are not neutral or value-free but are instruments of power, and that means political power. **1984** *Times Educ. Suppl.* 30 Nov. 3/2 Europe Singh, a maths teacher..believes maths and the sciences have wrongly been considered to be neutral and value-free.

1959 P. RIEFF *Freud* viii. 299 Scientific energies, by the facile transformation of the objectivity necessary to science into.."value-freedom", are easily enlisted to the aims of society, whatever these may be.

1892 J. ORR in *Thinker* II. 146 Two kinds of knowledge are distinguished by Ritschl – the one, religious knowledge which moves solely in the region of what he calls worth or value-judgments. **1899** A. E. GARVIE *Ritschlian Theol.* 176 The theoretical judgments cannot give an intelligible unity to the world~[sicl] whole, but the value-judgments can. **1941** J. S. HUXLEY *Uniqueness of Man* xi. 229 Even in natural science, regarded as pure knowledge, one value-judgment is implicit *belief in the value of truth.* **1961** *Listener* 30 Nov. 912/1 The decision depends on what may..be called policy considerations; that is, where the court has to make a value judgment. **1975** *Amer. N. & Q.* XIV. 53/2 Robert Frost's penchant for "the fact" (as in "Mowing") provides a useful measuring stick for determining the worth of value judgments about him. **1980** *Times Lit. Suppl.* 3 Oct. 1085/2 The method adopted here is a detailed interpretative analysis of poetic language and structure, liberally sprinkled with value-judgments.

1971 *Ibid.* 13 Aug. 958/4 For them, even the internal content of science is value-laden, and to some extent ideologically determined. **1977** *Jrnl. Politics* XXXIX. 24 The growing acceptance of the thesis that political science is necessarily a value-laden discipline.

1978 M. HESSE in Hookway & Pettit *Action & Interpretation* 8 A distinction between two sorts of "value-ladenness" in social science.

1951 D. RIESMAN *Individualism Reconsidered* (1955) 33 Obviously, the very term "masses" is heavily value-loaded. **1974** tr. *Wertheim's Evolution & Revolution* 35 To state that a given situation shows "progress" or "evolution".. in relation to another situation implies the use of value-loaded criteria.

1946 GERTH & MILLS tr. M. Weber in *From Max Weber* (1947) ix. 247 Even a pirate genius may exercise a "charismatic" domination, in the value-neutral sense intended here. **1979** *Dædalus* Winter 55 "Excellence" is not a value-neutral concept.

1951 G. W. ALLPORT in Parsons & Shils *Toward Gen. Theory Action* IV. i. 365 Prejudice is manifestly a value-orientation. **1968** W. E. LAMBERT et al. in J. A. Fishman *Readings Sociol. of Lang.* 488 In general, value orientations do not play an important role in predicting who will or will not do well in French. **1980** N. ABERCROMBIE et al. *Dominant Ideology Thesis* ii. 48 System integration is defined in terms of the processes whereby value-orientation patterns are institutionalised at the social level via the mechanism of social roles with the effect of organising the behaviour of adult members of society.

1962 N. J. SMELSER *Theory Collective Behav.* iii. 49 Behind a vast array of religious and political value-oriented movements lie the same kinds of strain. **1977** *Bull. Amer. Acad. Arts & Sci.* Oct. 16 It is at this point that value-oriented parameters for assessing progress become necessary.

1936 *Mind* XLV. 288 Persons who are not *Buerger* (citizens)..like the Jews in Nazi Germany, or the bulk of the Bantu in the Union of South Africa. For such as these, the relation to the value-system embodied in the state is of the most tenuous and indirect kind. **1969** *Listener* 3 July 3/1 Two American sociologists examined the value system of a small rural town in the American Mid-West. **1980** *Jrnl. R. Soc. Arts* June 416/2 A society in which there are overlapping different value systems which create different structures.

In purely descriptive terms, therefore, Himmelfarb's argument seems to be correct. The term *value* seems to have taken over from *virtue* as the central one in twentieth-century ethical and moral discourse.

Before we can accept her argument in full, however, we need to answer a further question. Does growth in the length of a word's OED entry correlate with its importance for the general public, or – in other words – has *value* registered a comparable increase in discourse frequency in non-technical registers? Table 3.12, with the frequencies for *virtue*, *value*, and those of some related terms for the OED Baseline1900 corpus, LOB and F-LOB, suggests that it has not.[38]

These figures need to be taken with a grain of salt. Uses of *virtue* in which the word is not used in its literal senses – e.g., complex prepositions such as *by*

---

[38] The figures do not include obviously irrelevant uses such as the proper name *Lady Virtue*.

Table 3.12. *Discourse frequency of* virtue(s), value(s), *etc. in selected twentieth-century corpora*

	virtue(s)	of which idiomatic	*value(s)*	*value/ moral*	*moral(ly)*	*ethical(ly)*
OED Baseline	21	4	261	1	74	12
LOB	25	7	388	1	85	6
F-LOB	63	21	282	1	116	14

virtue of, *in virtue of* or idiomatic expressions such as *make a virtue out of* (necessity, etc.) – are listed separately in column 3, but no attempt was made to classify the occurrences of *value(s)* semantically. A context search for any occurrence of *value(s)* together with the adjective *moral* in a span of ten words to the right or left, which was intended to target clear judgmental uses, yielded insufficient returns, as can be seen in column 5.[39] The table reveals some surprising if puzzling trends, for example the steep rise in the frequency of idiomatic uses of *virtue* from LOB to F-LOB, which might be worth following up in larger corpora, but overall the figures represent random fluctuation rather than any clear trend.

What the comparison between the OED entries and the corpus figures shows is that the lexical options available for formulating ethical judgments may well have changed in the twentieth century, but that ordinary usage as reflected in word frequencies in text has not been much affected by this. There is thus no systematic link between a lexical change and a change (or, in Himmelfarb's view, a decay) in contemporary social ethics. The rise of a new core term in ethical discourse, *value*, may reflect a modern tendency to ground moral precepts on scientific findings in sociology or psychology, rather than traditional religion or metaphysics. This will change the lexical profile of technical writings on ethics and moral philosophy considerably, but whether this change is reflected in ordinary discourse about moral issues is doubtful. Certainly, the launching of a new term will not cause ethical confusion in the ordinary speaker of English, who will continue to frame his or her value judgments in terms of "good" and "bad," or "good" and "evil," as has always been done, regardless of the notoriously vague meanings of these adjectives.

Similar caution about the alleged link between lexical and social change is inspired by the following elegantly formulated and hence intuitively appealing claim made by Eric Hobsbawm in his history of the twentieth century:

> When people face what nothing in their past has prepared them for they
> grope for words to name the unknown, even when they can neither

---

[39] For comparison the fluctuating frequencies of *moral(ly)* and *ethical(ly)* are given in columns 6 and 7.

define nor understand it. Some time in the third quarter of the century we can see this process at work among the intellectuals of the West. The keyword was the small preposition "after", generally used in its latinate form "post" as a prefix to any of the numerous terms which had, for some generations, been used to mark out the mental territory of twentieth-century life.   (1994: 287)

Hobsbawm clearly has a point as far as the astounding productivity of the prefix/combining form *post-* in present-day English is concerned. A randomly selected annual edition of *The Guardian on CD-ROM* from 1995 yielded hundreds of examples. Some of the more colorful ones with a second element beginning in *a* include:

- post-army (Elvis Presley) movies
- post-adolescent antisocial personality disorder
- post-Acid House (dance music)
- post-Andreotti generation of Mafiosi
- post-antiquity (on the style of Mario Botta's architecture)
- post-acned adults.

The majority of tokens are, of course, provided by more regular coinages such as *post-apartheid* (South Africa) or *post-apocalyptic*. Where Hobsbawm errs, however, is in assigning the start of the fashion to the third quarter of the twentieth century and probably also in the implicit negative judgment (*post-* signifying intellectual confusion). The reason is probably that he isolates the one development that has caught his attention from its linguistic background. *Post-* is just one instance of a phenomenon that is much more widespread: the creation of combining forms from analyzable parts of mostly Latin or Greek terms. Thus, the *super-* in *superlative* and *superfluous* is the basis for the "English" morpheme *super-* in *superimpose,* which in turn paved the way for the extremely productive and freely combinable emphasizer *super-* in *supermarket* or *supertasty.* The story repeated itself in the case of *hyper-*, *mega-*, *cyber-*, and many others. Thus, an accident of linguistic history – the fact that English happens to have an etymologically very mixed vocabulary – is the ultimate basis for the development noted by Hobsbawm, and a check in the OED Baseline 1900 corpus reveals that speakers did not wait until the 1960s to avail themselves of the opportunity. The forms attested in this corpus include:

post-operative, post-traumatic, post-Kantian, post-larval, post-bellum, Post-Millennialists, post-graduate, post-influenzial, post-Darwinian, post-meridian, post-Raphaelite, post-mediaeval, post-exibic, post-Reformation, post-reproductive, post-Pentecostal   (and numerous others)

Linguistically speaking, the issue is thus not that language reflects people's confusion or has a lack of required terminology but that this particular word-formation strategy is now available as a potential resource, enabling overshooting creativity and flowering linguistic experimentation. That an occasional individual result of this creative potential is silly should not be a cause for concern, much less be seen as a sign of the decay of the language.

But even if *post-* words in themselves are not the lexical sign of the times that Hobsbawm makes them out to be, the relationship between the words and the times is a real if more indirect one. *Post-* forms, alongside similar forms with *cyber-*, *mega-*, and related combining forms, are one aspect of a fundamental development in the recent history of the English vocabulary – namely, the popularization, semantic bleaching, and trivialization of scholarly terminology which, as has been argued above, is a necessary coping strategy for speakers of English in the modern world.

The two examples discussed above – the rise of *value* as a moral term and the growing productivity of the combining form *post-* – should be sufficient to caution us against short-circuiting lexical and social change. It is not linguistic-ally responsible procedure to base such links on one word, or even a small number of related terms. The lexicon is an immensely rich network of choices, with the added complication that in actual use the meaning of any given word is enriched in context. What do we call a "virtue" at a particular time, in a particular situation? Do we consider the term technical, formal, poetic, or common? Do we use it facetiously, with a sense of ironical distance?

Raymond Williams' classic *Keywords: a vocabulary of culture and society* (1976), and – on a more popular level – Martin Jay's *Cultural semantics* (1998) show cultural and social historians taking the important step from isolated words to the systematic study of conceptual-lexical networks, and among professional linguists Geoffrey Hughes has explored the role of social factors in shaping the development of the English lexicon in three major studies (Hughes 1988, 1991, 2000). In tracing systematic links between social and lexical developments Hughes focuses on earlier stages of the language. The rise of capitalism from the Middle Ages onwards, for example, is shown to have led to a systematic change in the lexicon of English, as new "financial" meanings were added to a large number of words which did not have them before (e.g., *purchase*, *debt*, *credit*, etc.). Similarly, words in the religious vocabulary have tended to widen their meaning to cover the secular domain or have been trivialized, which is quite plausibly attributed to the secularization of society (e.g., *worship*, *orthodox*, *propaganda*, *sermon*).

Hughes' major concern for the present is the abuse of language in politics, advertising, and the media, for which he gives pointed but occasionally polem-ical illustrations. Beyond such often superficial instances of "verbicide" in public discourse, there are certainly some deep semantico-cultural trends in the vocabulary of present-day English which deserve investigation.

Chief among them is the domestication of various scholarly, scientific, and technical terminologies for the purposes of everyday communication – a linguis-tic coping strategy which helps us come to terms with the effects of technology and science on everyday life. At no time in human history did technology and science have a more profound impact on everyday life than in the twentieth century, and one of the most important linguistic effects of this influence is that ordinary spoken English today cannot do without words which were coined as technical terms in some field of scholarly inquiry and were then generalized, usually broadening and even blurring their meaning in the process. The following citation from the British National Corpus shows the process in action.

Kath: <--> Well Sophie's <--> er bloody erm <pause> allergic to alcohol and Heidi, she was so funny okay, she had, what, two Martini Rossos and she was fucked, totally. <--> It was very funny. <-->
Claire: <--> Allergic to alcohol? <-->
Kath: She's allergic to alcohol, she ge— she gets really pissed on like one, two glasses of wine.
Claire: Yeah but allergic means you come up in something.
Kath: No it means, basically it means that <pause> it gets to her head really quickly <pause> like one, two glasses of wine <pause> and she's off her trolley. <pause>
Claire: Oh I couldn't handle that.
Kath: Nor could I.

(KPH 999–1006)

This is two 17-year-olds chatting, and obviously grappling with a narrower and looser meaning of the medical term *allergic*.

We use anthropomorphic metaphors to talk about computers (*memory*) and we use computer metaphors to talk about the human brain (*wetware*, *hard-disk*, *storage*) or communication (*thanks for your input*). We frame our emotions in words which are trivialized fragments of various psychological and psychoanalytical theories (*inferiority complex*, *oedipal*, etc.). We create endless ranges of new *syndromes* in the hope of turning ill-defined malaises into problems manageable in medical institutions, and – as has already been pointed out – we export the use of acronyms and initialisms, which originated in technical and institutional discourses, to the domain of ordinary communication, creating forms such as *BYO*, *snafu*, and *SOB*, and – not least – *TLC*.

4 Grammatical changes in twentieth-century English

4.1 Introduction

Grammatical change differs from lexical and phonetic/phonological change in at least two important respects. First, it generally unfolds much more slowly, often taking hundreds of years to run its course to completion; and second, it tends to proceed below the threshold of speakers' conscious awareness (which makes introspection-based statements on ongoing changes in English grammar particularly unreliable). A third, but relatively more manageable, problem is caused by the fact that, from among the vast number of grammatical changes going on in the language at any one time, a very small selection is strongly stigmatized. This has led to a bias in the scholarly literature towards the discussion of these high-profile instances – at the expense of developments which are, arguably, far more comprehensive and important in the long run. Examples which come to mind include the use of *like* as a conjunction (e.g., *tell it like it is*), the use of *hopefully* as a sentence adverb (e.g., *hopefully, they'll bury the hatchet soon*), or text-type-specific stylistic mannerisms such as noun-phrase name appositions of the type *veteran newspaper pundit Brian Miller*. Considering that some of these phenomena are not as recent as is often alleged[1] and that, moreover, they are often unsystematic in nature, it is surprising to see the inordinate amount of expert and lay comment which they have generated. Certainly, it is not appropriate to treat them as being on a par with long-term,

---

[1] Among the three examples mentioned, it is only the second case which represents a genuine innovation – with a first OED attestation from 1932 (s.v. *hopefully*, adv. 2). The use of *like* as a conjunction can be documented from the Early Modern English period onwards, and the only new thing about it in the twentieth century is that it is losing the stigma attaching to it in the eyes of many writers. The articleless noun-phrase name construction is difficult to attest before the twentieth century outside the established pattern "honorific + name" (*King George, President Jefferson*). Bell (1988: 339) traces the first British instances of the phenomenon back to the 1920s and plausibly suggests (1988: 326, 338) a somewhat earlier American origin. Whatever the age of the construction may be, however, it shows little sign of spreading into general spoken usage, so that it must be assumed to have stabilized as a style marker in certain written genres (on which, see Jucker 1992).

systematic and comprehensive changes in the core grammar of English, such as the increase in the discourse frequency and functional range of the progressive or the spread of gerundial complements at the expense of infinitival ones.

For the purposes of the present book, "twentieth-century" changes in English grammar will be defined as those developments for which solid documentation can be obtained in the predominantly written corpora providing the empirical basis of the present investigation. This means that the focus will be less on early phases of linguistic experimentation, which by and large would be expected to take place in speech, than on the spread of innovations which are attested as marginal options in the eighteenth and nineteenth centuries and have been generalized since.

Modeling of grammatical change in current linguistic theory tends to proceed along two lines. Where the focus is on the evolution or transformation of decontextualized linguistic systems (in the sense of Saussurean *langue*) or on diachronic changes in individuals' biological-psychological language faculty (in the sense of Chomskyan competence), change is often seen as an abrupt or dramatic reorganization of structures, rules, and constraints (cf., e.g., the Generativist tradition embodied in the work of David Lightfoot from 1979 to 1999). Where the starting point for the analysis is the study of recorded performance data in their linguistic and social context – as, for example, in grammaticalization theory (Hopper and Traugott 2003) or the budding field of historical sociolinguistics (cf. Nevalainen and Raumolin-Brunberg 2003) – the picture that emerges will be one of smooth and gradual transitions rather than abrupt changes, and syntactic changes will be seen as embedded in contexts in which semantic, pragmatic, and sociolinguistic factors are important as causes or determinants of change. However, even those scholars who focus on the causes and consequences of syntactic change in the individual speaker's competence (and might therefore emphasize discontinuity among individuals and between successive generations) will agree that the spread of a linguistic innovation throughout the community is a gradual phenomenon. In the time span of the one century covered in the present book, we are thus unlikely to see any one change run out its full course, from inception in particular genres, registers, or discourse communities, to full establishment in the core grammar shared by the whole community. What we will definitely be able to note, though, is shifting frequencies of use for competing variants which – over the course of a century – often build up into significant statistical trends.

As a point of departure we will take mid-twentieth-century standard American and British English as documented in two widely known and widely used matching reference corpora – namely, Brown and LOB. To cover developments in the second half of the twentieth century, we will use the Frown and F-LOB corpora, which match Brown and LOB as closely as possible in size and composition but contain texts published not in 1961, as the originals, but in 1992 and 1991 respectively. The corpora are available as plain texts and in versions tagged for part of speech, thus making it possible to compare frequencies both for individual words or phrases and for grammatical categories, such as verbs or proper nouns (or combinations, such as adjectives preceded by adverbs). For medium- and low-frequency grammatical structures the results obtained from a systematic comparison of these four corpora often are suggestive but not conclusive. In such instances, additional digitized corpora and textual databases have been used. Chief among them is the "Baseline1900" Corpus assembling all OED quotations from 1896 to 1905 and intended to represent the state of the language at the turn of the century.[2] Apparent-time evidence will be provided from the British National Corpus, newspaper databases or World Wide Web in those instances in which the real-time corpus-linguistic working environment provides insufficient data.

4.2   Review of the literature

The present book is not the place to systematically review the large number of polemical "decay-of-English" treatments of current change, usually aimed at a lay readership and not always written by linguistic professionals (cf., e.g., Howard [1984] or most of the contributions to Ricks [1991]). Some popular surveys (such as Barber 1964 or Potter 1969/1975), on the other hand, are rather well informed and largely free of open polemic. Even these works, however, suffer from an implicit bias. First, they tend to focus on phonetic and lexical rather than grammatical change; and second, what little attention is paid to grammatical changes is usually reserved for phenomena which have aroused the concern of prescriptivists. A typical list of changes suspected to be going on in present-day standard English is the following one, which is largely based on Barber (1964: 130–144):

 — demise of the inflected form *whom*
 — use of *less* instead of *fewer* with countable nouns (e.g., *less people*)
 — regularization of irregular morphology (e.g., *dreamt → dreamed*)
 — a tendency towards analytical comparison of disyllabic adjectives (*politer, politest → more polite, most polite*)
 — spread of the *s*-genitive to non-human nouns (*the book's cover*)
 — revival of the "mandative" subjunctive, probably inspired by formal US usage (*we demand that she take part in the meeting*)
 — elimination of *shall* as a future marker in the first person
 — development of new, auxiliary-like uses of certain lexical verbs (e.g., *want to → wanna*; cf., e.g., *the way you look, you wanna see a doctor soon*)[3]

---

[2] This is a total of 66,619 quotations (if the complete time span is searched as a whole) or the marginally different sum of 66,626 if the totals for the individual years are added up – see Appendix 2 for the detailed calculations.
[3] While it is not referred to as such in the literature aimed at wider audiences, this is, of course, an obvious case of ongoing grammaticalization.

- further auxiliation of semi-auxiliaries and modal idioms such as *be going to* (→ *gonna*) or *have got to* (→ *gotta*)
- extension of the progressive to new constructions (especially modal, present perfect, and past perfect passive progressives of the type *the road would not be being built/ has not been being built/ had not been being built before the general elections*)
- use of *like*, *same as*, and *immediately* as conjunctions
- omission of the definite article in combinations of premodifying descriptive noun phrase and proper name (e.g., *renowned Nobel laureate Derek Walcott*)
- increase in the number and types of multi-word verbs (phrasal verbs, *have/ take/ give a* + verb)
- placement of frequency adverbs before auxiliary verbs (even if no emphasis is intended – *I never have said so*)
- *do*-support for *have* (*have you any money?* and *no, I haven't any money* → *do you have/ have you got any money?* and *no, I don't have any money/ I haven't got any money*)
- spread of "singular" *they* (*everybody came in their car*) to formal and standard usage.

In popular works such as Barber's, or the similarly designed Potter 1969 [1975], these phenomena are usually illustrated with more or less unsystematically collected examples. More rigorous corpus-based testing usually reveals that, while such educated guesswork is rarely off the mark completely, important qualifications are required. For example, unsystematic observation routinely overestimates the speed of change. *Whom*, whose alleged disappearance is commonly presented as a "current" phenomenon, has been optional in most of its uses since the Early Modern English period. By the nineteenth century, it was a marker of formal style, really obligatory only if preceded by a preposition. This is very much the situation today, and any attempt to demonstrate the rapid loss of the form in the recent past in corpora will fail (on which, see section 4.9.1 below). Another problem with anecdotal observation is that commentators tend to focus on the "visible" tip of the iceberg of a change, while the drift in which a particular salient phenomenon is embedded generally tends to go unnoticed. A case in point is the use of *shall*. As all commentators on the topic agree, this modal has been receding as a marker of futurity for some time, and this observation is, of course, correct (see corpus figures in section 4.3). However, what commentators usually fail to note is that this particular change is embedded in a broader development, in which the frequency of *shall* is decreasing in all its functions, which in turn is part of a yet more comprehensive trend for many modals in general to become less common (see section 4.5).

Of course, information on current change in English grammar is not only found in popular surveys. There are many detailed studies of individual phenomena in the scholarly literature, many of them additionally relevant to the present study because they are based on corpora or at least partly rely on corpus-based methodology. Rickford et al. (1995), for example, have traced the recent emergence of the topic-introducing preposition *as far as* (e.g., "as far as my situation, I am less than optimistic . . ."), which they see as having been derived from clauses of the type "as far as X is concerned" through a process of grammaticalization. Some time before that, and without mentioning the technical term "grammaticalization" – the heading under which such processes would almost certainly be subsumed in current work on syntactic change – Olofsson (1990) traced a similar development, namely the emergence of prepositional uses of *following* splitting off from the "normal" use of the form as a participle in nonfinite clauses, as is illustrated in the following example from the 1991 British reference corpus F-LOB:

> The Sunday Mirror reported the following week that thousands of readers had responded to a phone-in poll – voting by 12 to 1 in favour of the Prince giving up the "sport". **Following** the story many Sunday Mirror readers contacted the League to protest at the Prince's abuse of his pony.   (F-LOB E15 27ff.)

The highlighted participle is not the nucleus of a clause here; a paraphrase of the type "after/as they had followed the story, many readers contacted the League . . ." is hence not possible. A paraphrase with prepositional *after* ("after the story"), on the other hand, makes perfect sense.

The emergence of *be like* as a quotation-introducing verb (e.g., *she's like: "Wow! I never thought that!"*) in some registers of American English is the focus of a study by Romaine and Lange (1991). These two studies, like many similarly detailed ones, are very valuable. What they cannot do, however, is to place the highly specific phenomena under study in the broader context of change. The results obtained are difficult to generalize from, and individual case studies are not the place to raise the questions which, ultimately, are probably the major ones: Which of the many ongoing changes recorded are part of major, systematic, and comprehensive developments? Are selected parallel developments interrelated? And, if they are, how precisely do the interactions work?

In the large body of published work on grammatical change in progress, an obvious point of reference for the present study is Denison (1998), a magisterial survey of developments in English grammar since 1776, which is unrivaled both in its methodological awareness and in the breadth of its empirical coverage. Beyond the consensus list of topics based on Barber (1964; see above), the following phenomena dealt with in Denison (1998) would seem to deserve additional attention, because they show a clear diachronic dynamic in the past century:

– plural reflexive pronouns without number marking (*ourself, themself*)
– concord for collective nouns, where grammatical or otherwise obligatory concord might be replacing variable "notional" concord

- the progressive form, where (in addition to a long-noted general increase in the frequency of the forms as a whole) the few remaining structural gaps in the system might be being filled (in principle, all those forms containing three or more auxiliaries incorporating two instances of *be* such as *been being* or *be being*, from "might be being V-ed" to "would have been being V-ed")
- a number of developments in the field of modal verbs and related phenomena (e.g., changing uses of *may* and *might*, emergence of epistemic *have got to* and progressive forms for deontic *have to*)
- rapid spread of indirect passives beyond the original core verbs of the *give*-type (e.g., *I was found/got a chair, the children were read stories*, etc.).

Chief among the grammatical phenomena which are not covered adequately in any source on current change is probably the use of nonfinite complement clauses – an area in which a vast, complex, and patchily described system has evolved over the past few centuries (see section 4.8).

All in all, it seems that, in spite of a sizable body of previous work, the study of ongoing grammatical change is an area in which even more remains to be done. At the outset of his survey, Denison points out that "the topic of syntactic change in late Modern English is only just beginning to get its share of serious scholarly attention" (1998: 92). He himself bases his work on two reasonable and related assumptions: (1) the past two hundred years have seen no dramatic typological reorganization of the grammar of the language comparable to what happened in the transition from late Old English to Middle English; and (2) most observable change has therefore been a matter of different statistical preferences in an existing inventory of choices and options:

> Since relatively few categorial losses or innovations have occurred in the last two centuries, syntactic change has more often been statistical in nature, with a given construction occurring throughout the period and either becoming more or less common generally or in particular registers. The overall, rather elusive effect can seem more a matter of stylistic than of syntactic change, so it is useful to be able to track frequencies of occurrence from eModE through to the present day.   (1998: 93)

Among the "relatively few" categorial innovations, Denison includes the spread of the progressive to the passive and to certain types of copular construction. On the one hand, the picture he paints is an encouraging one from a corpus-linguistic point of view because it is only through the detailed analysis of corpora that changes of the type described by Denison will be verified and documented. On the other hand, it complicates matters considerably, because grammatical change is accessible only indirectly, through changing stylistic fashions which govern people's expectations of what constitutes good or appropriate usage in specific text types or communicative genres. It seems that the history of English grammar in the recent past has to be written against the background of changes in traditions of speaking and writing and, ultimately, of the cultural history of the English-speaking peoples – an idea which will be taken up again in Chapter 6.

From such a broader perspective, many of the individual changes which will be discussed below appear less as direct grammatical change than as symptoms of over-arching sociocultural developments. For some time now, for example, and increasingly so since the 1960s and 1970s, an egalitarian and informal communicative culture has been promoted in the public domain which has brought the norms of writing closer to the norms of spoken usage. In grammatical terms this has favored the rapid disappearance of archaisms such as *upon* for *on* or the subjunctive in all but its mandative use, and led to a decrease in the popularity of typical markers of formal and written style such as the passive voice. On the other hand, it has facilitated the spread of informal grammatical options such as contractions, the *going to*-future, or certain types of progressive into domains in which they used to be rare.

The following sections of this chapter will present corpus-based case studies of grammatical change in progress in present-day English, starting with developments in the finite verb phrase, then moving on to nonfinite clauses, and ending with a few observations on the noun phrase. This order of priorities reflects the fact that in the recent history of the language the grammar of the verb has shown considerable diachronic dynamic, while the grammar of the noun phrase has remained stable in its basic outlines, with a few developments at the margin and some fluctuation in the choice of variants.

4.3   Aspect: twentieth-century changes in the structure and use of the progressive

While there have not been any dramatic changes in the use of the present, past, and perfect tenses in the twentieth century, verbal aspect in English is still rapidly developing. As Denison points out, late Modern English here continues a long-standing historical trend:

> The progressive construction, as in *I was swimming*, has undergone some of the most striking syntactic changes of the lModE period. By early in the ModE period the BE + -*ing* pattern was already well established, and its overall frequency has increased continuously ever since. Dennis (1940) estimates an approximate doubling every century from 1500, though with a slowing down in the eighteenth century and a spurt at the beginning of the nineteenth (Strang 1982: 429). Arnaud, working from a corpus of private letters and extrapolating to the speech of literate, middle-class people, estimates a threefold increase during the nineteenth century alone (1983: 84).   (1998: 143)

Changes affecting the progressive are of three types which need to be kept distinct, although they are often treated as one and the same phenomenon. First, many uses of the progressive which were already fully established around

1900 have increased their discourse frequencies since then. Second, new progressive forms have been created to fill the few remaining niches in the verbal paradigms – such as the present perfect passive – for which they were marginal or completely unavailable in the nineteenth century. Third, and on much weaker grounds, it has been suggested that there is currently a greater readiness than before to use the progressive form with stative verbs such as *want* or *understand*. A common misperception is that the second and third changes are the causes of the first, the statistical increase in the discourse frequency of the progressive (cf. Potter [1969 [1975]: 118–122] or Aitchison [1991: 100], who both suggest such a link). As can easily be shown through the analysis of corpora, this is not so.

Let us deal with the three separate developments in the order they were mentioned. Corpus evidence shows that the increase in the textual frequency of the progressive has largely occurred **within the existing framework of forms and rules**. Both the new forms (e.g., the present perfect passive progressive) and the suspected new uses (progressive for stative verbs) are far too infrequent to account for the frequency shifts that can be observed. Mair and Hundt (1995) have obtained the figures in Table 4.1 in a manual analysis of all progressive forms in the press sections (A–C, around 176,000 words each) of the four corpora providing the starting point for the present analysis.

As can be seen, the increases observed are statistically significant both in the British and the American data, which is not the case for the regional contrasts to be observed between British and American English at any one time. Further research on the (tagged versions of the) two British corpora was carried out by Nicholas Smith (2002), who noted an increase of 28.9 percent – from 980 to 1,263 – for the present active progressive and of 31.3 percent – from 198 to 260 – for the past active progressive in the complete versions of the two British corpora. Twentieth-century developments, it should be pointed out in conclusion, continue the long-term statistical trend mentioned by Denison (1998) above and documented in the sources he quotes.[4]

If the fact that there has been a significant increase in the frequency of progressives in the course of the twentieth century seems beyond doubt, what is more difficult to provide is a convincing explanation. Are we dealing with an instance of grammatical change directly, or are we seeing one grammatical symptom of a stylistic change, in which the norms of written English have moved closer to spoken usage, where the progressive has always been more common than in writing (see, for example, the figures in Biber et al. [1999: 461–463])?

As for the second type of change, the twentieth century has seen **the creation of new progressive constructions** in the few remaining niches of

---

[4] Additional sources could easily be added. Probably the most elegant way of making the point is the treatment in Jespersen (1909–1949: IV, 177), who used Bible translations from various periods as parallel historical corpora. More fine-grained and differentiated statistical evidence is provided by Nehls (1988), among others.

Table 4.1. *Progressive forms in the press sections (A–C) of four reference corpora*

	1961	1991/1992
British English (LOB/F-LOB)	606	716
American English (Brown/Frown)	593	663

Significances: LOB: F-LOB $p < 0.01$, Brown: Frown $p < 0.05$; LOB: Brown and F-LOB: Frown not significant

the verbal paradigm in which the form did not used to be current in the recent past – in the main forms such as the present or past perfect passive progressive ('*I have been being interviewed*'), the future/conditional/modal passive progressive ('*I will/would/might* (etc.) *be being interviewed*') or the future/conditional/modal perfect passive progressive ('*I will/would/might* (etc.) *have been being interviewed*'), which all involve sequences of *be being* or *been being* and the use of three or four auxiliaries alongside the main verb. The filling of structural gaps in the verbal paradigm that we are witnessing today builds on previous such episodes; for example, the replacement of the present and past "passival" (*dinner is/was preparing*) by the passive progressive (*dinner is/was being prepared*) in the late eighteenth and early nineteenth centuries. These new progressive forms are, of course, highly salient to observers and interesting for a theoretical analysis, but statistically they are insignificant and certainly do not account for the global increase observed in the discourse frequency of the progressive. In fact, they are so infrequent that the four corpora fail to yield conclusive results. For example, the present perfect passive progressive, one of the suspected late nineteenth/early twentieth-century additions to the paradigm, is attested in none of them. Nor is the past perfect passive progressive. The British material yields three instances of modalized passive progressives – two from LOB and one from F-LOB:

> To ridicule them only pushes them farther into themselves, so that they become unable to speak about it to anybody and the seeds of any amount of trouble are sown, the harvest of which **may still be being reaped** at forty or fifty.   (LOB, D6: 16ff.)

> We have also to notice that while the entropy of our given system will increase with external or given time, this relation is not reciprocal, for, if we first choose our time, a rare state in our stationary process **will just as likely be being approached** as **being departed from**.
> (LOB, J18: 197ff.)

> So the news that a second park-and-ride route **could be being intro-duced** for a trial period at Clifton Moor north of the city should be welcomed, especially as Christmas is approaching.
> (F-LOB, B18: 109ff.)

The first thing to note about these examples is that the progressive is not obligatory yet in such constructions, which is a sign that they are recent. Second, the return of examples from the four corpora, while clearly not conclusive in itself, is not entirely fortuitous. Modal forms of the type illustrated in these three examples are fairly common in the 100-million-word British National Corpus at around 60 instances. The present perfect passive progressive, on the other hand, which is absent completely from LOB and F-LOB, is attested no more than once, even in the much larger BNC:

> That er, er, little action has been taken in the last thirty forty years since this **has been being discussed**, erm, I think the first international conference erm, produced their own report in nineteen sixty.
>
> (BNC, JJG 542)

Tellingly, this example is from a spoken text and produced spontaneously. Again, as was observed for the related "modal" forms above, the use of the progressive is not obligatory yet.

Summarizing the corpus data on the currency of the "new" progressives, we can say that the forms in question can be attested if the database is sufficient, and that the spread proceeds considerably more smoothly in the modal environments (*be being*) than in the perfective ones (*have/had been being*). This robust result from the BNC can be replicated in the much more risky circumstances of Web-based corpus-linguistics, as is shown by the results of the regionally stratified searches in Table 4.2.[5]

Even taking into account the considerable margin of uncertainty of the search, it is remarkable that, as predicted, the *be being*-forms are consistently more frequent than *been being* in all varieties. In addition, there is a more specific result. In all British and British-influenced varieties – Irish, Australian, New Zealand, South African – the proportion of *been being/be being* hovers very roughly around 1 in 10; in the dominantly Northern American material of the domains .us, .ca, .edu, .gov, .nasa.gov it approximates values between 1 in 3 and 1 in 6. Given the risks besetting the statistical analysis of such Web-derived data and the caution required in the interpretation of apparent-time data, it would be foolhardy to claim that these figures prove anything, but they do provide a hint that British and British-derived varieties of English

---

[5] The searches were restricted to English-language pages. The frequencies obtained are subject to the qualifications necessary when using the Web as corpus (on which, see the Appendix). In addition, no manual analysis of hits was undertaken to separate instances of chance proximity (*the weirdest experience of my life has been being at the mercy of such a terrible boss* or *another thing you might consider would be being polite for a change*) from genuine instances of progressive forms. However, spot-checks undertaken on selected samples revealed that the proportion of genuine hits tended to be between 60 percent and 80 percent of instances and that, more importantly, the error rate was comparable in both columns.

Table 4.2. Been being *and* be being *on the English-language Web (Google, 23 July 2003)*

Database	been being	be being
www/total English language	21,200	80,700
.uk	960	10,900
.ie	36	264
.au	368	4,210
.nz	80	862
.za	37	236
.us	330	783
.edu	1,320	4,640
.gov	190	913
.nasa.gov	20	50
.ca	333	1,710

might be leading the way in the establishment of the modal passive progressive – a view which would have to be corroborated in further corpus-based analyses.

Corpus-evidence on the third development, the suspected spread of non-canonical uses of the progressive with stative verbs, is conflicting. On the whole, it seems plausible to regard the use of progressives with stative verbs as an instance of contextually/pragmatically licenced rule-breaking for specific rhetorical or expressive effect – an option which has been available ever since the present system of rules emerged in the eighteenth century. The reason that the phenomenon seems more in evidence today than in the past is simply that the type of informal context in which it happens is less likely to have been preserved in the past.

To underscore this point, let us have a look at the type of example which would typically be used to illustrate the alleged trend towards a new "stative" progressive. Here is a passage from an interview with novelist David Lodge, who comments on the difficulties involved in reading to non-English-speaking audiences:

> When you are reading comic fiction you will very quickly find out whether they are understanding you, by whether they laugh or not.
> ("David Lodge in interview with Rüdiger Ahrens,"
> *Anglistik* 1 [1999]: 21)

Under normal circumstances, we would indeed expect the simple form here, as *understand* is a typically stative verb of inert mental perception. The use of the progressive might be due to the fact that Lodge is making what is normally subconscious and automatic (i.e., understanding a joke) the focus of conscious reflection (after all, the passage is about understanding jokes in another language, which might require some conscious effort). On the other hand, it is usually futile to erect complicated ad hoc explanations around such occasional instances of contextually licenced rule-breaking, because they merely illustrate a truth which is obvious to most grammarians – namely that (in the words of Edward Sapir) "all grammars leak" and that, hence, grammatical rules should not be seen as natural laws but as conventions which can be flouted occasionally for good rhetorical effect in specific contexts.

Progressive *understand*, however interesting any individual instance might be for elucidating the complex interplay of syntax, semantics, and pragmatics in the use of aspect in present-day English, is a phenomenon which is completely insignificant from a statistical point of view. This becomes clear immediately if one consults the 100-million-word British National Corpus. A search for any form of *be* followed by *understanding* in a span of two words revealed a total of 12 instances (8 written, 4 spoken). All four spoken ones are, interestingly enough, produced by people in the teaching field and of the following type:

> If you get the right answers you know that they are with you and you know they are understanding what you have to say.   (BNC, JSA 568)

Admittedly, even if the examples are few, they might at least be new. But again a cursory look at older texts reveals that precisely the same amount of irregularity can be attested for the early twentieth century and even for the early nineteenth century. Compare, for example, the following extracts from novels by Evelyn Waugh, George Eliot, and Jane Austen, which either offer fictional dialogue or at least represented speech and show the progressive at play in more or less exactly the way it would work in standard English today whenever normally subconscious activity is made the object of reflection or bald statements are to be made less peremptory and more polite:

> "That's excellent, Jane. You're just the sort we want. How soon can you sail?"
> "How soon would you be wanting me to?"
> "Well, there's a vacancy in Rio I'm filling at the end of the week. I'm sending two very nice girls. Would you like to be going with them?"
> (Waugh, *Decline and fall*: II, v)

Note here the nice contrast between the first, simple use of *want* ("the sort we want"), and the second, progressive and polite one.

> It must be my own dullness. I am seeing so much all at once, and not understanding half of it.   (Eliot, *Middlemarch*: Chapter 21)

> "I can see what you are thinking of as well as can be, Dodo," said Celia, "you are wanting to find out if there is anything uncomfortable for you to do now, only because Mr. Casaubon wished it."
> (Eliot, *Middlemarch*: Chapter 50)

He was not intending, however, by such action, to be conveying to her that unqualified approbation and encouragement which her hopes drew from it. It was designed only to express his participation in all that interested her, and to tell her that he had been hearing what quickened every feeling of affection.   (Austen, *Mansfield Park*: Chapter 34)

Fanny estranged from him, silent and reserved, was an unnatural state of things; a state which he must break through, and which he could easily learn to think she was wanting him to break through.
(Austen, *Mansfield Park*: Chapter 35)

Note that in Austen's case such uses occur at an early stage in the development of the progressive in which it is not yet completely obligatory in many of its modern standard uses:

"Have you breakfasted? – When shall you be ready? – Does Susan go? – were questions following each other rapidly.
(Austen, *Mansfield Park*: Chapter 46)

Here it is difficult to see a modern writer/speaker not using the progressive: *Is Susan going?* In sum, the examples show that the "stative" progressives are thus not the recent innovation they are considered to be by many commentators.

However, this does not mean that the progressive attained its final and definitive functional load in the eighteenth century and that there have been no functional changes since. As Comrie argues from a cross-linguistic and typological perspective,

it may well be that English is developing from a restricted use of the progressive, always with Progressive meaning, to this more extended meaning range [i.e., progressive form indicating contingent state], the present anomalies representing a midway stage between these two points.
(1976: 39)

There is the "interpretive" use of the progressive identified best in Huddleston and Pullum's reference grammar (2002: 165), which might be a recent result of the development predicted by Comrie. Not surprisingly, it is attested fairly unambiguously in F-LOB and Frown:

I can only add that when Paul Gascoigne says he will not be happy until he stops playing football, he **is talking** rot.   (F-LOB, A09: 81f.)

When he speaks of apocalypse, however, he **is not speaking** of it in the literal and popular sense.   (Frown, D02: 120f.)

This use may well be spreading, though not at a rate sufficient to show up in the overall statistics. In fact, attempts at statistical analyses in this case might even be self-defeating, because in a situation in which for the majority of cases the "interpretive" reading is one option alongside others only collecting the clear instances means under-reporting the phenomenon, whereas including all possible instances in the counts will lead to clear over-reporting.

4.4   The *going to*-future

The *going to*-future is clearly not a recent innovation in English grammar. Nevertheless its use has not stabilized yet. In the four one-million-word corpora, there is stability in the British data, while the form continues spreading in American English, as is shown in Table 4.3.

This is an unexpected finding because the *going to*-future, and especially its phonetically reduced variant conventionally spelled as *gonna*, are often seen as American innovations spreading into British usage. In view of this, it is particularly surprising to see *going to* at a lower level in American English in the early data. However, the apparent paradox is resolved as soon as one looks into the reason for the frequency increase: almost all of it is due to instances in reported speech (cf. the figures in brackets). The figures thus say little about the development of the grammar of American English in the period under review but show that 1990s American writing contained more direct speech than 1960s writing, with direct-speech passages obviously providing a more hospitable environment to a traditionally informal construction. In other words, what changed was not the grammar but the textual structure of written texts, which became more oral or more colloquial.

Thus, the results of the search for the *going to*-future illustrate a general point made in the introduction. The investigation of change at close range is made difficult by the fact that it is embedded in synchronic regional and stylistic variation, which is sometimes more drastic than the short-term diachronic shift. This is instantly evident from an analysis of the BNC.[6] The average overall frequency of the form is c. 280 instances per million, which is in the range of the values obtained from the four written corpora. The frequency for the spoken texts alone, however, is c. 888 per million, and this is even before the many instances of *gonna* missed in the search are included. At the other extreme, the frequency of the *going to*-future descends as low as c. 36 per million for the natural and pure sciences category or c. 100 for social science texts (which has to be seen against the average of c. 207 per million for all written texts).

To assess the status of the *going to*-future in the twentieth century a two-pronged approach will be taken, which combines a survey of the form's long-term diachronic development with an investigation of its synchronic

---

[6] *Going to*-futures were targeted through a tag-sequence search for *going to*, followed immediately by a verb. This obviously misses the many instances of *gonna* in the spoken texts.

Table 4.3. Going to-*futures in four corpora (examples from direct speech in brackets)*

	1961	1991/92
British English (LOB/F-LOB)	233 (122)	236 (120)
American English (Brown/Frown)	185 (85)	294 (197)

Significances: Brown: Frown $p < 0.001$; LOB: Brown and F-LOB: Frown $p < 0.001$.

distribution in samples of late twentieth-century spontaneous speech, the text type presumably representing the most advanced stage in its development.

The rise of the *going to*-future since the Middle English period is a textbook example of grammaticalization, and treated as such in many standard works on the subject, for example Hopper and Traugott (2003: 69, 93, 125). While, strictly speaking, there is no precise end-point to a grammaticalization process – after all, phonetic reduction and morphological incorporation can always proceed further after the most important semantic and syntactic settings have been decisively and irreversibly switched – the grammaticalization of *be going to* from "progressive of a motion verb followed by infinitive of purpose" to "indicator of future" was completed long ago. Joshua Poole's *English accidence*, published in 1646, explicitly recognizes *going to* as a future marker, which strongly, if indirectly, suggests that grammaticalization was well under way by that time (see Danchev and Kytö [1994: 67] for a quotation and discussion of the relevant passage of the work). According to Jespersen, the grammaticalized use "began towards the end of the 15th c., but is not yet frequent ab[out] 1600" (1909–1949: IV, 217). The relevant OED entry (47b) gives a first good example for the year 1482[7] and provides continuous documentation from the late seventeenth century onwards.

Quantitative data is available on the subsequent spread of the *going to*-future, usually obtained by calculating the proportion of *going to*-futures and *shall/will*-futures in a given work of literature (cf. the review of such work in Danchev and Kytö [2001]). In addition, there are specialist corpus-linguistic studies of *going*

---

[7] The oft-quoted "thys onhappy sowle ... was goyng to be brought into helle for the synne an onleful lustys of her body" of the Monk of Evesham. The example has the advantage of being a truly diagnostic one, as both the semantics of the verb *bring* and the passive of the infinitive are incompatible with a literal interpretation of the verb *go* as a motion verb. Note also that the *going to*-form is used in the past tense, illustrating the future-in-the-past use that has remained common to the present day. The example is a free translation from a Latin original, which, however, does not seem to have any direct impact on the use of *going to* (see Danchev and Kytö [1994: 61] for a discussion). Danchev and Kytö cite a potential earlier case from 1438, in which the verb *go* could with some justification be read in its literal, motion-verb sense. On possible French influence on the rise of the construction in English, see Danchev and Kytö (2001).

OED / *going to*

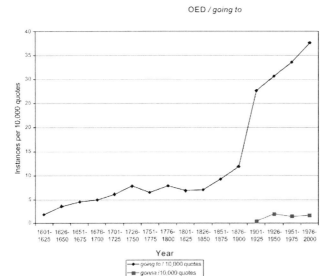

Figure 4.1 *Going to* and *gonna* 1600–2000 – frequency as n/10,000 citations

to – in particular, Danchev and Kytö (1994) for the earliest period (based on the Helsinki Corpus) and Mair (1997b) for the very recent past (based on Brown, LOB, and their Freiburg updates, Frown and F-LOB). However, as the corpora sampled are either too small or too heterogeneous to allow easy comparison, no coherent historical record emerges from these studies. It is here that a full analysis of the OED quotation base from the year 1600 – that is, the period when *going to*-futures cease being marginal oddities – comes in useful.

Figure 4.1, which indicates the occurrence of *going to* per 10,000 quotations, shows that a marked rise in frequency did not occur until the end of the nineteenth century, but has continued unabated since then.

In order not to be misled by purely quantitative measures, I singled out the attestations from the last quarter of each of the four centuries surveyed for close analysis, separating instances of prepositional and infinitival *to*. This yielded the differentiated picture shown in Table 4.4.

Judging from the language-historical evidence surveyed above, grammaticalization was complete by the end of the seventeenth century. This was at a time when (see Figure 4.1) the increase in the discourse frequency of the form in the OED quotation base had not even got under way. But it was also the time at which infinitival *to*, the relevant environment for grammaticalization, already accounted for more than half of all instances of *going to*. It may well be this latter statistical fact which is the crucial indicator of grammaticalization occurring/having occurred, while the subsequent rise to near saturation point (90+ percent for the present), accompanied by the drastic increase in the overall

Table 4.4. Going to – *manually post-edited output for four quarter-centuries*

	Going + infinitive (absolute frequencies)	Going + infinitive (as n/10,000 quotes)	Going + infinitive (as % of all instances of *going to*)
1676–1700	20	2.5	51.3
1776–1800	37	4.7	59.7
1876–1900	234	9.1	76.5
1976–2000	158	34.2	90.8

Table 4.5. Will/shall *and* going to-*futures in four spoken corpora (percentages, adapted from Szmrecsanyi 2003: 303)*

	CSAE	CSPAE	BNC-DS	BNC-CG
will/shall	52.8	68.9	72.3	72.6
going to	47.2	31.1	27.7	27.4

absolute frequency of *going to*, documents the relatively rapid spread of a successful innovation through different styles and genres.[8]

As announced above, we will now turn from long-term coverage of this process of grammaticalization to the use of the *going to*-future in late twentieth-century samples of British and American spontaneous speech. The most interesting question here is whether *going to* might have become the statistically most frequent option to refer to future time in spoken English and thus ousted *will* + infinitive in this function.

Szmrecsanyi (2003) has looked at (all realizational variants of) the *will/shall* and *going to*-futures in four corpora representing contrasting formality levels in spoken British and American English. The Santa Barbara Corpus of Spoken American English (CSAE) provides data on informal American speech, while the Corpus of Spoken Professional American English (CSPAE) illustrates US usage at a more formal level. For British English, he has compared usage in the spoken-demographic (informal) sample (BNC-DS) and contrasted it to the context-governed (more formal) parts of the BNC (BNC-CG). Table 4.5 gives the percentages for the two types of future.

[8] Part of the precise shape of the curve is undoubtedly due to the nature of the corpus, with its bias towards the written language. Assuming that the *going to*-future arose in the spoken language, and then started spreading into formal written discourse, we would expect a time-lag, indicating the period it took for the new form to lose its "informal" stigma and to appear in writing. It would, of course, be interesting to see whether the statistical facts reported here are unique to the case of *going to*, or whether comparable frequency patterns can be observed in other grammaticalization processes.

Table 4.6. Going to- *and* will-*futures in two age groups in the spoken-demographic BNC (normalized frequencies/words per million)*

	going to	gonna	will	'll	I'll	we'll	I will	we will	I shall	we shall	total
15–24	726	2,701	1,116	4,515	2,313	376	189	24	74	2	12,036
60+	1,114	1,024	1,246	4,011	1,721	496	145	31	174	37	9,999

The American data illustrate the expected trend: *going to* and *will* are about equally frequent in current informal usage, whereas *will* is still the preferred form in more formal registers. The formality factor is, somewhat surprisingly, not in evidence in the two British samples, which both offer a picture comparable to formal American usage as documented in the CSPAE.

However, the BNC, with its opportunities for apparent-time comparisons by speaker age, class, and genre, shows that the picture of apparent stability in British English is a misleading one, and that the highly systematic synchronic variation very likely reflects fairly rapid ongoing change. Table 4.6 above lists all forms of *going to*, *gonna*, *will*, *won't*, *'ll*, and *shall* with a future meaning in the 15–24 and 60+ age brackets. The table gives normalized frequencies per million words. This makes visible first trends, which will in some cases be accentuated considerably by further qualitative analysis.

In a number of respects the frequencies may be misleading. Looking for instances of *I/we shall* will under-collect relevant forms, because of possible ellipsis of subjects, not uncommon in spontaneous speech (e.g., *OK . . . shall do*). Similarly, this search fails to identify questions, and contracted negatives (*shall I/we win?*, *I/we shan't win*), and forms with adverbs intervening between the pronoun and the modal (*I always shall believe you*). The same is true for the corresponding patterns with *will*. It is unlikely, however, that inclusion of the lost instances would have decisively altered the results in either case. On the other hand, the searches for *will* over-collect, because they yield modal uses in addition to future ones. Disambiguation is laborious and frequently impossible even in context; it was not attempted here. Last but not least, the younger group seems more ready to refer to future time by means of any available device, as is reflected by the cumulative totals of 12,036 and 9,999 respectively.

In spite of these vagaries, the figures make several obvious points. First, they demonstrate the gradual decline of the *shall*-future even in British English. In comparison to *I/we will* or *I/we'll*, it is an exotic option even in the 60+ age group, and it has clearly receded further in the speech of the 15–24s. Second, the figures are impressive evidence of the growing popularity of the contracted form *gonna*, whose frequency has nearly tripled among younger speakers (a fact also noted on the basis of extended BNC material in Krug [2000: 174f.]). Third, they show that *gonna* still has some way to go before becoming the statistically normal way of coding future time in British English (even if, as was pointed out, not all of the instances of *will* and *'ll* are future uses).

Qualitative post-analysis of the output yields one further surprising result for *going to*. For the older group of speakers, 529 of 743 relevant forms are followed by a verb and hence instances of the future use. For the younger group it is 9 out of a total of 361. The grammaticalization of the *going to*-future has advanced to a state where there is a clean phonetic split between the movement-verb use providing the basis for grammaticalization and the grammaticalized future auxiliary which tends increasingly to appear in the contracted form. In her comparative analysis of *going to* and *gonna* in the BNC, Berglund (2000) is able to show consistent apparent-time patterning, with the percentage of *gonna* realizations being:

- 75 percent in the spoken-demographic sample (as against 41 percent in the context-governed, more formal one) (2000: 38)
- 81 percent in the "male" (as against 70 percent in the "female") portion of this sample (2000: 39)
- 87 percent in the 15–24 age group as against 53 percent in the 60+ one (same sample) (2000: 40)
- 85 percent for speakers marked for social class DE (as against 66 percent for those marked AB – 2000: 40).

4.5 Modality: *must* and *shall* – two modals on the way out, and possible replacements

As Table 4.7 (published originally in Leech 2003: 228; see also Mair and Leech 2006) shows, there have been fairly drastic changes in the discourse frequencies of some English modals in the course of a mere thirty years.

Dwight Bolinger has claimed that "the system of modal auxiliaries in English [is] now undergoing wholesale reorganization" (1980: 6), so that the observed shifts do not come as a complete surprise. Whether they reflect genuine grammatical change in the English modal system or whether they had better be interpreted against the background of their much greater synchronic-stylistic variability, which makes modals such prominent markers of textual genre or discourse type,[9] is a question which will be pursued below.

Here we are concerned with two modals from the list, namely *shall* and *must*, which have taken rather pronounced dips in frequency in both British and American English. Thereby, *shall* seems to provide the easy case. The

---

[9] See, e.g., the analysis of the tagged LOB corpus provided in Johansson and Hofland (1989: I, 7–39). MD (modal verb) peaks in categories B (press/editorial) and P (romance and love story), at frequencies of 20,148 and 20,292 per million respectively, whereas modals are rarest in C (press/reviews) at 9,353 per million. It is tempting to interpret this distribution in light of the possible worlds that – each in their own way – form the subject of press editorials and romance, and the definitiveness of the judgments put forward by reviewers.

Table 4.7. *Use of the modal auxiliaries in four corpora*

	British English LOB	F-LOB	Log likelihood*	Difference (%)**		American English Brown	Frown	Log likelihood	Difference (%)
would	3,028	2,694	20.4	−11.0	would	3,053	2,868	5.6	−6.1 %
will	2,798	2,723	1.2	−2.7	will	2,702	2,402	17.3	−11.1 %
can	1,997	2,041	0.4	+2.2	can	2,193	2,160	0.2	−1.5 %
could	1,740	1,782	2.4	+2.4	could	1,776	1,655	4.1	−6.8 %
may	1,333	1,101	22.8	−17.4	may	1,298	878	81.1	−32.4 %
should	1,301	1,147	10.1	−11.8	should	910	787	8.8	−13.5 %
must	1,147	814	57.7	−29.0	must	1,018	668	72.8	−34.4 %
might	777	660	9.9	−15.1	might	635	635	0.7	−4.5 %
shall	355	200	44.3	−43.7	shall	267	150	33.1	−43.8 %
ought (to)	104	58	13.4	−44.2	ought (to)	70	49	3.7	−30.0 %
need + V	87	52	9.0	−40.2	need	40	35	0.3	−12.5 %
Total	14,667	13,272	73.6	−9.5	**Total**	13,962	12,287	68.0	−12.2 %

*Log likelihood is a measure of statistical significance: a value of 3.84 or more equates with chi-square-based p values < 0.05; a value of 6.63 or more equates with $p < 0.01$.

**The column headed Diff (%) gives the increase (+) or decrease (−) in occurrences as a percentage of the frequency in the 1961 corpora.

Table 4.8. Shall-*futures in four corpora*

	1961	1991/1992
British English (LOB/F-LOB)	150	129
American English (Brown/Frown)	81	56

obsolescence of the *shall*-future (for the first persons singular and plural) is a well-known phenomenon much lamented by British language purists, for which corpus evidence from the BNC was provided in Table 4.5 and 4.6. A detailed look at the clear future uses of *shall* in the four corpora, however, shows that the decline of the *shall*-future accounts for no more than a small part of the overall decline in the frequency of this modal. Table 4.8 presents all instances of *I/we* followed by *shall/shan't* in a span of three words.[10]

This is a (statistically not significant) decrease of merely 21 cases in the British data and of 25 in the American data, whereas the total (and statistically significant) decrease to be accounted for is 155 and 117 respectively (see Table 4.7).

What the figures for the *shall*-future show is not so much that there has been a decline in the recent past but that the form was already moribund in both varieties even back in 1961. This is particularly obvious in the American material, where it seems to hold out as a marker of formality (two of the Brown examples are from speeches by President Kennedy). Some of the more recent examples from Frown are not even genuine but show the form being used consciously for specific literary effect.[11] Most of the remaining uses are formulaic discourse-structuring or metalinguistic devices of the type "as we shall see" or "[a word/concept] that we shall call . . .," which also is a symptom of an advanced stage of obsolescence of a form. The slightly greater residual vitality of the form in British English should not be taken as a basis for the claim that the form is a twentieth-century grammatical Briticism. It was too infrequent for that even in the 1960s.

The decline of *shall* in all its uses is corroborated further by evidence from the OED, which shows that the frequency of *shall* in its quotations has been decreasing steadily throughout the twentieth century – from 60/10,000 quotes in 1901–1920, to 50 for 1921–1940, to 38 for 1941–1960, to 22 for 1961–1980, and down to 9 per 10,000 quotes for the quotations from 1980.[12]

---

[10] This strategy is time-efficient but risks losing a small number of relevant cases (see comments on Table 4.6 above).

[11] "The Gräfin was partial to the word 'shall'," reads a passage from a novel (Frown N19 100f.), which makes it obvious that in the preceding text the *shall*-future was used to characterize the distinctly non-American speech of a continental European aristocrat.

[12] It seems that the twentieth-century decline of *shall* continues a trend already evident in the nineteenth century, for the corresponding normalized frequencies (n/10,000 quotes) are 106 (1801–1820), 89 (1821–1840), 69 (1841–1860), 66 (1861–1880), 49 (1881–1900).

It is difficult to square these findings with apparent-time evidence from the spoken-demographic samples of the BNC, where *shall* peaks at frequencies of c. 417 and 520 per million words in the age groups of 25–34 and 0–14 respectively, with the four other age groups (15–24, 35–44, 45–59, and 60+) varying relatively little between 328 and 370. These figures are probably best seen as a warning against the unsupported use of apparent-time data in the study of change in progress. What they show is: (1) that the incidence of modal verbs, individually and as a class, is strongly dependent on discourse type;[13] and (2) that *shall*, while receding, is not going to disappear completely because of its secure base in specific uses among the youngest age group.

The apparent-time evidence is stronger in the case of *must*, where the age groups pattern as expected, with the slight problem that the two oldest appear in reverse order: *must* has a frequency of only 353 per million words in the 0–14 age bracket, 670 in 15–24, 761 in 25–34, 775 in 35–44, 777 in 60+, and 887 in 45–59. In this instance it is the real-time evidence from the OED which makes it difficult to postulate a long-term trend toward the decline of *must*. A real-time decrease in the discourse frequency of *must* is evident in the OED quotation base for the second half of the twentieth century: while for the three periods 1901–1920, 1921–1940, and 1941–1960 the frequency of *must* hovers around 120 (126, 118, and 124 instances per 10,000 quotes respectively), it sinks to c. 112 for 1961–1980 and 92 for 1981–2000. But levels comparable to the second half of the twentieth century are also found in the nineteenth: 106 instances per 10,000 quotes for 1801–1820, 107 for 1821–1840, 93 for 1841–1860, 100 for 1861–1880, and 98 for 1881–1900.

In the case of *must* it is tempting to relate the decrease in the frequency of the modal verb to a corresponding growth of *have to* and *have got to*, for which there is solid long-term evidence (see Krug 2000: 74–83). Short-term support from the Brown quartet of corpora is somewhat more tentative. The developments documented in Tables 4.9 to 4.11, while going in the expected direction, are still below the level of statistical significance. Hundt (1998a: 201–203) presents results of a manual count of the tokens in the press sections (Table 4.9).

Based on an automatic analysis of the complete corpora, Leech (2004: 68, see also Mair and Leech 2006) finds fluctuation rather than directed change. Unlike Hundt, Leech lists *have to* and the less common *have got to* separately (Table 4.10 and 4.11).

Manual post-editing of the results obtained by Leech would probably lead to minor changes, but his main point – that, overall, *have (got) to* has not increased to such an extent as to compensate for the decrease of *must* in the four written corpora studied – seems to be beyond doubt. In accounting for this

---

[13] Many of the instances in the youngest age group are of the type *Daddy shall I show you*, common in adult–child interaction, for example.

Table 4.9. Have (got) to *in four corpora (press texts, section A–C only)*

	1961	1991/1992
British English (LOB/F-LOB)	130	172
American English (Brown/Frown)	97	137

Table 4.10. Have got to *in four corpora*

	1961	1991/1992
British English (LOB/F-LOB)	41	27
American English (Brown/Frown)	45	52

Table 4.11. Have to *in four corpora*

	1961	1991/1992
British English (LOB/F-LOB)	757	825
American English (Brown/Frown)	627	643

unexpected and puzzling result, Leech himself points out that written English may not be the ideal text type to document the growth of *have (got) to* and points to its firm entrenchment in recent spoken data.

A good source of data for the study of contemporary spoken English is the Santa Barbara Corpus of Spoken American English, which has the added advantage of conforming to extremely high standards of transcription. Not only is it possible, therefore, to see how narrow the functional range of *must* has become in informal late twentieth-century speech, but also how far the phonetic fusion of *have got to* into the single-word marker *gotta* has progressed. For purposes of comparison, Table 4.12 also lists the frequencies in the "direct conversation" part (c. 180,000 words) of the British component of the International Corpus of English (ICE-GB), which is material comparable to the Santa Barbara Corpus.

The table is intended to cover grammaticalized (= auxiliary and auxiliary-like) exponents of obligation and necessity, and not the many additional ways of expressing the concept (such as *be obliged to, feel the need to*, etc.). An exception was made for the verb *need* (as in *there needs to be a separate phoneline* or *that's what I'm needing to do*), because it allows auxiliary syntax (which is not attested in the Santa Barbara Corpus).

Table 4.12. *Obligation and necessity in the Santa Barbara Corpus of Spoken American English and the conversation component of ICE-GB*

Form:	Santa Barbara	ICE-GB
must	23	84
must not/ mustn't	—	4
need not/ needn't		1
NEED* to	31	43
NOT* *need to*	5	7
HAVE* *to*	131	189
NOT* *have to*	10	23
HAVE* *got to*	1	104
HAVE* *gotta*	4	1
got to	—	8
gotta	6	—

*CAPITALIZED forms stand for all morphological variants, in this case *need, needs, needed, needing,* and, for NOT, *do not, does not, did not, don't, doesn't, didn't, shouldn't,* etc.

Table 4.13. Must *and* have to *by function in ICE-GB (spoken), adapted from Depraetere and Verhulst (forthcoming)*

	Deontic	Epistemic	Unclassifiable	Total
must	153	139	4	296
have to	163	3	0	166

Generally, the figures correct any doubts one might have about the currency of the semi-modals on the basis of the results from the written corpora. *Have to* is the statistically most common form in both varieties, followed (in British English) by *have got to* and *must*, and (in American English) by *need to* and *must*. This is not only so because *have to*, etc. function as suppletive forms in those syntactic environments in which *must* is deficient (e.g., the simple past), but also because they directly compete with the auxiliary. Depraetere and Verhulst (forthcoming) have looked at the functions of *have to* and *must* in ICE-GB and noted an interesting asymmetry. As Table 4.13 shows, *have to* is replacing *must* in its deontic use, but not in its epistemic function.

Currently, epistemic *must* is secure in spoken British English, as *have to* in this function has a marginal status at best. In view of the lower overall frequency of *must*, this bastion may well have started to crumble in spoken American (cf. the Santa Barbara figures in Table 4.12).

A further interesting issue is raised by the syntactically reduced and phonetically contracted realisations of *have got to*. Assuming that the ICE-GB instances of *got to* (without *have*) represent a state in the grammaticalization process almost as far advanced as one-word *gotta*, there is broad similarity here: 10 such forms in the American material as against 9 in the British data (see Table 4.12).

The figures in Table 4.12, with the corresponding data, provide information on a few further issues. In the Santa Barbara Corpus the few remaining forms of *must* in their majority express epistemic necessity rather than deontic obligation, which is expected. Main verb *need* is the norm in both varieties, and *needn't* a minor presence in the British material, which is not surprising, either. Somewhat puzzling, however, is the role of *HAVE got to*.[14] As a full form, it is considerably more common in the British data,[15] whereas the coexistence of *HAVE got to*, *got to*, and *gotta* – a nice example of synchronic layering in an ongoing process of grammaticalization[16] – is more in evidence in the American material. Both the American and the British material provide interesting examples of self-correction, which might be seen as indirect psycholinguistic evidence of ongoing grammaticalization surfacing in unmonitored speech:

> Pamela: but, you g- you go you've gotta pull these ideas from your environment, and what's gone on before.
>
> (SBC)
>
> And it's like the same thing with the voice you got to while you're moving you've got to keep it there and the audience has got to see it up there.   (ICE-GB S1A 44: 324ff.)

It is interesting to speculate about the emerging conventions for the negation of single-word *gotta*: "natural" *ain't gotta* being avoided by some because of prescriptive concerns, the likely candidate seems *haven't/ hasn't/ hadn't gotta*, but *don't gotta* is also heard, and commonly attested as a written form on the World Wide Web.[17]

---

[14] In its non-modal sense of expressing possession, *have got* goes back to the seventeenth century and started adding the deontic modal sense of obligation (cf. *you've got to be silent*) early in the nineteenth century, to which epistemic uses (cf. *it's got to be true*) were added in the twentieth century (see Krug [2000: 61] for a conspectus of sources). Krug (2000: 76–88) also supplies impressive corpus evidence on the increasing frequency of *have (got) to* over the past two hundred years.

[15] Cf. the following assessment in Denison: "It is now thought to be more typical of BrE than AmerE (Quirk [et al.] 1985: 3.34). During our period it has increased greatly in frequency at the expense of HAVE, though in nonassertive contexts HAVE is fighting back in its non-operator form" (1998: 172).

[16] Assuming that the grammaticalization of *gotta* was dependent on the presence of *have got to*, it is interesting to speculate why this form, which arose only at the beginning of the Modern English period, disappeared from American English so rapidly.

[17] Readers unwilling to plow their way through several thousand attestations in the more informal reaches of the Web might want to think of John Hammond's famous "You don't

Like the negation with *do*, increasingly common combinations such as *gonna gotta* raise the interesting question of the finiteness of *gotta*, and its etymological ancestor *have got to*. Palmer (1990: 116) and, following him, Denison (1998: 172) rule out the form *to have got to* (except, of course, as an accidental combination such as might occur in *to have got to the city center so quickly surprised us*). A search of the Web (Google, 9 December 2002) for "to have got to go" (the common verb *go* being added in order to avoid spurious returns of the type *to have got to London at last!*) yielded one questionable instance of a nonfinite use ("Oh to be a comedy groupie again, and *to have got to go* to the launch party in a bar . . ."), in which it is not quite clear whether we are dealing with the modal idiom *have got to* or a perfective use of the inchoative construction *get to do something*. Three additional unambiguous instances found illustrated the sequence *going to have got to*, as in:

> I think we're going to have got to go further technologically and design-wise to bring more excitement into this game, with things like storylines.
> (www.dreamcastmagazine.co.uk)

This obviously represents the writer's attempt to honor the conventions of standard orthography in rendering the colloquial form *gonna gotta* (of which the Web contains rather more instances). A more general follow-up search for all combinations of *be going to* and *have got to* undertaken on 13 September 2003 yielded the following picture. With 24 genuine instances, *gonna gotta* was the most common realization of this combination, with the material not unexpectedly coming from fiction, transcription of pop-music lyrics, and chat and discussion groups. *Gonna got to* occurred twice, while the forms *going to have got to* (10) and *gonna have got to* (4) were almost exclusively restricted to British material.[18]

Coming back to the main lines of the development for the summary of the present section, we can draw the following conclusions. The discourse frequency of *shall* has declined further from an already low level during the past century. Its almost complete disappearance from the future paradigm is not much felt, as there are several alternative options available. The chief reason for its decline seems to have been that its historical core use – expressing strong obligation – dissolved, with this function being redistributed to other modals (e.g., *must*, *should*) or modal idioms (*be supposed to*, *be to*). It is likely to persist in questions and in a number of formulaic uses.

The obsolescence of *must* is a more recent phenomenon, which has triggered a number of compensatory developments. One well-known and well-described

---

gotta love me," from his album *Frogs for Snakes*. The form *didn't gotta*, while attested a few dozen times in Web material, is still very much rarer.

[18] The reader unwilling to check may think of the line "You gonna gotta get up to get DOWN" popularized by rapper Coolio. Similarly, the sequence "going to want to," which has markedly increased in the recent past, must be considered an orthographic realization of *gonna wanna*.

such development, to which the above discussion has added some details from the recent past and current spoken data, is the rise of *have to, have got to*, and, subsequently, *gotta*. A newer and so far largely unexplored phenomenon, however, is the drastic increase in the frequency of *need to*, which in spite of its main-verb syntax seems to be taking over increasingly modal functions (see Taeymans 2004: 112). Auxiliary *need*, on the other hand, is receding, as is shown by the corpus findings presented here, and results from related corpus-based work by others (cf. Smith [2003] for the Brown family of written corpora and Taeymans [2004] for the BNC).[19] What seems to make *need to* a particularly suitable substitute for *must* or *have (got) to* is the politeness benefits resulting from its use. Telling someone that they *need to pay attention* may be preferable to telling them that they *must* or *have to pay attention*, because it phrases an order in such a way that fulfilling it is presented as satisfaction of the recipient's "needs."

4.6   Further developments in tense, aspect, modality: a synopsis of current research

To complement the in-depth studies presented in sections 4.3 to 4.5, the present section will summarize corpus-based research by others on aspects of the grammar of the finite verb for which change is suspected for the twentieth century.

Chief among them are several further phenomena in the domain of modality. Whereas in general the subjunctive has been a moribund category since the Early Modern English period, there is one use which has made a surprising comeback since the early twentieth century, first in (formal) American English, but latterly also in other varieties (cf. Övergaard [1995] on developments in British English). Research on the "Brown quartet" of corpora undertaken by Hundt (1998b) and Serpollet (2001) supports this generally accepted view and fleshes it out for the second half of the century. Optional past subjunctives in subordinate clauses introduced by *if, as if* or *as though* (cf., e.g., . . . *if/ as if/ as though he were the boss here*) are shown to be on the decline. They may persist as formality markers in written genres for some time, but their future is bleak. The mandative use, on the other hand, as illustrated by forms such as *the committee requested that the report (not) be published*, is spreading. Serpollet (2001: 541) gives the following provisional frequency data for the mandative subjunctive from the four corpora: LOB 14 → F-LOB 33 occurrences; Brown

---

[19]   The spread (or otherwise) of main-verb *need* has been the subject of a dispute between Visser (1970–1973: III/1, 1429–1430), who assumes that main-verb uses of *need* are spreading in recent English, and Palmer (1990: 128), who claims that auxiliary *need* remains common and main-verb *need* is typical of written and formal language. Denison reserves judgment on the issue, saying that "until larger corpora become available it is not possible to verify either claim" (1998: 170). The figures for auxiliary- and main-verb uses of *need* reported here, especially those from the spoken corpora, generally support Visser.

91 → Frown 78 occurrences. Hundt (1998b: 163, 173), following a slightly different counting procedure, arrives at: LOB 12 → F-LOB 44.

More important in the expression of modality than the subjunctive in present-day English are of course the nine central modals and several functionally related marginal modals (*dare, need, ought to, used to*), modal idioms (e.g., *had better*), and semi-auxiliaries (e.g., *be able to, have [got] to*, and *be supposed to*).[20] For a surprisingly high proportion of them diachronic changes are suspected for the recent past. Denison (1998: 165ff.), for example, mentions the following developments affecting the use of *may* and *might*:

1 the demise of past deontic *might* (e.g., *I begged that I might stay*)
2 a tendency to replace *may* with *can*, both in its deontic and epistemic uses
3 a loss of the functional distinction between *may* and *might*, in epistemic uses (following Coates 1983: 153)
4 a tendency for *may* to be (mis?)-used for *might* (Denison 1998: 177f.).

The last-named phenomenon – illustrated, for example, by sentences such as *the victim may have been dead for days before police arrived on the scene* – is not very frequent but tends to arouse considerable prescriptive concern. Denison offers two possible explanations: a small-scale "local" one which sees such uses as hypercorrect responses to the disappearing contrast between *may* and *might*, and a large-scale one, which interprets this phenomenon as one specific symptom of a more general trend, namely the erosion of tense back-shift in dependent clauses. Assuming that the large-scale explanation holds, it would account for occasionally attested past-reference uses of *must*, which would otherwise have to be interpreted as inexplicable and unmotivated archaisms.

Another modal expression commented on by Denison is *had better* (1998: 173). Current developments affecting this expression are (1) a tendency to drop *had*, and (2) occasional recategorization of the remaining *better* as a core modal, as apparent, for example, in the use of enclitic negation, *bettern't* (for which Denison reports an early attestation in a representation of child language from 1895). The spoken-demographic material from the BNC reveals that the first tendency has progressed considerably. A search for "you better not," followed by verbs, yielded a total of 101 instances.[21] This is almost the same as the 103[22] instances of *you'd better*. In the smaller sample of negative forms, the simplified variant (*you better not*) even outnumbers the traditional one (*you'd better not*) at 9 to 4. A search for *bettern't* in the spoken corpus material consulted for the present study yields no results, and a Web search suggests that the form has remained restricted to child language, as it was in the late nineteenth

---

[20] The classification and terminology here follow Quirk et al. (1985: 137).
[21] The search was conducted using the tag-sequence search facility of the BNC World. Four instances of "hadn't you better" were subtracted from the raw total of 105.
[22] Composed of 99 returns on the lexical search, plus the 4 instances of "hadn't you better" subtracted from the preceding count.

century, the period from which Denison obtained his earliest example. The BNC spoken material also supports Denison's claim that enclitic negation for *used to* (*usedn't to*) is disappearing fast in British English (1998: 175f.). Unlike operator negation (*didn't used to*), of which there are 20 instances, it is not attested at all.[23]

Most of the research on current changes in the English modal system has focused on changes in the form, function, and frequency of individual modals or modal expressions. A new departure is presented in recent work by Leech (2003), which has looked at changes in the discourse frequency of the category of modals as a whole – with a surprising result. Modals, which until recently were a high-growth area in English grammar, decreased significantly in the time span covered by the Brown quartet of corpora. This represents a U-turn in a consistent contrary drift since Old English and requires an explanation. Some of this decrease is probably not significant in grammatical terms because it is due to a change in contemporary stylistic norms, which favor informal and direct expression over formal, polite, and indirect phrasing. An expression such as *this would seem to suggest . . .* might strike a writer as too pompous and might be replaced by the blunter *this suggests . . .* However, grammatical factors are no doubt involved, as well. The easy explanation – central modals being replaced by modal idioms and semi-auxiliaries – does not seem to hold. As Mair and Leech (2006: 327) put it in a summary of the relevant findings:

> The least frequent modals – *shall, ought to* and *need* (in auxiliary construction) have plummeted, and the mid-frequency modals *must* and *may* have also declined drastically. On the other hand, the most common modals *will, can* and *would* have maintained their position robustly.
>
> Interestingly, it appears that the modals have lost frequency by around 10% in both sets of corpora, but the decline is a little sharper in AmE; also, that in AmE the frequency both in 1961 and in 1992 is lower. This looks like a follow-my-leader situation, in which BrE is following in the track of AmE.
>
> . . .
>
> Perhaps what is most striking, however, is that the semi-modals in aggregate are so much less frequent than the modals: added together they are less frequent than the single modal *will*! From this evidence it is obviously difficult to mount a general argument that the semi-modals are increasing *at the expense of* the core modals.

The proportional frequency of the other modal expressions is somewhat greater in the spoken material, but it seems that after a period of expansion, in

---

[23] *Usedn't to* is not attested even once in the whole corpus (although there are 11 instances of *used not to* in the written material). *Did not used to* is not attested and, in addition to the 20 instances of *didn't used to* in speech, there are 4 more in writing, 3 of which are from fictional dialogue.

which new forms emerged and their functional range and discourse frequency kept expanding, the system of English modal verbs may now be facing a period of retrenchment, in which core members persist but some of the more marginal members of the class are being eliminated.

In comparison to aspect and mood/modality, the tense system of present-day English has remained rather stable for the past century. One exception may be the use of the present perfect, which in some of its functions is less frequent in American English than in British English. In addition, in American English past tense is possible for "recent indefinite past" expressions which usually require the present perfect in British English, such as *did you eat yet?* (for *have you eaten yet?*) or *did you go to England?* (for *have you been to England?*). This is an accepted contrast in regional preferences, but its diachrony is unclear. Is American English more conservative, in having been more resistant to the spread of the present perfect since the Early Modern English period, or is American English more advanced, with the decline of the present perfect representing a recent, and possibly spreading, innovation? These questions have been the subject of corpus-based analyses in a number of publications by Elsness (in particular, Elsness 1997, forthcoming). In his investigation of the four corpora he notes that, as expected, the incidence of the present perfect is significantly lower in Brown than in LOB, that there is little diachronic change from Brown to Frown, but a considerable drop from LOB to F-LOB, which has brought British English closer to American English. Seen against the background of the long-term development, the most likely scenario is that, after expanding for several centuries in frequency and functional range, the present perfect has now entered a phase of slow decline, which set in somewhat earlier in American English than in British English.

4.7   Current changes in the English voice system

4.7.1 The get-*passive*

There is agreement in the literature that the *get*-passive[24] is among the faster-spreading recent grammatical innovations in English;[25] what precisely the *get*-passive is, or whether indeed it is a true passive at all, on the other hand, is a matter of some debate. It is not possible in the scope of the present book to explore this controversy in detail (on which see, e.g., Givón and Yang [1994] and Hundt [2001]), but it needs to be emphasized that the structure *get* + past participle subsumes several grammatical constructions, of which the *get*-passive

---

[24] This section incorporates findings from an unpublished Freiburg MA thesis submitted by Ms. Stefanie Rapp in 1999.

[25] For a somewhat hyperbolic claim, compare, for example: "A shift to the *get*-passive appears to be one of the most active grammatical changes taking place in English" (Weiner and Labov 1983: 43).

is historically the youngest one. There are some idiomatic constructions such as *get lost*, *get rid of*, *get shot of*, or *get acquainted with* (the last one with a history dating back to at least 1652 – cf. OED, s.v. *acquainted* and Visser 1970–1973: III, 2, 2032), for which active analogues are rare and/or artificial.[26] Then there are inchoative uses such as *get married* or *get started*, which present a type which shades into the true passive. For example, it is difficult to arrive at an unambiguous analysis of a sentence such as *the workers in the factory got organized*. It can be seen as inchoative, patterned on present-participle or adjectival uses such *as the workers got going* or *the workers got ready*, or as one passive variant of *the union organized the workers in the factory*. True passive uses are represented by cases such as the following one, from one of our four reference corpora:

Calamari gets grilled and served with beans, garlic and tomatoes.

(Frown C15 54f.)[27]

Note that this example contains little of the semantic import usually attributed to the *get*-passive; namely, that the subject has some responsibility for what happened to him or her (*he got shot, the idiot!*) or that what happens is a negative event presented with some emotional involvement (*he got kicked out*). What is left of the semantico-stylistic baggage of the construction is a touch of stylistic informality.

It is cases such as this one, where there is a clear active analogue – *people grill and serve calamari with beans, garlic and tomatoes* – and where the auxiliary *get* can easily be replaced with *be* – *calamari are grilled and served with beans, garlic and tomatoes* – which are regarded as instances of the *get*-passives here. Marginal and doubtful cases were included if they met most or all of the criteria posited for "central passives" in the typology of Quirk et al. (1985). Such core instances of the *get*-passive should be seen as true passives, which is not to deny the fact that the "middle" semantics traditionally attaching to *get* + participle-constructions still play an important role in many more marginal instances.

These clarifications are necessary to place the figures presented in Table 4.14 in their proper context. It lists the manually post-edited output of

---

[26] That phrases such as the ones listed above should not be included in a discussion of the *get*-passive is additionally made clear by the fact that they are themselves passivized as a whole even before the genuine *get*-passives became current in the mid-nineteenth century. Compare, for example, the following citation from Baseline1800:
  "That it should be got rid of by the whiffing way of an adjournment!" (1800).

[27] For a more striking illustration of the fact that the paths of the lexical verb *get* and the homophonous passive auxiliary have diverged, consider the following double occurrence from the additional material: "It's not that you know the hero is going to get the girl, or rather get got by the girl, nor even that the thought processes and articulations enjoined by this procedure would disgrace a children's TV programme, simply that the obstacles placed in their way are as flimsy as matchwood" (*Private Eye* 983 [20 August 1999]: 25).

Table 4.14. Get-*passives in four corpora (examples from direct speech in brackets)*

	1961	1991/1992
British English (LOB/F-LOB)	34 (15)	53 (22)
American English (Brown/Frown)	35 (13)	64 (23)

Significances: LOB: F-LOB $p < 0.05$, Brown: Frown $p < 0.01$; LOB: Brown and F-LOB: Frown $p > 0.05$.

a search for all forms of *get* followed by past participles or, in other words, the uncontroversial instances of the *get*-passive in the four corpora.[28]

As can be seen, the increase is not restricted to uses in direct speech but proceeds across the board, which is a sign that *get*-passives are no longer the markers of colloquial style that they used to be at an earlier stage of their development.

At 42 instances, the *get*-passive is surprisingly common even in the OED Baseline1900 corpus. However, the semantic and stylistic constraints associated with the construction – agent's responsibility, adversativeness, and informal style – are much more strongly in evidence than in the recent past. Some examples are from slang glossaries or reports from the underworld, such as the following:

> You get lagged for loiterin' wiv intent. (1899, from Rook's *Hooligan Nights*)

Practically all have human subjects in adversity, often sharing responsibility:

> A boy got drawn into the chain-gearing of the wheels. (1897)

> A goodly number of these yawping lads went to the front to get shot at. (1899)

> On the average stupidity in the Church gets better paid than brain at the Bar. (1896)

There is one example of a "secondary" or "personal" passive with *get* (i.e., a passive in which the "personal" indirect object rather than the direct object has been made the subject of the passive clause) in these early data:

---

[28] Obviously, there is a large number of potentially ambiguous examples, but an independent count undertaken by Hundt (2001: 87) comes very close to the figures given in Table 4.14, which can be read as a sign of their reliability. She lists the following frequencies: *Get*-passives in four corpora 35 (LOB), 31 (Brown), 51 (F-LOB), 64 (Frown) – cf. Hundt (2001: 87).

The figures for ambiguous constructions are 27, 22, 12, and 19, and those for clearly adjectival participles 21, 42, 30, 57, in LOB, F-LOB, Brown, and Frown respectively.

Every man that drops anything into the bins gets docked an hour's pay.
(1901)

In an "OED Baseline1800 Corpus" constructed on similar principles to the Baseline1900 one, on the other hand, *get*-passives are very rare indeed. There is only one clear instance,[29] accompanied by two further doubtful ones which are probably best analyzed as instances of the (by then) firmly established inchoative *get* + participle-construction.[30] This suggests the following development. The nineteenth century saw the establishment of the *get*-passive as a construction with a fairly specific semantics partly determined by related constructions which featured *get* as an inchoative, causative, or reflexive-causative verb;[31] in the twentieth century this new passive was grammaticalized further, with the semantic and stylistic constraints on its use lessening to the point that it is now a serious rival to the *be*-passive. This is shown by a close-up analysis of the subjects in the *get*-passive citations from the British LOB and F-LOB corpora. Of the 34 examples from LOB, 6 have an inanimate subject, while the proportion in F-LOB is 12 out of 53 (with a further indeterminate case), which not only means that inanimate subjects are far more common than in Baseline1900, but also that there has been a consistent increase between 1961, the sampling year for LOB, and 1991, the sampling year for F-LOB.

Corroboration of this account based on "real-time" data can be provided by "apparent-time" results obtained in an analysis of the spoken-demographic and spoken-context-governed components of the BNC, for which speakers are tagged for age. Figure 4.2 shows that there is one group of young speakers who uses *get*-passives (as defined here) more than all the others, but that we do not observe the decrease in proportion to speakers' age which we would expect if we were dealing with an incoming form.[32]

An analysis of the rich BNC data also helps answer the question to which extent the *get*-passive is losing the semantic overtones of agent involvement and adversativity traditionally associated with it, and hence becoming an alternative to the *be*-passive. As a first indicator, consider the frequency of *by*-agents, the possibility of adding such a phrase being one of the criteria of central-passive status in Quirk et al. (1985). *Be*-passives of a judgment sample of six verbs (*tell*, *take*, *kill*, *put*, *pay*, *make*) were retrieved from the spoken BNC material and classified according to whether they appeared with or without an agent phrase. It turns out that an agent is present in 97 out of a total of 1,091 *be*-passives

---

[29] It is: "get snubb'd i' th' nose – or haply singe our beards" (1796 – note the informal ring).
[30] They are: "Take care to fix the stake firmly, and to tie the tree so with a firm hay-band that it may not easily get galled" (1796) and "The only way a quack-medicine gets very celebrated, is, by its being constantly puffed off in advertisements" (1799 – note the modifying *very* preceding the participle *celebrated*).
[31] These uses are illustrated by the following ideal-typical examples: *she got ready/started/ going, she got him to talk/talking, she got herself (to be) introduced to the Duke.*
[32] There is also hardly a difference between the frequency of *get*-passives in male (181.2 per million words) and female (189.6 per million) speech in this material.

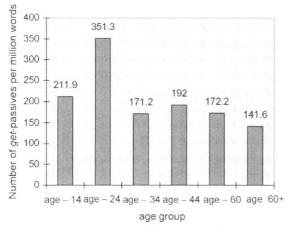

Figure 4.2 *Get*-passives according to age in the BNC

(= 8.9 percent). In a total of 1,104 *get*-passives (based on a larger judgment sample of verbs), on the other hand, there were only 45 agents (= 4.1 percent). While this is certainly less than for the *be*-passive, it is nevertheless more than the literature on *get*-passives would lead one to expect, in which agents are described as rare or, according to some sources, even as ungrammatical (cf. the review in Matthews [1993: 22–25]).

To assess the status of the *get*-passive in present-day English, it is necessary to compare its discourse frequency with that of the traditional *be*-passive. For selected verbs a frequency index was computed on the basis of BNC data, using the following formula:

$$\frac{number\ \text{get} + verb}{(number\ \text{get} + verb) + (number\ \text{be} + verb)} \times 100 = frequency\ index$$

This frequency index ranges between the values of 100 (only *get*-passives attested for a particular verb) and 0 (only *be*-passives). Table 4.15 gives the actual figures for 52 common verbs, listing separate indices for the spoken and written texts, and the total.

The table is instructive in many ways. The frequency indices are consistently higher in speech than in writing, which supports the traditional classification of the *get*-passive as an informal variant of the *be*-passive. In addition, the vast majority of the top-ranked verbs denotes the kind of negative or adverse event considered typical of the *get*-passive, while, at the other end of the scale, there is a cluster of largely those stative and cognitive verbs which are incompatible with the traditional semantics of the construction. This suggests that little has changed in the course of the twentieth century with regard to the constraints limiting the use of this construction. However, the picture is not all stability. Especially in the mid-frequency range of verbs, we find stative or

Table 4.15. *Frequency indices for* get-*passives in the BNC*

Verb	Frequency index spoken	Frequency index written	Frequency index total
caught	52.29	12.87	15.53
paid	40.46	4.63	8.65
smashed	39.29	6.18	10.68
hit	36.00	4.82	6.18
damaged	33.33	2.02	3.37
promoted	31.25	3.60	4.87
fucked	30.00	18.61	22.22
killed	29.68	2.55	4.00
hurt	29.63	16.57	17.06
shot	28.57	4.34	5.39
beaten	28.57	4.18	5.28
eaten	26.32	3.08	4.00
stopped	21.69	1.31	2.08
sacked	18.37	3.00	4.46
accused	17.78	0.09	0.79
served	9.30	0.74	1.00
written	8.00	0.71	1.15
played	7.41	0.31	0.58
invited	6.61	0.98	1.31
destroyed	5.88	0.00	0.16
saved	5.34	0.00	0.67
told	5.13	0.44	0.94
asked	4.65	0.62	0.92
put	4.17	0.72	1.17
called	4.03	0.48	0.79
rejected	3.70	0.09	0.18
bought	2.86	0.16	0.30
taken	2.42	0.72	1.17
kept	1.79	0.03	0.11
built	1.49	0.12	0.19
given	1.46	0.03	0.09
thought	1.37	0.00	0.30
brought	1.21	0.04	0.12
said	1.14	0.04	0.08
found	1.11	0.08	0.11
made	1.08	0.07	0.11
talked	0.00	1.52	1.23
born	0.00	0.18	0.16
tried	0.00	0.14	0.14
remembered	0.00	0.10	0.10
heard	0.00	0.06	0.05
seen	0.00	0.03	0.03

Table 4.15. (*cont.*)

Verb	Frequency index spoken	Frequency index written	Frequency index total
needed	0.00	0.02	0.02
considered	0.00	0.02	0.01
watched	0.00	0.00	0.00
invented	0.00	0.00	0.00
hated	0.00	0.00	0.00
created	0.00	0.00	0.00
wanted	0.00	0.00	0.00
liked	0.00	0.00	0.00
meant	0.00	0.00	0.00
felt	0.00	0.00	0.00

cognitive verbs (e.g., *think*) or verbs unlikely to be used in the *get*-passive for other reasons (e.g., *get born*[33]), which might be an indication that the force of the constraints is lessening.

4.7.2 Voice: summary and synopsis of further relevant research

A typologically salient characteristic of Modern English, especially in comparison to other major European languages, is the prevalence of unmarked middles of the type *weather reports translate easily* (meaning "weather reports can be translated easily"). Such forms are relatively recent (the earliest genuine attestations going back no earlier than the eighteenth century) and widely assumed to be spreading rapidly. The assumed cause is the ponderousness of the English reflexive, which allegedly makes people prefer forms such as *this material molds to your body shape* to *this material molds itself to your body shape* (see, e.g., Jespersen 1909–1949: VI, 112). Hundt (forthcoming) has confirmed received opinion with regard to the first assumption but not found any evidence for a causal link between a loss of reflexives and the increase in middles.

Taking her cue from the fact that middles are a highly text-type-sensitive phenomenon, Hundt focuses on advertising texts, where they are noticeably frequent, helping to create the impression of a world in which – to play on some of her examples – air cleaners "wall-mount," sofabeds "fold out for comfortable sleeping in a pinch," and drapery hooks "adjust easily" to whatever length is

---

[33] What is found is, obviously, not sentences such as **I got born in 1958*, but iterative uses such as the following example from a novel, which incidentally features the *get*-passive in variation with a following *be*-passive: "A baby would get born and an upstairs window be lit: an old man would die and the hearse arrive" (BNC HGJ 896).

desired. While usually it is not advisable to short-circuit grammatical form and the cultural climate of an era, in this particular case Hatcher's considerations ring true:

> [Middles] conjure up a utopian world where all the material and mechanical factors of our civilisation "operate" smoothly, easily, to the end that man shall be more comfortable – a world where the pass-word is "easy". Thus the ideal of comfort characteristic of our age has found its grammatical reflection; if all verbs of manipulation could become hypothetical intransitives the world would be perfect!   (Hatcher 1943: 13)

Through a systematic comparison of American mail-order catalogs covering the years from 1897 to 1986 – a very unusual but highly effective type of manually compiled text-type-specific diachronic corpus – she is able to show that the relevant forms started taking off seriously between the late 1920s and 1950s (and that, as has been pointed out, this had nothing to do with a concomitant decrease in reflexive uses of the verbs in question). On the basis of data from the Brown quartet of corpora, Hundt is able to show that there has been a lesser and more patchy increase in middles in the written language in general.

In its extreme affinity to a specific textual genre, this verbal grammatical construction has a clear analogue in the nominal field, namely noun phrase–name appositions of the type *bearded Cuban revolutionary leader Fidel Castro* (on which, see section 4.9 below). These are likely to be of twentieth-century origin and have spread extremely rapidly in journalistic language, while their currency in ordinary speech and writing is still limited.

A further example of diachronic dynamism in the voice system of twentieth-century English is presented by "personal" or secondary passives of the type *I was given a present*, which – if one can believe the claims in the relevant literature – were restricted to a rather small number of verbs until recently. Describing such personal passives in 1927, Jespersen writes that "it would probably be difficult to find examples like these: he was *written* a letter, *sent* a note, *telegraphed* the number, or she was *got* a glass of wine, or *done* an injustice" (1909–1949: III, 309). Writing half a century later, Barbara Strang finds these forms "all normal, except the third, which is not only grammatically improbable" (1970: 99).

In fact, the form questioned by Strang can be easily attested from the Web (which is not self-evident, as telegraphy today is not a normal mode of communication any longer):

> On the 14th of August, 1868, Governor Crawford was telegraphed the situation at midnight, and in four hours he was in Salina.
> (www.kancoll.org/books/cutler/ottawa/ottawa-co-p2.html)

> To add insult to injury, President Kruger declined its services when he was telegraphed the news.   (www.rapidttp.co.za/milhist/vol062jc.html)

The father, who was at Terrill with his train, was telegraphed the awful news. (www.rootsweb.com/~txtarran/obits/obits09c.htm)

It is ironic that the last example first appeared in the *Arlington Journal* of 8 October 1909 – that is, many years before Jespersen and Strang denied the possibility that such forms could exist.

That the productivity of personal passives derived from newly coined ditransitive verb phrases is currently unrestricted is proved by the hundreds of instances of constructions of the type *I was e-mailed the code*, which can be turned up in Web searches.

A minor subplot in this broader story may be the creation by analogy of personal passives for the few verbs for which they are ruled out in theory – for example, *explain*. The double object construction – *explain somebody something* – is not available for this verb, and neither is the corresponding personal passive. An investigation of this issue takes us to the limits of traditional corpus-linguistics. A search in the 100-million-word British National Corpus for the sequence "explain* me the" and the corresponding passives "I am/was explained the" yields no results. No such cases are attested in the OED quotation base. However, several hundred examples can easily be found in Web material. A fair number of them are probably from non-native speakers, but many of them seem to have been produced by native speakers in routine communication. This situation suggests that the forms might be coming in. On the other hand, the Web is a corpus of a magnitude that places it outside the frame of traditional corpus-linguistic reference, so that a conservative analysis would have to proceed from the assumption that these apparently irregular uses represent the type of performance slip which surrounds any grammatical rule if its instantiations are investigated in a database of sufficient size.

4.8 Nonfinite verb forms: some twentieth-century developments in the field of clausal complementation

Nonfinite verb forms – infinitives, gerunds, and participles – are a grammatical category that has become more functionally prominent, and correspondingly more frequent in discourse, since the Middle English period. In spite of the relative lack of attention that these forms have received in the literature on change in progress in English, there is no indication that the diachronic dynamic that characterized these forms in the Early Modern English has abated in the recent past. This will be demonstrated in two ways below: (1) through a comprehensive comparison of the recent development of one constructional type, infinitival clauses with notional subjects introduced by *for*; and (2) through detailed studies of a number of individual matrix verbs and their constructional potential.

4.8.1 The strengthening of a nonfinite grammatical construction in recent English: for + *NP* + to-*infinitive*

Infinitival clauses with an explicit notional subject introduced by *for* – e.g., *they arranged for their guest to be met at the station* – represent one of the faster-spreading syntactic innovations in the history of English.[34] Not only have they become more frequent overall since the Early Modern English period (Denison 1998: 256), but they have also diversified functionally – to the extent that they are now represented in all major functional classes of subordinate clauses. Consider the following examples from recent British English (F-LOB):

> *Subject clause*: Under the circumstances, for Laura Herbert to encourage his courtship was an act of most uncharacteristic rebelliousness. (G 12 104f.)
>
> *Subject clause/extraposed*: It would be possible for religion to come down out of the heavens and from the world beyond death so as to occupy again its primal place. (F 28 137f.)
>
> *Subject complement clause*: The only guarantee is for there to be a federal state and for the UN to recognise that. (A 04 189f.)
>
> What we want is for the Government to force the brewers to either allow us to buy the pubs in a competitive market, or to rent them at a commercial rent. (A 29 119f.)
>
> *Extraposed object clause in complex transitive construction (SVOC → SV it CO-clause)*: All of these factors weaken the ties that such businesses have with the communities in which they are located and make it less difficult for them to close down and/or relocate if and when business conditions deteriorate in one country relative to other countries. (J 26 104ff.)
>
> *Object clause*: . . . and she could only wait for his rage to exhaust itself. (L 22 35f.)
>
> *Complement of adjective*: The verb means that the priests welcome it when the people sin and are anxious for it to happen more often because it means more sacrifice and, since they share the offered meat, more food for them. (D 03 155f.)
>
> *Complement of noun*: In this technological age, there is a tendency for people to forget that humans are mammals, just like zebras and gorillas. (E 33 7f.)
>
> *Relative clause*: She has made it a subject for us to study. (P 22 140f.)

---

[34] The long-term history of the construction has been described by Jespersen (1909–45: V, 299–315), Visser (1970–73: II, 957f., III, 2, 244–2, 248, et passim), and more recently by Fischer (1988). Rich empirical demonstration of contemporary usage in British and American English is given in Erdmann (1997).

Adverbial clauses: *Carry On* star Barbara Windsor made a 500-mile round
trip to bowl the first ball in a charity cricket match – only for rain to stop
play. (A 42 143f.)

The policeman was shouting above the roar, holding his warrant-card
up for the pilot to see. (N 01 117f.)

If a population does not grow enough, or grows too fast for agriculture
to respond, then production is likely to remain extensive. (J 03 214f.)

Other: It is not for us to say how and when change will come. It is for us to
speak our minds and at the same time reason with those who govern
China. (A 01 225f.)

As is typical of complex nonfinite clausal constructions, many individual
examples are difficult to classify, either because they are ambiguous and the
context is such that both alternative interpretations make sense, or because they
are vague, representing, for example, non-canonical or transitional structures
which combine features of several of the ideal constructional types set out
above. Consider the following examples:

So something had to be done; either new markets had to be found for the
gut rot wines, or the outmoded wine-making traditions had to be over-
turned to make room for "new style" wines to develop – wines capable of
holding their own in the international market.   (E 20 153ff.)

This opened the way for the development to begin.   (G 51 1 45f.)

The normal system of exploitation is to invite in a logging company, who
buy the timber rights and clear the land for the local people to cultivate.
(E 27 111f.)

The *for*-clauses in these examples can plausibly be analyzed as relative
clauses postmodifying the nouns *room*, *way*, and *land* respectively: "room in
which new-style wines could develop," "the way which development might
begin on," "the land that the local people could cultivate." On the other hand,
all three also allow an adverbial-clause reading and the corresponding finite
paraphrases – "clear the land so that the local people can cultivate it," "open
the way so that development could begin," or "clear the land so that the local
people can cultivate it." Note that in the third example the noun phrase *the
land* could easily be replaced by the pronoun *it* – "clear it for the local people
to cultivate" – a paraphrase for which a relative-clause interpretation is ruled
out. A rather unusual adverbial clause is instantiated by the following example:

The big reservoirs take many weeks for the water to reach a comfortable
temperature.   (F 38 23f.)

Here the main clause – "the big reservoirs take many weeks" – is structurally
incomplete, and the apparent adverbial clause is not an optional circumstantial
addition to the main clause but rather fills the semantic gap in it. On the other

hand, there is no clean way of relating the sentence as it is to a fully spelled-out underlying form "It takes many weeks for the water to reach a comfortable temperature in the big reservoirs" (such as we could relate *the reservoirs take many weeks to fill* to *it takes many weeks to fill the reservoirs* or *to fill the reservoirs takes many weeks* via extraction and/or fronting). If we were dealing with a case of extraction from the subordinate clause and fronting, the sentence would have to read, "The big reservoirs take many weeks for the water to reach a comfortable temperature **in**," with preposition stranding.

The following two examples display overlap between *for*-adverbial clauses and *for*-clauses functioning as noun complements:

> We believe that the time is now right for us to distribute the product directly.   (E 30 99f.)

> There is no scope within the procedure for the operator to recover his error.   (J 72 133)

In the next example, finally, the syntax suggests a relative clause postmodifying *thing* (note the coreferential gap), but the semantics is closer to *for*-subject clauses of the type *it is odd for a man to say that kind of thing* or *for a man to say that kind of thing is odd*.

> That's an odd thing for a man to say.   (P 28 160f.)

Note also that especially the "adverbial" category is internally very heterogeneous as a whole, containing as it does prototypical adverbial clauses which are semantically optional additions to the higher clause (cf. illustrative example 1: Carry On *Star Barbara Windsor made [the trip] – only for rain to stop play*), but also structurally reduced clauses (cf. illustrative example 2: *The policeman was shouting above the roar, holding his warrant-card up*).

It is not a priority in the present study to detail all the syntactic complexities that surround the various types of *for*-clauses. It should be pointed out, however, that difficult-to-categorize examples are not mere accidents in an otherwise straightforward system. Rather, they point to a fundamental typological characteristic of Modern English grammar which John Hawkins has referred to as a "loose fit" between propositional form and syntactic structure (cf. Hawkins 1986). In contrast to many historically related languages (e.g., German and, more distantly, French or Russian), the recent evolution of English grammar has led to a system which allows a speaker to code multiple underlying meanings very efficiently by conflating them into common surface realizations, while some extra effort is required from the hearer in order to arrive at the intended or contextually most relevant interpretation. In tight-fit languages, on the other hand, there is little tolerance for surface ambiguity of the type illustrated, and speakers are under pressure to map propositional content unambiguously on to syntactic forms.

The distribution of *for* + NP + *to*-infinitival clauses seemed a suitable phenomenon to study in the four one-million-word reference corpora used as a database for the present study mainly for two reasons. First, the construction, though common enough, is not extremely frequent – so that quantitative and qualitative methods of analysis can still be combined usefully. Second, the literature contains many – mostly unsupported – statements about the variable geographical spread of the construction. An analysis of matching British and American databases covering a span of thirty years should be sufficient to determine whether the pattern is more common in American English, as is sometimes alleged, or whether it is spreading in the language as a whole.

The search carried out over all four corpora was for instances of *for* separated from an infinitival *to* on the right by no more than five words. The raw returns were post-edited manually to identify the relevant constructions. The search obviously misses all those instances of *for* + NP + *to*-infinitive in which the NP is longer than five words,[35] but represents a reasonable compromise between completeness of coverage and labor required for post-editing. Table 4.16 gives the frequencies of the relevant constructions in the four corpora, grouped broadly into the functional classes defined and illustrated above. Ambiguous and vague cases, which – as will be remembered – are quite numerous, were assigned to the class which they fitted best in the context, and every attempt was made to classify similar cases consistently.

As can be seen, the evidence from these figures is conflicting. Somewhat surprisingly in view of contrary statements in the literature, the construction overall is more common in the British than in the American data, although the disparity is not significant in the chi-square test. There has been stability in US usage, and a slight rise in British usage, again not significant statistically. Many cells in the table are so small that no statistical interpretation is possible, but among the better-filled ones the fairly drastic rises (both significant at the $p < 0.01$ level) in the category "adverbial" for British English (from 44 to 74) and in the "object" category for American English (from 33 to 70) should be pointed out. Globally, however, the construction can be expected to display a frequency of c. 300 per million words throughout the latter half of the twentieth century, without dramatic shifts either regionally or diachronically.

In view of this picture of stability in the short term, it will be instructive to establish mid-term trends in the OED Baseline corpora, presented in Table 4.17.

For those who assume that syntactic change is rapid, this is a sobering picture. The whole functional range of the construction was available even in 1700, and there have not been very drastic changes in the relative importance of the various sub-types. What was common in 1700 tends to be common now,

[35] Compare, for example, "But it is a primary task for anyone who aspires to a self-conscious understanding of mathematics to say what a set is" (C 12 149f.), in which *for* and the infinitival *to* are separated by nine words. This example did happen to be captured in the original search because of the accidental presence of a second, prepositional *to* in the noun phrase but was not included in the counts.

Table 4.16. *For + NP + to-infinitival clauses in four corpora*

	LOB	F-LOB	Brown	Frown
Subject/initial	5	9	7	2
Subject/extraposed	94	74	91	74
Subject complement	4	13	6	6
Object/extraposed	12	22	10	16
Object	50	50	33	70
Complement of adjective	3	4	7	2
Complement of noun	51	58	42	39
Relative clause	21	23	28	26
Adverbial	44	74	45	39
Other/unclassified	10	7	4	1
Total	294	334	273	275

Table 4.17. *For + NP + to-infinitival clauses in three OED Baseline Corpora*

	Baseline1700	Baseline1800	Baseline1900
Subject/initial	4	1	1
Subject/extraposed	33	19	60
Subject complement	2	—	4
Object complement	1	1	7
Object	2	2	9
Complement of adjective	1	1	1
Complement of noun	4	5	11
Relative clause	17	6	15
Adverbial	23	13	22
Other/unclassified	3	4	5
Total	90	52	135

and what was rare then is, on the whole, still rare now. As for diachronic trends, these raw figures say little, as the Baseline corpora are not of equal size. For the necessary normalization of the figures ("x/1,000,000 words") I assume a size of c. 403,000 for Baseline1700, c. 486,000 for Baseline1800, and c. 933,000 for Baseline1900.[36] Table 4.18 presents the normalized frequencies for the totals of the three Baseline corpora and F-LOB and Frown (representing late twentieth-century usage), and normalized frequencies for selected individual sub-types. Relative clauses and adverbial clauses are grouped

[36] See Appendix 2 for detailed calculations.

Table 4.18. For + NP + to-infinitival clauses in three OED Baseline Corpora and F-LOB and Frown (normalized, as instances per million words)

	Baseline 1700	Baseline 1800	Baseline 1900	F-LOB	Frown
Subject/extraposed	82	39	64	74	74
Object	5	4	10	50	70
Complement of noun	10	10	12	58	39
Relative clause and adverbial uses	99	39	40	97	65
Other	27	15	19	55	27
Total	223	107	145	334	275

together because of the semantic affinities between these two uses and the resulting considerable structural overlap found in the data.[37]

A look at the totals serves as a first important warning. Had we restricted the period of observation to the nineteenth and twentieth centuries (Baseline1800 to F-LOB), the impression would be one of a steep and continuous increase in the discourse frequency of the construction. However, the figures for Baseline1700 show that the development must have been more complicated – a slower and more gradual increase punctuated by temporary reversals and much fluctuation. The analogy which comes to mind in the field of nominal and adjectival grammar is the comparison of di-syllabic adjectives (see section 4.9.4 below), where a long-term trend towards analytic forms since c. 1200 is not reflected consistently in many individual sub-periods.

As for the developments of individual sub-types of the construction, two uses seem to have undergone remarkable expansion during the twentieth century: for + NP + to-infinitival complement clauses functioning as object

---

[37] Compare "On each hand of every seat were placed Crutches for the Priest to lean upon" and "Such a man, truly wise, creams off nature, leaving the sour and the dregs, for philosophy and reason to lap up," from Baseline1700. Like many similar structures these could be regarded as relative constructions ("crutches which the priest could lean upon" and "the sour and the dregs, which philosophy and reason can lap up") or as adverbial clauses of purpose or result (". . . so that the priest could lean on them" or ". . . so that philosophy and reason can lap them up"). The examples as they are suggest a relative-clause analysis for the first because there is no comma or intervening material setting apart the head and the relative clause, and an adverbial-clause analysis for the second, because of the comma. On the other hand, while nonfinite relative clauses are less common in non-restrictive uses, they are by no means ruled out – quite apart from the fact that a syntactic analysis should not depend on the vagaries of historical spelling and punctuation. This means that a relative-clause interpretation remains possible also for this example. Conversely, it is easy to replace the head noun crutches by a pronoun in the first example ("they were placed on each hand of every seat for the priest to lean on"), which then requires an adverbial interpretation and rules out the relative-clause one.

clauses depending on transitive verbs (e.g., *arrange/wait/pressure/signal . . . for something to be done*) and as complements to nouns (*a tendency for something to happen, a petition for something to be granted*, etc.).

4.8.2 The spread of nonfinite clauses: further illustrative case studies

4.8.2.1 Remember (his/him) doing something..

Gerundial complement clauses have been spreading consistently since the Early Modern English period, both at the expense of other types of nonfinite clauses (such as infinitival clauses) and finite subordinate clauses (see, e.g., Fanego 1996a, 1996b, Vosberg 2004). In some cases this has led to a replacement of one type of construction by another, in others to a functional differentiation between two or more competing complement types in present-day English.

In this connection it is interesting to note how recent some of the apparently rock-solid Modern English contrasts between infinitives and gerunds actually are. This is well illustrated by the verb *remember*. The data for the case study in Table 4.19 is provided by the quotation base of the OED (second edition on CD-ROM). Three constructional types are distinguished: (1) prospective *to*, as in *I must remember to fill in the form*; (2) retrospective *-ing*, as in *I remember filling in the form*; and (3) the now defunct retrospective construction with the (perfect) infinitive, as in *I remember to have filled in the form*. Since the number of quotations available for the three centuries under review varies, frequencies are given as "n occurrences/10,000 quotations".

The table reveals random fluctuation – and structural stability – for prospective *to*, but a clear reversal of preferences for the retrospective uses, as is visualized in Figure 4.3.

This diagram makes obvious another important fact about the change. The spread of the gerund was not a zero–sum game in which one nonfinite form took over the functions of another while the overall frequency of nonfinite complements remained constant. Rather, the gerund became more frequent in excess of what would have been needed merely to compensate for the obsolescent infinitival uses, and this means that it must have additionally encroached on finite complement clauses introduced by *that*, *whether*, etc. (which were not counted) or plain noun-phrase objects. In other words, what has changed is not merely this particular matrix verb and its associated constructions; what has happened to *remember* is a sign that the category of nonfinite complementation has been strengthened as a whole.

An additional complication in the complementation of *remember* is that gerunds following this verb may have explicit notional subjects of their own, for which traditional prescriptive grammar has generally recommended the genitive or possessive rather than the objective case – hence *I remember Peter's/ his filling in the form* rather than *I remember Peter/him filling in the form*. Many commentators on ongoing change in English grammar have suggested that in the current climate of permissivism the objective forms are gaining ground.

Table 4.19. *Gerunds and infinitives after* remember *in the OED quotation base – normalized frequencies ("n/10,000 quotations," rounded to the first decimal, absolute frequencies in brackets)*

	Prospective *to*	Retrospective *–ing*	Retrospective *to*
18th century	5.5 (15)	1.8 (5)	4.8 (13)
19th century	2.2 (17)	4.1 (31)	2.1 (16)
20th century	5.8 (28)	12.0 (58)	0.8 (4)

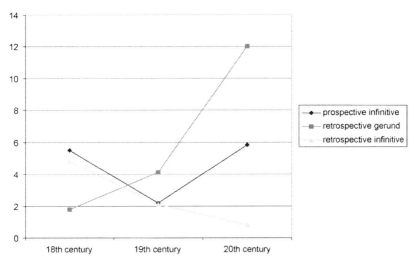

Figure 4.3 Nonfinite complements of *remember* in the OED quotation base by century – normalized frequency as n/10,000 quotations

Here the OED evidence for the past two centuries (Table 4.20) is instructive, but clearly not in the way expected.

The figures show that, at least for this particular matrix verb, the prescriptive recommendation has never had a strong foundation in actual usage. Prescriptivists seem to have based their calls for preserving traditional usage on a fictitious norm.

4.8.2.2 Begin to do/doing something; start to do/doing something.. For a medium-frequency verb such as *remember* it was necessary to use the masses of data provided by the OED quotation base as a basis for an historical investigation. For another verb, however, namely *begin*, the four corpora

Table 4.20. *Notional subjects in gerundial constructions after* remember *in the OED quotation base*

Period	Objective case (NP)	Objective case (pronoun)	Possessive (NP)	Possessive (pronoun)*
1801–1825	2	—	—	2 (1)
1826–1850	4	1	—	3 (1)
1851–1875	1	—	—	3
1876–1900	4	1	—	1
1901–1925	3	—	—	—
1926–1950	6	—	—	—
1951–1975	12	4	1	—
1976–2000	6	—	1	1 (1)

* Figures in brackets give instances of ambiguous *her* included in the totals

Table 4.21. *Proportion of infinitival and gerundial complements after* begin *in four corpora*

	1961	1991/1992
British English (LOB/F-LOB)	260:23	204:20
American English (Brown/Frown)	230:53	202:95

BrE vs. AmE 1961 $p < 0.001$, BrE vs. AmE 1991/1992 $p < 0.001$, BrE diachr. not significant, AmE diachr. $p < 0.001$

providing the usual starting point for the present study are sufficient to attest an increase, so far confined to American English, in the frequency of gerundial complements.

Close analysis of the data (Mair 2002) reveals that, as expected, the diachronic development documented in the table is just one strand in a complex fabric of factors, in which grammatical context, the partly contrasting semantic import of the gerundial and infinitival complement types, text-type specific preferences, and, (obviously) regional origin of a speaker/writer play an equal part.

The long-range history of aspectual *begin* is not without its complexities (see Mair [2001] for a detailed analysis), but the basic facts seem to be the following. *Begin to* has been a part of the grammatical inventory since Old English times. From the late eighteenth century, as part of the general spread of the verbal gerund, *begin V-ing* is attested as well. However, the gerundial forms remain rare throughout the nineteenth century. The distribution in the

Table 4.22. *Infinitive vs. gerund complements with* begin *in selected British databases*

	To-infinitive	Gerund
Guardian on CD-ROM 1996: first 100 relevant cases	86	14
Guardian on CD-ROM 1996: first 50 relevant cases of *began*	38	12
Guardian on CD-ROM 1996: first 50 relevant cases of *begins*	48	2
London-Lund Corpus of Spoken British English	52	5
British National Corpus/Spoken-Demographic Sample	79	8

Baseline1900 Corpus (*begin* + *to*-inf.: 169; *begin* + *V-ing*: 14) is representative, and similar proportions are obtained from virtually all spoken and written British samples to the present day, as is shown in Table 4.22.

As can be seen, the infinitive is the statistically normal form both in the newspaper style of the *Guardian* and in two spoken corpora sampling different periods in the twentieth century. It would be interesting to speculate why the gerund is somewhat more common with the past tense form *began*, but all in all the figures do not show any development away from the situation documented in Baseline1900. Comparable figures obtained from American data show a different picture (Table 4.23).

The nineteenth- and early twentieth-century American fictional texts and the present-day spoken data from the Longman Corpus show no difference from British usage. It is only in the recent newspaper data that the gerund complements are gaining. Whether changing newspaper usage will influence community norms and ultimately erode the dominant position of the infinitive after *begin* is as yet an open question, all the more so as other American written material does not seem to be sharing in the trend.[38]

Complement usage is different for a close synonym of *begin*, the verb *start*. Gerund complements have been very common for this verb ever since it became a verb of inception through semantic change in the eighteenth century – probably because by that time gerund complements had already emerged as a fully fledged structural alternative to infinitival ones. In addition, the use of gerunds after *start* may have been helped by the fact that the gerund is the only complement type found with its antonym *stop*. It is thus not surprising to see the gerund complements well represented in all four corpora.

[38] Compare the following breakdown of the Brown and Frown written data. In the press texts (A–C), the proportion of *to*-infinitives to V-*ing* forms is 22: 10 in Brown and 19: 26 in Frown, i.e., the preferences have been reversed. There is no such reversal in categories D–J (other non-fiction), where the figures are 126: 25 for Brown and 88: 37 for Frown, and in K–R (fiction; 82: 18 in Brown and 95: 32 in Frown).

We see that the infinitival complements remain dominant both in fiction and the non-press nonfiction genres.

Table 4.23. *Infinitive vs. gerund complements with* begin *in selected American databases*

	To-infintive	Gerund
Los Angeles Times 1992: first 100 relevant cases	55	45
Boston Globe 1992: first 100 relevant cases	57	43
Miami Herald 1992: first 100 relevant cases	24	76
LA Times 1992: first 50 relevant cases of *began*	21	29
Boston Globe 1992: first 50 relevant cases of *began*	19	31
Miami Herald 1992: first 50 relevant cases of *began*	10	40
LA Times 1992: first 50 relevant cases of *begins*	34	16
Boston Globe 1992: first 50 relevant cases of *begins*	38	12
Miami Herald 1992: first 50 relevant cases of *begins*	30	20
Faulkner, *Light in August*	157	2
Cather, *O Pioneers!*	51	6
Thoreau, *Walden*	48	1
Whitman, *Complete Prose*	42	1
Emerson, *Essays*	67	—
Longman Corpus of Spoken American English	122	14

Table 4.24. To-*infinitive: V*-ing *after start in four corpora*

	BrE	AmE
1961	36:52	47:49
1991/1992	49:59	59:110

AmE diachr. $p < 0.05$, all others not significant

As the figures in Table 4.24 show, nothing much has taken place with regard to the complementation of *start* in the period under study. Disregarding for the moment the weakly significant increase in Frown, there is a near even split between infinitives and gerunds in British and American English.

4.8.2.3 Prevent somebody (from) doing something.. Changes in the complementation of *prevent* represent one of the rare instances in which the grammars of the British and American standard have definitely moved apart in the course of the twentieth century. At the beginning of the century three types of construction were available in both varieties.

Table 4.25. *Nonfinite complements of* prevent *in the OED Baseline Corpus*

Type	Frequency
prevent X *from* V-*ing*	28
prevent X V-*ing*	17
prevent X's V-*ing*	2

i) How can we prevent a reviewer from selling his free copies?
ii) How can we prevent a reviewer selling his free copies?
iii) How can we prevent a reviewer's selling his free copies?

Option (iii), with the notional subject of the gerund in the genitive/possessive, was marginal even in 1900 and has further declined in importance since. The Baseline1900 corpus shows the distribution of the variants shown in Table 4.25.

One structural factor which seems to have a bearing on the choice of complement type is passivization, both of the matrix verb *prevent* and the complement verb. Of the 28 instances of the first constructional type (with *from*), 2 have the matrix verb *prevent* in the passive. Passivization of *prevent* in the *from*-less construction, on the other hand, is not attested in this corpus or any other consulted for this study and seems to be exceedingly rare. The use of the second constructional type (without *from*), by contrast, seems to be encouraged by the passivization of the dependent nonfinite clause. There are 5 instances of the type "prevent the free copies being sold" as against a single token for "prevent the free copies from being sold."

Unfortunately, it is not easily possible to differentiate between American and British sources in the OED Baseline corpora. However, there is a lot of independent evidence to show that in nineteenth-century English variation was not confined to British English only, where it persists today. Instances of the *from*-less construction can be attested from early American prose (cf., e.g., the examples from the works of Benjamin Franklin discussed in Mair 2002: 115). As for twentieth-century sources, all three constructional options are recognized without qualifying comments in the entry for *prevent* in *Webster's third*. *Webster's dictionary of English usage* (1989), while noting that the *from*-less construction is rare in American English, does not rule it out entirely (1989: 770). On the basis of corpus-evidence, even this seems to overstate the presence of the *from*-less variant, because by mid-century it is virtually eliminated from American English. In British material, by contrast, it is on the increase during the same period, as can be seen from the figures from the Brown, LOB, Frown, and F-LOB corpora shown in Table 4.26.

Within one century, the construction *prevent* NP V-*ing* has developed from a regionally neutral minority variant to a grammatical Briticism. This instance of a British-led differentiation deserves particular mention, as grammatical change in standard English today is all too often seen as homogenization on the

Table 4.26. *Ratio of* prevent *NP* from *V*-ing *vs.* prevent *NP V*-ing *in four corpora*[a]

	BrE	AmE
1961	34:7	47:0
1991/1992	24:24	36:1

[a] One of the seven instances of *prevent* NP V-*ing* in LOB has *her* as the notional subject of the gerund and could thus have been excluded as representing the "archaic" type (*prevent my leaving*) disregarded here. The sole American attestation of the "British" pattern (in Frown) is from a work of military history dealing with, significantly, the Battle of Britain.
BrE diachr. $p < 0.01$; all other contrasts not significant.

Table 4.27. *Ratio of* stop *NP* from *V*-ing *vs.* stop *NP V*-ing *in four corpora*[a]

	BrE	AmE
1961	6:4	5:0
1991/1992	3:12	7:0

[a] The following ambiguous cases involving *her* as NP in *stop* NP V-*ing* were included: 1 in LOB, 2 in F-LOB.

American model. Also, the difference is not a trivial one, related to the idiosyncratic complementation patterns of one verb only. A similar trend seems to be affecting the entire semantic class of what could be called verbs of prevention.

In all varieties of English, such verbs take a gerundial construction with *from*. Huddleston and Pullum's (2002: 657) *Cambridge Grammar* gives the following list:

> *ban, bar, block, delay, discourage, disqualify, dissuade, distract, divert, enjoin, exclude, exempt, forbid, hinder, hold back, inhibit, keep, preclude, prevent, prohibit, protect, restrain, restrict, stop* (somebody from doing something).

With the exception of *keep*, which has a completely different meaning when used in the V NP V-*ing* pattern ("keep them from selling review copies" vs. "keep them selling review copies"), *from*-less variants are possible in theory, and – on the strength of the *prevent* model – expected in British English. None of the verbs, however, is as common in the relevant construction as *prevent*, and only one, namely *stop*, is frequent enough for analysis in the four corpora (see Table 4.27).

The result is as expected: *stop* NP V-*ing* has emerged as a syntactic Briticism in the past half-century. The contrast is all the more salient as, unlike *prevent* NP V-*ing*, the corresponding structure with *stop* never seems to have had a foothold in older American English. It is explicitly ruled out in a survey article on British/American grammatical differences (Algeo 1988: 24), and how unusual it is in contemporary US usage is also illustrated by the fact that Clement Attlee's famous dictum that "democracy means government by discussion but it is only effective if you can stop people talking"[39] is regularly misquoted as ". . . if you can stop people from talking" by Americans.[40] A historical study of the long-term history of the construction on the basis of the OED Baseline corpora is not possible for lack of material. In Baseline1900 *stop* X *from* V-*ing* happens to be unattested, while *stop* X V-*ing* and *stop* X's V-*ing* occur once each.

All the other verbs in Huddleston and Pullum's (2002) list are too rare or recent in the construction in question for systematic corpus-based research, but a few relevant data and observations are worth mentioning. Here is a list of *from*-less constructions, all of course from British sources:

discourage
. . . aim to discourage Britain returning to the exchange rate mechanism.   (BNC CEK 2355)

block
. . . it became possible that the relatives of the dead, the soldiers, or both, would seek a judicial review to block the findings being published . . .
(*Private Eye* 1046 [25 January 2002]: 13)

Back at the top I helped Duncan carry the police barrier across the road so that it blocked traffic coming up.   (BNC HML 500)[41]

ban
. . . the editorial I wrote for *Palatinate* over the banning of our ice hockey team visiting Communist East Berlin . . .
(*Private Eye* 1053 [3 May 2002]: 4)

Smoking, eating sweets, playing CDs, listening to the radio, scratching your head, talking to your passenger . . . An interesting list. Because it's the list of things they're going to ban you doing in your car.
(*Sunday World*, 2 September 2001: 18)

A verb interesting in the present connection which is not in Huddleston and Pullum's (2002) list is *save*. *Save* NP *from* V-*ing* is attested in modest

---

[39] From a speech held at Oxford, 14 June 1957; cf. *Times*, 15 June 1957.
[40] Compare, for example, a Montgomery County (Maryland) Public Schools website at http://www.mcps.k12.md.us/schools/churchillhs/departments/ss/apeur.../democracy. htm, accessed on 4 October 2002.
[41] This example allows an alternative analysis in which "coming up" is a relative clause postmodifying the preceding noun.

quantities throughout all four corpora, whereas the *from*-less variant is currently still too rare or too colloquial to show up even once in F-LOB. However, it is richly attested in the BNC, more richly in fact than the corresponding structure with *from*, as is shown by the results of the following searches for *saves you* and *saves you from*, followed by V-*ing*. Here are the 3 instances of *saves you from* V-*ing*:

> It saves you from becoming under-insured as a result of inflation, with the risk of having to find thousands of pounds out of your own pocket in the event of a serious claim.   (BNC, AYP 1603)

> He saves you from a beating with remarkable ease and skill, yet you remain as blind and dull-witted as an earthworm.   (BNC, C85 1656)

> You can also print documents in the background while editing a second document which saves you from waiting around while your printer catches up with your typing speed.   (BNC, HAC 8936)

And here are the 13 returns for *saves you* V-*ing*:

> His text explains: "And with this funeral goes a rented coffin – it saves you buying one."   (BNC, CES 1202)

> "It saves you weaving through all those tables and chairs," Kolchinsky replied.   (BNC, ECK 2037)

> Oh well, it saves you penning.   (BNC, GYT 157)

> Because er i– from the management point of view if you have got four hundred people and you work a lot of overtime that saves you having six or seven hundred people.   (BNC, HO 3329)

> This saves you having to exit one program to start another, and you can move freely between open programs using either the Hot Keys or CTRL + ESC keys.   (BNC, HAC 3755)

> Saves you buying one.   (BNC, KB6 1427)

> It saves you having a holdall <unclear>, organise it more <pause> to heavy if we put that in there, right, what about, will they fit in the bag?
> (BNC, KBF 9660)

> Saves you carrying it in the bag.   (BNC, KCA 2765)

> Yeah that saves you making a payment don't it?   (BNC, KD2 2203)

> It saves you running into the living room.   (BNC, KE4 2264)

> <pause dur=11> I mean, that thing is with Argos Mick it saves you walking round the blasted town!   (BNC, KE6 3147)

Table 4.28. Save *NP V*-ing *in selected top-level Web domains*

	.gov	.uk	.us
Saves you having	1	759	3
Saves you from having	38	208	39
Saves you paying	—	10	—
Saves you from paying	1	1	1
Saves you getting	—	41	—
Saves you from getting	—	18	3
Saves you being	—	21	—
Saves you from being	—	12	2

Yeah, but then it saves you getting all the bits and . . .

(BNC, KP1 3465)

Saves you leaving all them taters.   (BNC, KSU 245)

From-less forms such as these are not attested in the American corpora used for this study. A search of the English-language Web for "saves you (from) having" (Google, accessed on 6 June 2003) supports the impression that we are dealing with an emerging Briticism (see Table 4.28).[42]

The almost total absence of the *from*-less variants from the American ".gov" and ".us" domains is conspicuous. As can be seen from the extrapolations in Appendix 3, these two domains must each be assumed to contain roughly a third of the amount of text in ".uk."

4.8.2.4 Help (somebody) (to) do something: the corpus as discovery procedure? A corpus is a database and therefore cannot really be a discovery procedure in the literal sense. In a looser sense, however, the sifting of concordance output and the comparison of frequencies across corpora, usually the first stages in most corpus-based descriptive work, have the characteristics of a discovery procedure because the open-ended and provisional nature of hypothesis formation in such data-driven analyses may alert the linguist to possibilities of explanation not yet explored or simply unavailable in the closed universes of specific theories and models.

In the following analysis of patterns of infinitival complementation with *help*, usually regarded as a minor example of different regional preferences in British and American English, it will become apparent that the twentieth century has seen a dramatic diachronic change which has gone entirely unnoticed both by descriptive linguists and prescriptive commentators. Within this overarching

---

[42] Of course, the construction itself is not twentieth-century. Compare, for example, "It will save you cutting into my talk," c. 1890, from Kipling, which the OED contains – s.v. *cut* (55d).

Table 4.29. *To- vs. bare infinitives with* help *in four corpora*

	BrE	AmE
1961	94:27	55:125
1991/1992	77:122	44:203

BrE vs. AmE 1961 $p < 0.001$; BrE vs. AmE 1991/1992 $p < 0.05$; BrE diachr. $p < 0.001$; AmE diachr. $p < 0.001$

Table 4.30. *Complementation of* help *in the "spoken-demographic" BNC*

	Without following NP/object	With following NP/object	Total
help + bare infinitive	34	92	126
help + *to*-infinitive	22	44	66

change, the extensively investigated regional variability is merely a minor and temporary side effect. In an analysis of the four corpora, the results shown in Table 4.29 were obtained – the figures for *to*-infinitives comprising the types *he helps to build the house* and *he helps us to build the house* (with their passive analogues) and the figures for bare infinitives giving the frequencies for the types *he helps build the house* and *he helps us build the house*.

As can be seen, in 1961 the *to*-infinitive was the statistical norm in British English, whereas the bare infinitive dominated in American English (cf. also Algeo 1988: 22; Kjellmer 1985). This is also the state of things recorded in Quirk et al.'s (1985) widely used reference grammar. Commenting on the variation between *Sarah helped us edit the script* and *Sarah helped us to edit the script*, the authors say:

> Of the two constructions with *help*, that with *to* is more common in BrE, and that without *to* is more common in AmE.
>
> (Quirk et al. 1985: 1205f.)

The results from the recent corpora show that this has changed, because now the bare infinitive has become the statistical norm also in British English.[43] This is not only so in written material but also in the spoken language, as is shown in Table 4.30.

---

[43] Since I have repeatedly argued above that participant observers unaided by corpora are in a weak position when monitoring ongoing grammatical change, fairness requires to draw attention to the following very perceptive analysis in Foster (1968: 204): ". . . the constructions accompanying certain verbs quietly change over the years without causing any great outcry. Some notable changes of this sort are once again products of American

In the British tradition, where the distinction is not always rigidly made between American, informal, or uneducated usage,[44] it has been commonplace to consider the bare infinitive as in some way informal or nonstandard, as opposed to the formal or standard construction with *to*. Particularly instructive in this connection are changes to the relevant OED entry, where in the first edition of 1933 the bare infinitive figures as dialectal and obsolete, whereas the new edition of 1989 lists it as a common colloquial form.

All analyses proposed so far – including those that correctly diagnose the disappearance of a regional contrast between British and American English – have disregarded a second important fact. It is not only British English which has been changing by moving closer to American English, as American English itself has also been developing. Infinitival complements after *help* do not form a closed system in which the proportion of bare and *to*-infinitives may change but the overall frequency of the relevant instances remains constant. Even in the course of the very short period documented in the four corpora studied here, instances of *help* governing (any kind of) infinitive have increased significantly – from 121 to 199 in the British corpora, and from 180 to 247 in the American ones (see Table 4.29 above).

This increase is not a statistical fluke but part of a long-term trend, as is obvious from Figure 4.4 (overleaf), which presents the frequencies of the constructions in question in the OED quotation base since 1600.

Barring some fluctuations in the proportions of bare and *to*-infinitives, nothing happens for the first two and a half centuries of the period under review. Instances of *help* + infinitive never exceed a very low frequency of 5 per 10,000 citations. From the mid-nineteenth century onwards, however, uses of *help* with infinitival complements start mushrooming.[45] Thereby, the increase is faster for the bare infinitives than for the *to*-infinitives, which of course explains why the former must have overtaken the latter in the recent history of British English.

It is one thing to observe and document an increase in frequency, and another to explain it. Increasing frequency of a word in a corpus might

---

idiom, a typical example being seen in the omission of the preposition 'to' after 'help'. Now this phenomenon was not unknown in poetical and somewhat archaic language . . . . But only in the late nineteen-thirties and early 'forties did the construction really make headway in Britain. Its acceptance into the standard language was very rapid and J. Hubert Jagger, writing his *English in the future* (1940), commented on 'the speed with which the American habit of omitting *to* after *help* has invaded Britain' (p. 55). But in spite of the speedy acceptance of the new form the old one is still well entrenched and the two rivals seem destined to battle it out for some time to come." The 1930s and 1940s were indeed important in the spread of the bare-infinitive construction in British English (cf. the frequency distributions in the OED discussed below), and one wonders about the role of the common contemporary collocation *help us (to) win the war* in the process.

[44] As one source graciously puts it, "*Help* followed by an infinitive without *to* . . ., once condemned as an Americanism, is now accepted in British English . . ." (Wood 1962: 107).

[45] As the twentieth century is plotted by decades rather than twenty-five-year intervals, the "real" rise is even sharper.

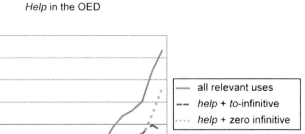

Figure 4.4 *Help* + infinitive 1600–2000 – frequency as n/10,000 citations

correspond to increasing salience of the related concept in the community. This explanation is not plausible here, as we would not want to claim that ours is a more caring society in which the concept of helping has become more prominent. Increasing frequency of one word might also correlate with decreasing frequency of its synonyms, such as when the proportion of *persons* grows at the expense of informal/neutral *people* in formal and technical registers. This does not seem to be an explanation here, either. The higher frequency of *help* is not related to a corresponding drop in the frequency of synonyms such as *support* or *aid*. Focusing on the construction as a whole, we could argue that infinitives might have encroached on *that*-clauses (as was observed above for the relation of gerundial and finite complements with *remember*). This does not seem to be the case, as finite complement clauses depending on *help* are rare in Old and Middle English and absent from the Early Modern period onwards. The only plausible explanation that remains to account for the increase in frequency is that the meaning of *help* has broadened from "somebody lends support to somebody else in performing some task" to a more general notion of "contribute to/provide a favorable environment for." It will be noted that, while the first meaning is compatible with inanimate subjects or objects only in metaphorical diction, such constraints are absent for the second. In fact, the latter meaning is so general and abstract that it approaches those typically associated with grammatical categories. The verb *help* might thus be said to be in the process of taking over quasi-auxiliary function in complex verb phrases (see Mair 1995, 2002 for a proposal of this kind).

Reviewing research by Benveniste and others, Brinton points out that the creation of new auxiliaries by grammaticalization:

> crucially involves three kinds of reanalysis:
>
> a.   of a full verb as an "auxiliary",
> b.   of a participle or infinitive as an 'auxiliate', and
> c.   of a loose concatenation of main verb plus verbal complement as a unified or "frozen" form.
>
> (Brinton 1988: 96f.)

Given the grammatical facts of English, in which true auxiliaries are a closed class of anomalous finites with a large number of clear morphosyntactic properties, avenue (c) is the pertinent one here. The *help* + verb combination is about to be added to the large number of modal idioms and catenatives already in existence in Modern English. The fact that the reduced form of the infinitive (typically, but not exclusively, found with modals in Modern English) has become the statistical norm is a telling sign that the process is already well under way.

By way of conclusion, a few typical examples will be discussed of the kind of use which is responsible for the increase in the frequency of *help*. They are taken from the quotation base of the OED:

> 1941 *Punch* 2 July 13/3 Sir Kingsley Wood . . . asked the House for another £1,000,000,000, to help pay for the next three months of war.

> 1961 L. Mumford *City in History* xv. 479 Nor have they eliminated the unburned hydrocarbons which help produce the smog that blankets such a motor-ridden conurbation as Los Angeles.

> 1968 *National Observer* (U.S.) 8 Apr. 5/4 Negro cabbie John W. Smith, whose arrest for "tailgating" a police car . . . helped spark five days of rioting . . ., was found guilty of assaulting a policeman.

> 1976 *Alyn & Deeside Observer* 10 Dec. 5/2 Part of the fun of the game comes in "sooping". This is when the players sweep the ice with special brooms in front of a moving stone to help it go further.

The first example illustrates the pseudo-prepositional use of the infinitive. "[Money] **to help pay for** the next three months of war" is "[money] **for paying** for the next three months of war." Formulated as it is, the sentence suggests a structure in which an instrument has been promoted to the syntactic role of subject: it is the money that pays for the war, and we do not think about the actual agent who spends the money in order to pay for the war. Inserting *to* before *pay* in this example would not only be stylistically clumsy because of the repetition involved; it would also produce a slight shift in perspective, from the instrument (money) to the agent who spends it. In "Sir Kingsley Wood asked the House for another £1,000,000,000, **to help to pay** for the next three months of war," the relevant semantic frame for the interpretation of *help* is more likely to be that associated with the literal three-place predicate: by granting the money, the House helps Sir Kingsley/the government to pay for the war. The next two examples feature negative effects – smog and rioting – which are not compatible with the core semantics of *help:* nobody is helped/supported in order to produce smog or spark off a riot here, which is why adding *to* before the infinitives would be slightly incongruous. Rather, inanimate entities create a favorable environment for the negative effects. The last example is a fairly clear case of a purely causative use of *help*, equivalent to *make* ("make it go further"). Again, adding *to* before the infinitive is problematical.

4.8.2.5 Concluding remarks.. One area of instability in the recent history English has been the interaction between nonfinite clausal complementation and the voice system. Denison (1998: 184ff.) notes that variability is suppressed in two directions for infinitives. Passives have tended to be generalized in the type *what's to be done* (with a few remaining fossils such as *who is to blame* or *the house is to let*), and the active has become the norm in the type *that's pleasant to hear* (fossils: *fit/ ready to eat/ to be eaten* "and others", 1998: 186). All of these types would certainly repay analysis on the basis of corpora.

What remains to do (or be done) here is to summarize and point out that what John Algeo has remarked about contrasts between the grammars of British and American English – namely, that "[p]erhaps the most fertile area of divergence between British and American is the complementation of verbs" (1988: 22) – is no less true for the study of the recent history of the language as a whole. In relation to their importance, changes in the function and use of the various types of nonfinite complement clauses remain an under-explored area of research.

4.9   Nouns, pronouns, adjectives

Unlike the tense/aspect/modality-complex or the system of nonfinite clausal complementation, the basic structure of the noun phrase – "determiner(s) + modifier(s) + head + postmodifier(s)" – has remained remarkably stable over the late Modern English period. In the words of Denison:

> This overall structure holds good for the whole of our lmodE period, with significant change confined to the internal structure of the Determiner position, and to greater freedom for former postmodifiers to be used in premodification.   (1998: 96)

This stability is not unexpected, as after a complete restructuring in the late Old English and early Middle English periods the nominal grammar of English had reached a stable state. Number marking in Modern English, for example, is so transparent that – short of shedding this inflectional category altogether – few changes can be imagined which go beyond eliminating the few remaining irregular plurals (*children, oxen, lice, mice, sheep*, etc.) or replacing opaque foreign plural endings on borrowed words with the more transparent native ones (e.g., *phenomena* → *phenomenons*).[46] But, even if there are no systematic drifts of interconnected changes, there have been many individual developments, some of which shall be treated below.

4.9.1 Inflection

The collapse of the Old English inflectional system in the noun phrase has caused the remnants to sit uneasily in the new, radically analytical grammar of Middle and Modern English and made them obvious focal points for synchronic variation and diachronic change. Three different phenomena will be discussed below to illustrate the point. A fourth, which might have been included under the heading of "inflection," the comparison of disyllabic adjectives, is treated independently in section 4.9.2.

A demise of whom? One important role of corpora in the study of ongoing grammatical change is "negative" or "corrective" in the sense that they provide evidence that some suspected change has not actually been proceeding in the assumed direction in a given period of time. A good case in point is the alleged demise of *whom* – assumed to be inevitable by many ever since Sapir put the case for it in his classic *Language* (1921: 166–174).

On the basis of a small and generically biased corpus of 180 *Times* editorials covering the period from 1900 to 1985 in five-year intervals, Bauer finds:

> The decrease in the use of *whom* marking a direct object as a percentage of all relative clauses with human antecedents in *The Times* corpus for 1900–1980 and with the inclusion of the figures from 1989 is significant at the 0.05 level, but it is not clear that this is a relevant measure.
>
> (1994: 76)

His skepticism is justified, as an across-the-board decrease of *whom* in the twentieth century cannot be substantiated by findings from larger and more

---

[46] Now, in the age of megacorpora and the practically unlimited availability of English-language text online, it is tempting to start hunting for instances of regularized *mans* or *mouses*, or to determine the proportion of *wharfs* and *wharves* in a particular variety. The return of such research is not unrewarding. For example, it will reveal that *mans* is common in forms like *Walkmans* and *Discmans* rather than those compounds in which it refers to male human beings, and that *louses* is more common in derogatory metaphorical usage (*those dirty little louses of my neighbors's kids*) than in its literal use. In terms of the long-term linguistic history of English, such observations are trivial. The same discrepancy between the amount of public interest and language-historical significance can be observed in the case of accidents which happen in the course of the assimilation of foreign plurals – such as when speakers recategorize plurals such as *data* and *criteria* as singulars, sometimes compounding the offense by adding the English plural suffix to the foreign one (*criterias*).

Table 4.31. Whom *in four matching corpora*

	1961	1991/1992
British English (LOB/F-LOB)	217	177
American English (Brown/Frown)	144	166

balanced corpora. In the four corpora providing the starting point for the present study the figures in Table 4.31 were obtained.

If anything, such figures show that there is fluctuation, or even convergence between the two major regional standards, rather than a directed diachronic change.[47] Apparent-time results based on the 100-million-word British National Corpus (BNC) are also instructive. At a total frequency of 12,596, or around 129 words per million, *whom* cannot exactly be called a rare word in contemporary English. Its function as a style marker, however, becomes obvious as soon as one looks at the frequencies in different textual genres: 141 per million, with outliers beyond 200 in the more formal genres, for written English, 26 overall for spoken English, and as low as 5 instances per million words in the spontaneous dialogues.

The apparent disagreement about the vitality of *whom* thus finds an easy solution. *Whom* is moribund as an element of the core grammar of English, but still very much alive as a style marker whose correct use is acquired in the educational system. A closer look at the spoken BNC examples reveals two telling indications of this state of affairs. *Whom* is not used at all by speakers from the under-14 age group, and the one instance in which it is used by a lower-class speaker (BNC marking "DE") shows the person reading from a written text. There are indications, as is to be expected given that the use of *whom* is not acquired naturally but taught in the educational system, that the prescriptive rules are often broken – both directly, by people using *who* where it is in theory ruled out (e.g., after prepositions, as in *to who? from who?*), and indirectly, by using the well-known hypercorrect forms of the type *the woman whom I believe is waiting*.

Going on from the BNC to even larger databases, it is possible to document the spontaneous use of *whom* in informal English even today – provided that one looks in favorable syntactic contexts. In .uk Web material (Google, accessed on 6 November 2003) a search for the phrase *who are you kidding?* yielded 233 hits, whereas there is only one case of *whom are you kidding?* This is what one would expect given that *to kid* is not a verb that goes well with very formal syntax. However, in *who's kidding who(m)?* the inflected form is attested 28 times (as against 108 times for the uninflected form *who*). This is still a minority of cases,

---

[47] This goes against previous research based on other corpora, in which results did point towards a decline in the discourse frequency of *whom* in spoken and written English in the late twentieth century (Aarts and Aarts 2002: 128).

but the greater proportion of *whom* is here motivated by the presence of *who* in the immediately preceding context.

All things considered, *whom* now seems to have reached the tail end of the characteristic S-shaped curve of progression in linguistic change. Its use today is highly restricted, but, rather than disappear entirely, the form is likely to remain in use for some time to come because of its overt prestige in writing.

Twentieth-century realignments in the use of case-marked personal pronouns.. Unlike the inflected form *whom*, which has been on the decline for a long time, case-marked forms of personal pronouns (*me*, *him*, *her*, *us*, *them*) have been spreading in the recent history of English. The English personal pronoun is the only grammatical category in which there is still a distinction between a nominative (subject) and an oblique (object) form. However, as inflection ceased to be a factor in determining subject and object status in the transition from Old English to Middle English elsewhere in the noun phrase, inflectional marking on the pronoun became redundant and is in some instances even a source of confusion for speakers and writers.

The most obvious example of this is presentational structures of the type *it is I*, long defended by language purists because a subject or subject complement in inflectional Germanic languages, including Old English, was marked by nominative case. Nominative forms of the pronoun no longer fitted easily into positions after the finite verb in the word-order-based logic of Modern English grammar, so that variability became endemic.

The use of objective-case forms in presentational structures (*it's me/him/ her/us/them*) or comparatives (*he's taller than me*) is now uncontroversial in standard English, and the traditional forms are not seriously defended by anyone today. "LIFE STORY OF KING EDWARD/The Man Who Said 'Why must it be I?'" was a headline in the *News Chronicle* of 11 December 1936 (p. 7), the day after King Edward VIII had renounced the throne. Even given the speaker and the formality of the occasion, it is difficult to imagine the same construction being used in similar circumstances today.

In informal and nonstandard usage, developments have even gone further, and there is now considerable scope for using the object forms even in pre-verbal position, especially in coordinated subject noun phrases (e.g., *me and my Dad used to have fights all the time*). A response to the possible stigmatization of such forms is occasional hypercorrection, in which nominative forms are transferred to post-verbal position (cf. *it is a great pleasure for Mary and I*).

However, the almost exclusive focus of the debate on *it is I* vs. *it is me* – that is, the presentational structure in its bare or pure form – has not done justice to the full complexity of the changes involved. An unprejudiced sifting of twentieth-century corpus evidence shows that (a) there are many contexts in which forms such as *it is I* are still found, and (b) that the shift to a preference for object forms of pronouns was not simultaneous for all persons. In the BNC,

Table 4.32. *Nominative vs. objective case for pronouns in specific syntactic contexts (BNC)*

	that	*who*	*whom*
it was I	1	45	—
it was me	16	33	—
it was he	10	204	3
it was him	11	9	—
it was she	1	90	1
it was her	7	3	—
it was we	—	—	—
it was us	1	3	—
it was they	—	60	1
it was them	4	1	—

forms of the type *it is I* are well attested in the favorable structural contexts illustrated by the following examples:

> The point of the story is that it was I that programmed the computer.
> (BNC J52 1259)

> It was I who decided to remove our troops from the Gulf, because I thought they'd become more of an irritant than a stabilizing factor.
> (BNC G2J 112)

As Table 4.32 shows, at 46 instances *it was I who/that . . .* is still almost as common in late twentieth-century British English as *it was me who/that . . ..* A complicating factor is that the likelihood of *it is I* is greater before following *who* (45 out of 77) than following *that* (1 out of 16).[48] Table 4.32, however, also shows an even more interesting trend: the distribution of the variants found for *I/me* is not paralleled for the other pronouns.

Interpreting the distribution as apparent-time data, we can infer a considerable time-lag between the spread of object case forms to "subject" position between the first and third persons. On the basis of the BNC evidence, a "modern" variant such as *it was them who did it* is positively daring even today.

A revival of the 's-genitive? A residual inflectional category in the English noun is the *'s-genitive*.[49] It is in variation with an analytical *of*-genitive: *their*

---

[48] *It was I/me whom. . .* is not attested.
[49] It has been suggested that the modern *'s*-marker should not really be regarded as a direct continuation of the genitive inflection of the Old English strong masculine class of nouns, but as a clitic. Among other things, the possibility of group genitives of the type *the king of*

children's problems → *the problems of their children.* Variation is, of course, not free but subject to a number of strong semantic, discourse, and idiomatic constraints which are well described in standard reference grammars. Referring to what they call a "gender" scale (in fact, a version of the typological animacy hierarchy), Quirk et al. (1985), for example, claim that:

> the genitive is favoured by those gender classes which are highest on the gender scale, in particular where N1 [the noun carrying the genitive inflection] is a personal name, a personal noun, and a noun with personal characteristics, i.e. animal nouns and collective nouns . . . With inanimate, in particular concrete, nouns, the *of*-construction is normally required.   (1985: 1277)

At the beginning of the twentieth century, Jespersen was among the first to note a tendency for the genitive to spread to concrete inanimate nouns. As the following quotation shows, he saw this development being led by journalistic style:

> During the last few decades the genitive of lifeless things has been gaining ground in writing (especially among journalists); in instances like the following the *of*-construction would be more natural and colloquially the only one possible.   (1909–1949: VII, 327f.)

Among the examples he cites are expressions such as the "sea's rage," "the rapidity of the heart's action,"[50] or "the room's atmosphere." Two further important treatments of change in progress in twentieth-century English do not see this particular change as being restricted to the language of the press, or indeed to the written language, anymore (Barber 1964: 132f.; Potter 1969 [1975]: 105).

'S-genitives with inanimate nouns do not seem to be very common in spoken English today. A search for *sea's*, *heart's*, and *room's* (i.e., cases similar to those provided by Jespersen) yielded five instances – all in one and the same passage of the text JST – of *to your heart's content*, which is not very good evidence as the genitive is not in variation with an *of*-phrase in this idiom, and the following, from a relatively informal board meeting:

> The other period erm the other thing I would like your advice on erm <pause> did you, you didn't note all this?
> Oh I'll give you all that, it's alright.

Sweden's wife or *it's not my car, it's the guy over there's* is invoked as evidence of its status as a clitic. See Rosenbach (2002: 203–208) for a comprehensive review of the arguments for and against the analysis as a clitic.

[50] This example happens to instantiate a discourse/stylistic factor possibly encouraging the use of the genitive. It prevents the occurrence of two *of*-phrases in the same noun phrase ("the rapidity of the action of the heart").

Table 4.33. *'S-genitives in four tagged corpora*[a]

	BrE	AmE
1961	4,962	5,063
1991/1992	6,194	7,145

[a] Figures for LOB and F-LOB are based on the manually post-edited tagger output. As post-editing was still in progress for Frown at the time of writing, those for Brown and Frown are from the raw output. As automatic identification of the genitive is largely error-free, this will lead to very minor discrepancies only.
Significances for LOB: F-LOB and Brown: Frown $p < 0.001$

> Er the other thing I'd like your advice on is that the coffee room's franchise <pause> er is due for renewal in nineteen ninety three.
>
> (BNC F7A 812–814)

But, even if the suspected shift to the genitive were confined to the formal or written language, it would be a remarkable development: a partial reversal of a general drift towards analyticity in English grammar. As searches for *s*, *'s*, or *s'* in untagged corpora are beset with obvious problems, it is fortunate that the issue can be investigated on the basis of the tagged versions of the four corpora, which code the genitive separately on nouns. Indeed, the striking increase in the frequency of the genitive tag, both in the British and in the American material, seems to point to a rapid diachronic development at first sight. Table 4.33 gives the figures.

The rise is real, even if one factors in a 5.3 percent increase in the frequency of nouns from LOB to F-LOB, which has been noted in Mair et al. (2002: 249), and which makes the occurrence of genitives proportionally more likely. However, the genitive is clearly not an independent variable in other ways, as well. Corpus studies (Raab-Fischer 1995) and studies relying on a broader array of data-gathering methods (Rosenbach 2002) show that the determinants of synchronic variation in genitive usage interact in complex ways, and that it is very difficult to identify diachronic trends against a background of sometimes far greater synchronic variability. Raab-Fischer has undertaken a laborious qualitative analysis of genitive use in the press sections of the LOB and F-LOB corpora, paying particular attention to the semantic class of nouns and the alternation between the inflectional genitive and the *of*-paraphrase. Table 4.34 presents her results.

As there is only an insignificant increase of 0.8 percent in the frequency of nouns from LOB to F-LOB, the frequency shifts are genuine. They add up to an increase in the frequency of the genitive particularly for collective nouns, and for nouns – both proper and common – referring to location and

Table 4.34. *Use of genitive and* of-*phrase in the press sections (A–C) of two corpora (compiled from Raab-Fischer 1995)*

	LOB genitive	LOB *of*-phrase	F-LOB genitive	F-LOB *of*-phrase
Human	702	661	937	530
Collective nouns	175	528	311	381
Higher animals	5	8	9	9
Location	159	478	286	331
Time	80	149	120	144
Others	38	2059	79	1984
Total	1159	3883	1742	3379

time (e.g., *England's, the city's, next week's*, etc.), which is in some instances paralleled by a corresponding decrease in the frequency of the *of*-phrase. Inroads made by the genitive at the lower end of the animacy scale (category "others"), however, are minimal, so that no major rewriting of current grammatical rules is required.

The following example shows that much of the current synchronic and diachronic variability can probably be handled entirely on the discourse level, without making adjustments to the underlying grammatical system:

> This [Handsel Monday] was the equivalent of England's Boxing Day, but took place on the first Monday of the New Year.
>
> (F-LOB F 34 159f.)

In this particular example, the use of the genitive is encouraged by the presence of another *of*-phrase: "the equivalent of the Boxing Day of England" would sound clumsy. In addition, owing to the different relative order of the nouns in the genitive and the *of*-phrase (*England's Boxing Day* vs. *the Boxing Day of England*) the two constructions lead to a different information structure in the phrase/clause. The genitive phrase has the extra advantage that it is shorter and thus a suitable device for compressing information – certainly not a negligible factor in genres such as press reportage. Its greater incidence in current written English might thus entirely be due to writers using the available – and stable – grammatical options to achieve a greater information density.

This is made clear by a generically stratified analysis of the BNC (shown in Table 4.35), where the genitive forms *country's* and *London's* cluster in information-oriented written genres and are largely absent from spontaneous speech.

A comprehensive qualitative analysis of the alternatives *of the country* and *of London*[51] is not feasible as the greater part of the huge output represents cases

---

[51] To exclude spurious hits of the type *move out of the country*, the search was restricted to occurrences following an immediately preceding noun.

Table 4.35. *Normalized frequencies (occurrences per million words) for selected genitives in spoken and written text types from the BNC*

	Country's	London's
Written-to-be-spoken	87	8
Written books/periodicals	39	18
Written miscellaneous	28	10
Spoken-context-governed	5	2
Spoken-demographic	0	1*
Average written	39	17
Average spoken	3	2

*Value based on a manual analysis of BNC World output after eliminating 4 out of 8 instances of *London's* in which a cliticized auxiliary was mistagged as a genitive.

in which there is no variation between the two constructions for structural, semantic or idiomatic reasons (cf., e.g., *another part of London, City of London*, etc.). A check on the spoken–demographic material, however, shows the *of*-genitives firmly entrenched in this register, with a minimum of 5 instances of *of the country* and 7 of *of London* displaying clearly genitival function on the basis of a substitution test.

4.9.2 Synthetic and analytical comparison for disyllabic adjectives

Seen against the background of the long-term history of English, the comparison of disyllabic adjectives is an area in which a tendency towards increasing use of analytical, periphrastic forms might have been expected in the course of the twentieth century. This is not what seems to have happened. The comparison of adjectives is pinpointed as an area of diachronic instability by Denison (1998) and practically all other sources on recent change in English grammar, and there is no doubt that the long-term development since Middle English has been away from the synthetic, inflection-based pattern (*-er, -est*) and towards the analytical one (*more, most*). But, however tempting it is to assume that such a development has persisted in the recent past, the facts tell another story.

Bauer, for example, is able to demonstrate that what the twentieth century has seen is not really a linear continuation of the trend but rather a cleaning-up of random variation: "the change in the course of this century appears to have been only incidentally an increase in the use of periphrastic comparison. Rather, the change has been a regularization of a confused situation, so that it is becoming more predictable which form of comparison must be used" (1994: 60). Other investigators go further and claim that the language is experiencing a (temporary?) revival of inflectional comparison. Surveying data from late Middle English to the BNC, Kytö and Romaine, for example, present the following conclusion:

> the older inflectional type has been reasserting itself since the Early Modern period. . . . Contrary to what one might predict from the general trend in English towards a more analytical syntax, corpus-based studies have since revealed that the majority of both comparative and superlative adjectives in present-day English are inflectional.
>
> (Kytö and Romaine 2000: 172f.)

The details of the two authors' research, however, generally support Bauer's assessment, as very clear and contradictory diachronic trends emerge for different classes of adjectives. The overall rise in inflectional comparatives and superlatives is thus largely due to "the relatively great proportion of adjectives ending in -y/-ly in this category" (2000: 181), whereas over the past few centuries inflectional comparison has practically been eliminated as an option for adjectives ending in -ful or -ous (Kytö and Romaine 1997: 344).

All in all, therefore, the spread of analytical constructions seems to have come to a halt in this fragment of the grammar, and a division of labor between the synthetic and analytical comparison of adjectives is emerging. With known and well-described exceptions (e.g., adjectives beginning with un- such as unhappy), synthetic comparison is now ruled out for trisyllabic adjectives, and analytical comparison is very rare for monosyllabic ones. For disyllabic adjectives, there is variation, with the dominant determinant of choice being the shape of the second syllable. Phonologically light second syllables seem to favor inflectional comparison, but the correlation between type of comparison and the phonological weight of the second syllable is far from perfect. Thus, adjectives ending in unstressed -ful or -ous never have inflectional comparison, whereas certain types of stressed second syllable (e.g., sincere, polite) still allow it. Within the individual classes, however, the tendency generally is, as assumed by Bauer, for variation to be cleaned up. This is shown well in Figure 4.5 (adapted from Kytö and Romaine 1997: 344), which follows four classes of adjectives from late Middle English to the present.

Late Middle English shows all four groups variable in broadly the same percentage range. In a first stage of development (EModE), the synthetic option is eliminated for two classes (-ous, -ful). The other two (-y/-ly and -le/-er), after remaining variable into the nineteenth century, have gravitated towards synthetic comparison since. The roughly one-fifth of analytical forms remaining in present-day usage are likely to be accounted for by complexity effects of the type described by Mondorf (2003); for example, analytical comparatives used in coordinated structures (cf., e.g., *this will make you look more handsome and happy*) or with structurally elaborated adjectival phrases (e.g., *he's more happy than anybody can imagine about the way things worked out*).

Percentage of analytical comparison

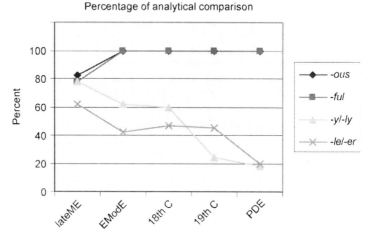

Figure 4.5 Analytical and synthetic comparison for four classes of adjectives (Kytö and Romaine 1997: 344)

4.9.3 Number in the noun phrase/subject–verb concord

Change in this fragment of the grammar manifests itself in two different instances. The first concerns an isolated word: *less*, the comparative of the adjective *little*, which is claimed to be increasingly used with countable nouns (and thus encroaching on territory traditionally occupied by *fewer*). The second is somewhat more general: a tendency frequently noted in nineteenth- and twentieth-century English, especially the standard British variant, for plural concord to be used with formally singular collective nouns if the context provides strong pragmatic or semantic support (cf. Depraetere [2003] for a synchronic description of the facts in late twentieth-century British English).

Let us first turn to *less*, as in expressions such as *more cabs is less cars*. As can be confirmed by a quick look at the relevant entry of the OED (s.v. *less*, a. [n.], adv., and conj., A 1.c.) the use of *less* with count nouns is obviously not the innovation it is commonly considered to be, but an established usage with a history going back to Old English. As the editors put it, it is "frequently found but generally regarded as incorrect." The question therefore needs to be rephrased from "Is this form a recent innovation and spreading in the language?" to "Has the form had the stigma removed from it in the course of the twentieth century and is it spreading in the standard language?" The corpora consulted present a picture which highlights the importance of genre as a determinant of linguistic change (Table 4.36).

The fact that F-LOB and Frown contain one case each of a construction that is absent from their 1961 counterparts is clearly not a solid statistical finding,

Table 4.36. *Fewer vs. less with count nouns in selected corpora* *

	fewer	*less*
1. Late twentieth-century spoken English		
ICE-GB, direct conversations	1	—
BNC spoken-demographic	5	4
Santa Barbara	—	—
Longman Corpus of Spoken AmE	14	16
Corpus of Spoken Professional AmE	18	6
2. The Brown quartet		
Brown	13	—
LOB	4	—
Frown	11	1**
F-LOB	12	1***
3. OED Baseline corpora		
Baseline1900	5	—
Baseline1800	—	2****
Baseline1700	2	—

*Search algorithms
(a) for Brown"quartet," Corpus of Spoken Professional AmE, and Baseline: *fewer *s, less *s*. This meant that some instances – for example, irregular plurals (*less children*) – were overlooked, but avoided massive over-collection of irrelevant instances of *less* (e.g., *this is less interesting than . . .*)
(b) BNC spoken-demographic: lexical searches for *less* and *fewer*, followed by tag for plural nouns
(c) Longman: lexical search for *fewer*; figure for *less* extrapolated from manual analysis of first 200 of 644 cases
***less accidents* (J 41, 151)
****Several hundred more or less manyears of work* (H 08, 192)
****Both instances of *take less pains*

and the picture suggested by these figures is that "*less* + count noun" is a stable style marker rather than a diachronically evolving variable. It is a regular presence in those spoken corpora which are big enough to yield relevant returns, but dramatic inroads into formal and written usage are not apparent.

Selected further searches of the World Wide Web do not substantially change this verdict: *take less pains*, which – interestingly – is attested twice in Baseline1800, is the one collocation found in which *less* is more common than *fewer* today. A Google search for the phrase *take less pains* yielded 27 instances as against 5 for *take fewer pains*. *Fewer cars* polled at 15,500 (against 5,780 for *less cars*), and similar ratios were obtained for nouns such as *opportunities*, *miles* and *dollars* (accessed on 17 September 2003 in all cases). The nature of Web material being what it is, an attempt to detect systematic relations between the semantic class or formal/informal stylistic value of the noun and the use of *less* and *fewer* soon had to be abandoned.

Probably as a result of the decreasing functional load of inflection in the history of English, the language has shown an increasing tolerance of "notional" or semantic concord alongside "grammatical" concord. In most cases, this has led to the treatment of grammatical plurals as singular (*the United States is ...*/*the news is ...*) or of grammatically singular collective nouns as plurals (*the police are ...*). In addition, there are some nouns, such as *information*, *advice*, or *heebie-jeebies*, which for arbitrary reasons admit either the singular or the plural only. In an otherwise very stable and transparent system of grammatical number marking these are predetermined breaking points encouraging regional variation in varieties of English around the world or diachronic change.

One obvious instance is variable concord, found with collective nouns such as *government*, *team*, *audience*, *family*, or *band*, where – in contrast to cases such as *police* – it is possible to use both singular and plural. Traditionally, variable notional concord was considered to be typical of the British rather than the American standard. As variable forms, such usages are ideally suited for investigation on the basis of corpora. Two very comprehensive recent studies of the phenomenon are Levin (2001) and Depraetere (2003), who – like most of the classic treatments of the issue (such as Liedtke 1910 or Dekeyser 1975) – are more concerned with synchronic (regional and stylistic) variability than diachronic change.

However, to the extent that sources do comment on diachronic tendencies in this area, they usually agree that variability is on the decline and the tendency is for variation to sort itself out by collective singular nouns either reverting to obligatory singular concord or, in exceptional cases, moving to obligatory plural (*police*, with very strong statistical preferences also for the plural for *pair* and *duo*). Sometimes the development toward obligatory plural is tied to a reanalysis of the grammatical structure of complex noun phrases – for example, the question of what the head is in phrases such as *a lot of people is/are* or *the majority of voters is/are*. Taking the cue from the hints provided by Liedtke (1910), Dekeyser (1975), or Siemund (1995), one could argue that variable concord with collectives, rather than portending fundamental simplification of noun–verb concord in standard English, at the end of the twentieth century reveals itself as a fading stylistic fashion typical of more formal varieties of British English during the nineteenth and early twentieth centuries – in other words, the equivalent of the *shall*-future in the nominal domain.

4.9.4 "Singular" they

Just as case, gender has disappeared as a major grammatical category from the grammar of the English noun phrase, again with a remaining residue in the third person singular pronouns (which, of course, are largely distributed according to the referent's natural gender). And again this has led to a conflict between rules long propagated by prescriptivists and the development of community norms. The most conspicuous issue in question is "singular" or generic *they* – as in *everybody came in their own car* – where prescriptivists have tended to insist on number concord between singular *everybody* and the anaphoric reference (*everybody came in his own car*). Language reformers of varying degrees of zeal and pedantry have recommended forms ranging from *everybody came in his or her own car* to *everybody came in shim's car*,[52] while the majority of speakers has probably gone on using singular *they* in their spontaneous usage (see Bodine [1982] for documentation).

The Brown quartet of corpora shows that singular *they* has indeed made a most impressive comeback in the written standard in a mere thirty years. In 1961, the so-called "generic" use of *he* for both male and female reference was well established, and hardly under threat. The efforts of the women's movement of the 1970s and 1980s, however, ensured that by 1991/1992, generic *he* was declining fast. Mair and Leech (2006) give the following figures: a sample of approximately 500 instances of *he/him/his/himself* from each corpus showed a decline of gender-neutral use from 32 (LOB) to 4 (F-LOB), and from 20 (Brown) to 7 (Frown). The opposite trend shows in a corresponding sample of *they* and its variants, with a rise in the use of singular *they* from 0 (LOB) to 9 (F-LOB), and from 7 (Brown) to 9 (Frown). Although rare in all four corpora, the gender-inclusive coordinated pronouns *he or she* (and their variants) rose in frequency for the entire corpora from 11 to 37 (LOB → F-LOB) and from 9 to 56 (Brown → Frown). The promotion of singular/generic *they* in formal and standard English is one of the very few examples of almost instantly successful feminist-inspired language planning, its success probably being due to the fact that language reform in this instance did not involve the promotion of a new usage but merely the removal of stigma from an existing one.

Ultimately, the need to plug the gap left by the demise of gender-neutral *himself* may lead to the establishment of a new pronoun, *themself*. Although Huddleston and Pullum (2002: 494) cite it as an innovation in standard English since the 1970s, the word form *themself* has a long history in English. The OED, which does not have an entry for *themself*, lists 41 mostly Middle English and Early Modern English occurrences in its quotation base, many of them with a distinctly nonstandard ring. The form has survived into the modern nonstandard, but in contemporary written English it is still too rare to show up in any of our four corpora. The BNC has 26 instances, 10 written and 16 spoken ones, which is sufficient for a first orientation as to its status. Here are two written examples, in which the generic/singular reference of *themself* is beyond doubt:

---

[52] The reader is recommended to consult the World Wide Web to get an idea of the community promoting *shim* as a gender-neutral third person pronoun.

You won't be the first or last man or woman who gets themself involved in a holiday romance.   (BNC, K4D 386)

Or the person who's trying not to drink so much and beats themself up when they slip back and get drunk!   (BNC, CDK 2464)

It is interesting to note that all written examples are of this type, whereas the spoken ones show a mix, with some uses of *themself* having generic/singular reference and others referring back to referential or anaphoric plural *they*. It seems that, from a situation in which *themself* appears in corpora as an occasional performance slip or infiltration from nonstandard usage, we are moving to a more focused one, in which the form gains a clear function at the margins of the contemporary standard. Singular *themself* can also be attested in contemporary spoken American English, as is shown by the following extract from the Longman Corpus. At two occurrences in the Longman Corpus and a further five attested in MICASE (Michigan Corpus of Academic Spoken English), the degree of currency (or marginality) of the form in the two varieties is at present comparable:

> It is, but the thing is like all of 'em there's this horrible death scene and this one was the first ones where the dead parent is on screen, you know the father lion is laying there and the little baby lion is poking at him and going daddy, daddy. I just thought, you know, how much gross are they going to get? Next thing you know, they'll have the kid accidentally killing the parent themself. Those things they put <unclear> They've been like that ever since.   (LCSAE)

An additional complication is introduced into the analysis by the form *ourself*,[53] which is attested 32 times in the BNC. Its complicated concord and reference patterns are occasionally discussed in the literature on pragmatics (cf., e.g., Levinson 1987: 70). In addition to the usual performance slips, it is editorial uses of *we* which seem to encourage the occasional use of the form *ourself*, because the editorial plural is, of course, an underlying singular. All in all, we can conclude that, given that *themselves* still vastly outnumbers *themself* even in the specialized generic use, we are certainly seeing the earliest stages in the curvilinear pattern typically associated with the spread of linguistic innovations.

4.10 Conclusion

The present survey has demonstrated that there has been noticeable grammatical change in the past century even in a rigidly codified language variety such

---

[53] And possible singular uses of *yourself*, which can, of course, not be extracted from corpora with reasonable effort owing to the homophonous singular reflexive.

as written standard English, and that the spread of individual innovations can be documented in language corpora. Further, it has been shown that those accounts of ongoing grammatical change in English which are based on anecdotal or impressionistic observation are generally unreliable, erring in three ways.

1   Directed diachronic changes have been assumed where in fact there is stable long-term variability.
2   Undue emphasis has been placed on the investigation of a small number of often trivial shibboleths important to prescriptivists.[54]
3   A focus on the study of isolated salient instances of change has led to a failure to notice the ever-present groundswell of linguistic change, apparent in important long-term developments in the core grammar.

Unsurprisingly, the analyses and case studies presented in this chapter have shown that diachronic change is embedded in regional variation in standard Englishes worldwide, and in the even greater stylistic variability which can be found within any one variety at a particular time.

---

[54] The qualification of some of these shibboleths as trivial does not imply that they are not worthy of serious linguistic study, nor that they are necessarily infrequent in actual usage. The problem is rather one of analytical perspective. Usually, such stigmatized usages are studied in isolation from each other and from their wider grammatical background, which makes it difficult to arrive at a balanced assessment of their place in the larger picture of ongoing grammatical change.

5 Pronunciation

5.1 Introduction

For a long time, standard English was a written language, defined through its orthography, vocabulary, and grammar. The development of standardized prestige accents for spoken communication is a comparatively recent phenomenon. In fact, there are linguists who claim that standard English can be pronounced in any accent even today (e.g., Trudgill 1999). This position is not an unattractive one for its internal consistency but will not be adopted in the present book. To take contemporary Britain as an example, it is true that standard English may come in several accents, but certainly not in all. Apart from RP ("Received Pronunciation"), the accent traditionally associated with it, standard English may be pronounced with a Scottish accent, a general Northern pronunciation, and others, but it is still difficult to imagine standard English in broad Cockney or Liverpool "Scouse." Such speakers are not found, and there are obvious sociolinguistic reasons accounting for this gap.

Two prominent sociolinguists have drawn attention to an apparent paradox besetting efforts to standardize speech. There is a mismatch between the desire to do so, which has been strong throughout the recent past, and an obvious lack of success in fully achieving the intended goal:

> For a number of reasons it is difficult to point to a fixed and invariant kind of English that can properly be called the standard language, unless we consider only the *written* form to be relevant. It is only in the spelling system that full standardisation really has been achieved, as deviations from the norm (however logical) are not tolerated there. When, however, we refer to "standard" spoken English, we have to admit that a good deal of variety is tolerated in practice, and scholars have often had to loosen their definition of a "standard" in dealing with speech. . . . Strictly speaking, however, standardisation does not tolerate variability. Thus it is best, in our view, to look at the question of "Standard English" in a different light, and to speak of standardisation as a historical process which – to a greater or lesser degree – is always in progress in those

languages that undergo it. Standardisation is motivated in the first place by various social, political and commercial needs and is promoted in various ways, including the use of the writing system, which is relatively easily standardised; but absolute standardisation of a spoken language is never achieved (the only fully standardised language is a dead language). Therefore it seems appropriate to speak more abstractly of standardisation as an *ideology*, and a standard language as an idea in the mind rather than a reality – a set of abstract norms to which actual usage may conform to a greater or lesser extent.   (Milroy and Milroy 1991: 22f.)

The present chapter is thus as much about the cultural and social history of the twentieth century as about the history of English sounds during this period. It will deal with phonetic changes in selected English accents during the twentieth century but it will also discuss the social motivation which makes people attempt to suppress the natural variability in spontaneous pronunciation through the standardization of prestige accents and, more specifically, address the question why – at least in Britain – such standardizing efforts were so energetically promoted from the late nineteenth century onwards. Raymond Williams, the cultural historian, who devotes an entire chapter to linguistic standardization in *The long revolution*, his classic account of the roots of modern British society, identifies the ideology of standardization as follows:

These and similar changes [e.g., the move from /æ/ to /ɑ:/ or the loss of post-vocalic /r/ in eighteenth-century London pronunciation] were spread by improved communications, but the main agency, undoubtedly, in fixing them as class speech, was the new cult of uniformity in the public schools. It was a mixture of "correctness", natural development, and affectation, but it became as it were embalmed. It was no longer one kind of English, or even useful common dialect, but "correct English", "good English", "pure English", "standard English". In its name, thousands of people have been capable of the vulgar insolence of telling other Englishmen that they do not know how to speak their own language. And as education was extended, mainly under middle-class direction, this attitude spread from being simply a class distinction to a point where it was possible to identify the making of these sounds with being educated, and thousands of teachers and learners, from poor homes, became ashamed of the speech of their fathers.   (Williams 1961 [1981]: 247)

Of course, we know from literary works and educators' comments that rustic and provincial pronunciations were frowned on in metropolitan London society even in the Early Modern English period, and the eighteenth century itself produced a wealth of pronouncing dictionaries of the English language which, in addition to giving advice on the proper pronunciation of Latin and Greek loanwords, also tended to caution against some perceived features of a lower-class accent. However, Williams is right in emphasizing that it was not until the mid-nineteenth and early twentieth centuries that the thrust towards the standardization of the spoken language gained coherence and direction. The way in which accent became a "social symbol" among sections of the English middle class and upper middle class has been traced in great linguistic detail for Britain in Mugglestone (2003). Not unexpectedly, her account of the developments is less passionately critical than Williams', but in its broad outlines the picture sketched by him remains intact:

> [W]hat could most clearly be said to have come into existence by the late nineteenth century was a set of regionally neutral "standard pronunciation features" from the [h] which it would be "social suicide" to drop to the [ɪŋ] which "polite speakers" all over the country might assimilate, alongside the vocalization of [r] in words such as *bird*, and the use of [ʌ] rather than [ʊ] in words such as *butter*. It was the sum of features such as these (as well as the connotative features with which they were liberally endowed) which served to create the most potent – if looser – perceptions of a "standard" which was to various degrees adhered to, as Ellis notes, by those who assumed, or attempted to adopt "the educated pronunciation of the metropolis, of the court, the pulpit and the bar." Rather than a rigidly monolithic norm, it was elements such as these which, bound to no region in isolation, tended to establish common signifiers of accent (and associated images of identity) all over the country. (2003: 264)

The standardization of pronunciation did not remain confined to Britain. With a delay of about half a century, a local prestige accent was consolidated in the United States (cf., e.g., Bonfiglio 2002), and similar developments are now to be observed in many parts of the ex-colonial English-speaking world, where local educated norms of speech are emerging in a three-way competition between an inherited, usually British, colonial norm, an American one which is currently dominant globally, and strengthening tendencies to assert local identity through the promotion of local accent features.

As in all standardization processes, there is a functionally motivated element which is non-controversial. Modern technology has extended the sphere of the spoken word far beyond the narrow limits of face-to-face communication, and this obviously calls for a levelling of some of the more extreme regional and social characteristics of pronunciation among speakers operating in this wider sphere. However, as both the Milroys and Raymond Williams have made clear, the standardization of pronunciation in the twentieth century has progressed far beyond what is required for purely practical purposes, and it is this ideological and cultural element in standardization processes which has led to sometimes bitter social controversies being fought out about trivial phonetic details.

For two obvious examples, consider the role of "aitch-dropping" or the glottalization of the voiceless alveolar plosive /t/ in recent British English. Both are minor changes if measured by their linguistic impact on the phonemic system of modern English. Aitch-dropping is a natural and expected development for the simple reason that it has been one of the most venerable long-term trends in the history of English pronunciation. The voiceless glottal approximant /h/ has been restricted to word- or stem-initial position since late Old English, which has reduced its functional load in the phonemic system and encouraged phonetic weakening. With the exception of the northeast and, possibly, East Anglia, /h/ has disappeared from all modern English dialect regions identified by Trudgill (1990), so that the normal vernacular pronunciation of a word such as *hill* has long been /ɪl/ in most of England. Even in educated speech, the use of /h/ was variable in words such as *historical, herb,*[1] or *hotel*, before a desire to differentiate vulgar and good usage led to an establishment of the spelling pronunciations. In sum, the preservation of /h/ in standard English cannot be seen but as the result of social forces postponing the advent of the very last episode in a thousand-year development. The very fact that in present-day English the loss of /h/ would be such a natural change probably explains the intensity of educated resistance to it.

The glottalization of /t/ is similar to aitch-dropping in that its impact on the phonemic system is minimal and certainly no explanation for the social stir caused by it. The difference is that this particular change is a recent innovation, originating in London and southeastern speech in the later nineteenth century and spreading rapidly into most British urban dialects. The social stigma attaching to these urban vernaculars is so powerful that the glottal stop, which is now part of the standard pronunciation in many non-salient environments (e.g., pre-nasally, as in *but not*, or with two successive *t*'s, as in *a bit tight*) is still strongly resisted in more salient positions (e.g., intervocalically, as in *party* or *lot of*).

Another area in which the excess ideological forces behind standardization are much in evidence is the placement of stress in di- and polysyllabic words of Latin or French origin. Considerable variability in the English stress system is to be expected in view of its history. Old English had the typical Germanic stress system, with a fixed stress normally falling on the root syllable. From the Middle English period onwards, thousands of loanwords were taken over from French, a language with largely word-final stress. The most common resolution of the conflict between two incompatible stress systems was for the loanwords to eventually adopt fixed stress on the first syllable (which was for convenience seen as the root), and hundreds of French words like *nature, virtue,* or *travel* now exhibit initial stress in English.[2] A further complication was presented by the Latin and Greek borrowings of the Renaissance, as the

---

[1] /ɜrb/ is, of course, the dominant current pronunciation of the word in American English.
[2] *Travel* has the semantically differentiated minor form *travail*, which – consistent with its formal stylistic value – preserves the French stress pattern.

movable-stress patterns of these languages were incompatible with either of the two systems coexisting uneasily already.

Not surprisingly, the stress pattern of present-day English is therefore a highly complex and only partially transparent one, as the assimilative power of the inherited Germanic "root" stress pattern has come to operate rather unpredictably and unsystematically. For example, families of etymologically and semantically related words have established arbitrary stress patterns which are stable, as, for example, *define* and *defining, definite, definitive*. In other cases, minor sub-regularities have been implemented – for example in noun–verb pairs such as *object* vs. *to object* or *import* vs. *to import*, in which the noun receives initial stress and the verb retains final stress. It is in the nature of a sub-rule that it will not generalize to all relevant cases, as is shown by pairs such as *comment/to comment, contact/to contact* or *a divide/to divide* in which both the nouns and the verbs have initial (or, in the last case, final) stress. In a good number of cases, particular variants have come to be associated with particular regional varieties. Thus, *laboratory*, with a stress on the second syllable, is the preferred British form whereas the initial stress is typical of American English. In *áddress* (noun), American English has an additional initial-stress option in addition to common *address* with a stress on the second syllable. Many of the words concerned[3] are very rare or unlikely to occur outside written texts.

In cases not covered by any of the categories illustrated above, variation seems to be free, and usually reveals itself as a symptom of obvious rule-conflict. For example, in *comparable*, initial stress would appear desirable globally (analogy to a large number of related cases in which the stress has moved left in French and Latin loans), but not locally (*compárable*, stressed on the second syllable, is in a transparent relationship with its root *compare*). In short, there are no rational arguments which prescriptivists or language planners might invoke to recommend one variant over the other.

Thus, hesitation as to where to place the stress in those rare instances in which one actually has to pronounce a word such as *prognathous* or similar "eye-words" should not cause a lot of concern even in an educated and linguistically aware community. Nevertheless, stress placement is dangerous territory in folk-linguistics. As one commentator has remarked:

> Nothing excites [readers] to write to *The Times*, proclaiming that civilization as we know it is coming to an end, more than the tendency of broadcasters to shift their accents forwards or backwards on such words.
>
> (Howard 1984: 16)

As a case in point, consider the noun *dispute*, historically derived from the verb *dispute* through conversion in Early Modern English. Early editions of Daniel

---

[3] Berg (1999) identifies 932 such cases (out of a total of around 75,000 entries) in Wells' *Longman pronouncing dictionary*, many of them being rarely used words or proper names.

Jones' *Pronouncing dictionary* unfortunately do not contain an entry for the noun, so that the OED first edition's *dispúte* probably represents the consensus pronunciation at the time. There is, however, the related adjective *disputable*, stressed on the first syllable, and a pronunciation *díspute* is additionally motivated by the fact that it would bring the word in line with those other pairs, such as *object* and *to object*, in which the verb has the stress on the second syllable and the noun has it on the first. Obviously, competing motivations support competing forms, in this instance as in many others.

Treatment of the issue in the linguistic reference literature is, accordingly, rather matter-of-fact. When Jones' *Pronouncing dictionary* first notes the new pronunciation in the 13th edition (1967), it does not make any value judgments and confines itself to the statement that the "stress pattern ´ - - is increasingly found for the noun." This comment is retained in the 14th edition, and dropped in the 15th, where *díspute* is given as the second alternative pronunciation in British English. A consultation of the *Longman pronunciation dictionary* (Wells 2000) and the 2001 *Oxford dictionary of pronunciation* reveals broad consensus. Longman follows Jones and even quantifies the preference for *dispúte* as 62:38 percent (based on a poll of an expert panel); Oxford concurs, and – as a new aspect not noted by the competition – accepts *díspute* as current also in American English.[4]

How a relatively trivial and by no means unusual minor change becomes a social marker is shown by occasional comments found in the prescriptive usage literature. At least in British English, the placement of stress in the noun *dispute* seems to have become a social symbol for some, setting off traditional standards of educated usage against perceived working-class vulgarity. While Greenbaum and Whitcut (1988: 214), authors of a usage handbook, merely hint that "the pronunciation of the noun with the stress on the first syllable is disliked by some people," Burchfield is more specific in identifying the agents of this particular change:

> The noun is often heard with stress on the first syllable in imitation of northern dialects where it is much more widespread than in the south and midlands. The influence of usage by northern trade union leaders is tending to bring the form with initial stress into prominence.   (1989: 13)

These few introductory illustrations should have given the reader a first idea of the workings of phonetic standardization, as regards both its linguistic and its social motivations. Section 5.2 will present a more systematic survey of the history of "Received Pronunciation" in Britain, showing that conspicuous change has occurred in the course of a century even in this most tightly

---

[4] As a matter of curiosity, the *COBUILD English dictionary* is out of line with the rest of the sources, and ahead of its time, in only recognizing *díspute* for the noun. While this may be the eventual end-point of the development, we have not reached it yet.

codified norm. Section 5.3 will look at the more informal but no less effective standardization of English pronunciation in the United States of America. It should be noted at the outset that, while the grammar and, to a lesser extent, the lexicon of standard English have on the whole tended to converge in the course of the twentieth century, there has been increasing divergence in the norms of educated pronunciation – not only between the prestige norms of Britain and the United States but also among the various new Englishes that have emerged in the post-colonial world and which cannot receive adequate treatment in the present book for reasons of space.

5.2   A history of RP in the twentieth century

5.2.1 Introduction

By the beginning of the twentieth century the accent which eventually came to be widely known as "Received Pronunciation" or "RP" had been established as a supra-regional norm in England and to a lesser extent the rest of Britain. It was influential in the British Empire, both as an educated norm for the native-speaking population of all settler colonies (with the possible exception of Canada) and as a teaching norm for those colonial subjects of non-European background who were offered promotion through education. In the early stages of this development, there was some terminological vacillation about the name of the accent. Daniel Jones, the influential phonetician, opted for "Public School Pronunciation" (PSP) in the early editions of his *Pronouncing dictionary* (from 1917). The term "Received Pronunciation" had been coined by Alexander J. Ellis before, in the 1860s, but it did not gain wider currency until Jones adopted it for his dictionary.[5] It is a paradox that Daniel Jones, whose mature work on the RP accent was informed by a robust descriptivism, should have produced one of the most influential works of prescriptive reference in matters of educated British pronunciation. But this was inevitable in the social context of the time.

How far Daniel Jones was ahead of his contemporaries becomes clear by comparing his own introduction to the first edition of the dictionary with that of Walter Ripman, the series editor. While Daniel Jones almost exclusively confines himself to the description of PSP in linguistic and technical terms, the ideology of standardization is very much to the fore in Ripman's paraphrase, which combines a facile sense for the supposedly practical with some late Victorian pieties on the role of women. Jones writes:

---

[5] Ellis (1869–1889: 23) describes "a received pronunciation all over the country, not widely differing in any locality, and admitting a certain degree of variety. It may be considered as the educated pronunciation of the metropolis, of the court, the pulpit, and the bar." Jones used RP to replace PSP from the 3rd (1926) edition of the dictionary onwards.

The pronunciation represented in this book is that most usually heard in everyday speech in the families of Southern English persons whose men-folk have been educated at the great public boarding-schools. This pronunciation is also used by a considerable proportion of those who do not come from the South of England, but who have been . . . educated at these schools. It is probably accurate to say that a majority of those members of London society who have had a university education, use either this pronunciation or a pronunciation not differing very greatly from it. The form of pronunciation recorded in this dictionary may be referred to shortly as "Public School Pronunciation"; it is indicated in what follows by the abbreviation PSP. Having stated what the pronunciation is, it may be as well, in order to avoid possible misunderstandings, to state what . . . it is not. It is not the pronunciation commonly used in declamation; still less is it that used in singing. It is not as a rule heard from Americans, South Africans or Australians; it is not used by a considerable proportion of those educated at day schools in the South of England. Least of all is it a product of the delusion under which many lexicographers appear to have laboured, viz. that all educated people pronounce alike. I should like here to state that I have no intention of becoming either a reformer of pronunciation or a judge who decides what pronunciations are "good" and what are "bad". The proper function of the phonetician is to observe and record accurately, to be, in fact, a kind of living phonograph. It may be as well to add that I am not one of those who believe in the desirability or the feasibility of setting up any one form of pronunciation as a standard for the English-speaking world.

(1924 [1917]: viii–ix)

It is the last sentence in particular whose message is subverted in Ripman's paraphrase:

It may be pointed out that this form of speech is very widely used by educated people in Southern England, and that those whose home is elsewhere, and whose dialect differs from it considerably, often make concessions to it, in order that they may be more generally understood. This has been the case, to a marked degree, in the "great public schools" where this kind of speech prevails; and the influence of these schools has been a very great (but, I believe, neither the only, nor even the greatest) factor in rendering acceptable what Mr. Jones calls "public school pronunciation." I am disposed to ascribe the considerable extension of this form of speech during the last fifty years chiefly to the influence of women in the home, to the increased attention paid to speech in our educational system, and to quickened intercourse among members of the English-speaking world.

There are many who think that for the purposes of social intercourse and of various kinds of public speaking (such as the pulpit and the stage), we require a "standard speech" and that, when a language is spread as widely over the world as ours is, a generally recognised form of speech is no less desirable than a common literary language. Every dialect has its interest and its appeal; but one who knows only his dialect finds himself at a disadvantage in social life, when once he passes beyond the limits within which that dialect is spoken, and it may well be doubted whether his æsthetic appreciation of our literature is not impaired.

(Jones 1924 [1917]: vf.)

The *Pronouncing dictionary* has become a classic work of linguistic reference which has been continuously updated and revised and is still in print today. From 1917, the first edition, to 1997, the year the current 15th edition of the work appeared, we have a reliable account of developments in RP. The description of the standard accent has also been one of the focal areas of academic research in phonetics in Britain. John Wells, one of Daniel Jones' successors as Chair of the Department of Phonetics and Linguistics of University College London, has focused on twentieth-century changes in RP. His overview of the internal development of this accent is widely accepted and will provide the foundation for the survey in section 5.2.2. What is more controversial is the social history of RP in the twentieth century and its position as a supra-regional but certainly not socially neutral or "classless" accent in Britain today (on which, see section 5.2.3).

5.2.2 The internal development of RP in the twentieth century

As has been pointed out, the main phonetic developments within RP in the past century have been documented by John Wells in a number of research papers and online materials (e.g., Wells 1997 and http://www.phon.ucl.ac.uk/home/wells/). Not unexpectedly, vowels have tended to be somewhat more unstable than consonants. "Older" vowel changes which were already under way at the beginning of the twentieth century are:

1   The transfer of the *cloth* lexical set from /ɔ:/ to /ɒ/
    Pronunciations of words such as *off*, *cross*, or *cough* with /ɔ:/ are now rare and heard in the speech of the oldest speakers only. This change affects a small number of words and has no impact on the phonemic system or the phonetic realization of the sounds concerned.
2   Merger of /ɔə/ and /ɔ:/
    Pairs such as *saw* and *soar*, or *flaw* and *floor*, are homophones for the majority of speakers today. As practically all instances of the /ɔə/-diphthong are historically due to the loss of post-vocalic /r/ in the late eighteenth century (note the presence of <r> in spelling in the relevant words), this change can be seen as a somewhat delayed "mopping-up" operation simplifying a possibly over-complex inventory of centering diphthongs in older RP

(/ɔə/, /ʊə/, /ɪə /, /ɛə/). When completed, the change will have brought about the loss of a phoneme from the total inventory, as /ɔə/ will no longer contrast with either /ʊə/ or /ɔ:/ in minimal pairs but merely live on as a realizational variant of the former.

3   Fronting of the onset in the *goal*-diphthong
This particular development caused A. C. Gimson, reviser for the 13th edition (1967) of the *Pronouncing dictionary*, to change the transcription symbol from the original /ɔʊ/ to /əʊ/. This change concerned the phonetic realization of a phoneme but, unlike the preceding one, did not have any impact on the phonemic inventory.

4   More open articulation of /e/ and /æ/
Unlike the preceding one, this particular change has not yet led to a different IPA symbol being used for the transcription of the two vowel phonemes concerned. Nevertheless, there has been noticeable development in the realization of the /e/ and /æ/ phonemes in the past century. Phonetically, words such as *bet* and *bat* would now best be rendered as [bɛt] and [bat], while the conservative early twentieth-century pronunciations – now current only in Southern Hemisphere varieties of Australia, New Zealand and South Africa – would have been [bet] (for *bet*) and [bɛt]/[bæt] (for *bat*). Not surprisingly, this change figures prominently in novelist Kingsley Amis's long list of gripes against current broadcasting usage:

> The sound of short A is now close to what used to be short U (as in *but*). A broadcaster now seems to talk about "the impuct of blucks' attucks on other blucks" in parts of Africa. . . . The sound of short E is now close to what used to be short A. A broadcaster now seems to talk about "lass attantion in the Prass" paid to something-or-other.   (Amis 1997: 169)

The following development is dated as "mid 20c" by Wells (see Figure 5.1).

5   Transfer of the *cure* set from /ʊə/ to /ɔə /and /ɔ:/
The development is obviously an extension of (2) above, a further stage in the "mopping-up" operation following the loss of post-vocalic /r/ in British English. Wells has monitored current usage for selected words in an elicitation experiment, whose results suggest that the change spreads by lexical diffusion.

As can be seen, the informants are grouped into four age brackets. With the exception of a very minor reversal for *yours*, the results represent a near-perfect apparent-time distribution, with the incoming forms dominating among the younger speakers. Unlike the /ɔə/-phoneme, /ʊə/ will probably not disappear in the near future as it still has a strong foothold in rare and formal words (e.g., *allure*, *lure*) and, more importantly, shows few signs of eroding yet in certain phonetic environments – for example, following non-initial /j/ (cf., e.g., *pure*, *obscure*). In all these cases, fully

/ʊə/ gradually gets
replaced by /ɔː/...

so that yours sounds
like yaws...

poor like pour (or
paw)...

and sure like shore

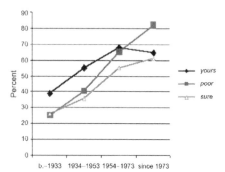

Figure 5.1 The decline of /ʊə/ (John Wells, http://www.phon.ucl.ac.uk/home/wells/)

monophthongal pronunciations such as /ljɔː/ or /əbskjɔː/ are not very common at present. Similar, if weaker, tendencies towards simplification are at work in the front pair of centering diphthongs, where /əə/ is increasingly realized as a long monophthong [əː]. In the absence of a corresponding long-vowel phoneme, however, this change has no impact on the phonemic system.

The most salient recent development affecting RP vowels, dated as "late 20c" by Wells, is probably:

6   A change in the quality of /ʊ/ and /uː/
The articulation of the tense and lax back high vowels (e.g., in *look at the moon*) is more front, and less rounded.
The two salient consonantal changes in twentieth-century RP are both due to continuing contact between RP and the popular accent of London and the Home Counties. They are *t*-glottalling and the vocalization of velar /l/.

7   /t/-glottalling
According to Wells (1997: 19–21), glottalling became common first (mid-century) pre-consonantally or, more precisely, before a following obstruent or sonorant consonant across a syllable or word boundary (as in *football* or *quite good*) and is now spreading to word-final position before vowel or pause (*it's too hot*; *quite easy, get it*). Glottal stops in intervocalic position, however (*party*), or before syllabic *l* (*bottle*) are (as yet?) firmly ruled out. This assessment has recently been confirmed with modifications in an extensive empirical study (Fabricius 2002), whose main result is that:

> speakers use *t*-glottalling at a uniformly high rate pre-consonantally in interview style. The utterance-final position (pre-pausal) shows greater variation between speakers, and this variation has been shown to be regionally determined. High rates of *t*-glottalling in

the pre-vocalic environment in interview style are restricted to London speakers.

In addition, pre-pausal and pre-vocalic *t*-glottalling is widely avoided in reading passage style. If we recognise London as the source of most innovations in the standard accent . . ., there is support for the idea that the pre-pausal environment will become the next "widely acceptable" environment for *t*-glottalling, perhaps within the next generation or two. However, this change has not yet occurred; pre-pausal and pre-vocalic *t*-glottalling have not yet come into more formal speech, as the style-shifting results showed.

(Fabricius 2002: 132–133)

Fine-grained statistical results of sociolinguistic research show current usage among educated speakers in various shades of grey; for example, by highlighting an interesting tie to London in a standard accent which in theory has non-localizability as one of its distinctive features. Seen as an ideological construct, however, RP is defined in terms of black or white, and performance either conforms to the expected norm or it remains "substandard." The question raised by such findings then is when *t*-glottaling in the controversial environments will reach a level which makes an updating of the idealized norm inevitable.

8   /l/-vocalization

For a long time there has been a tendency for the velar allophone of /l/ ([t]) to vocalize sporadically. This is the reason why the <l> is silent in words such as *walk* or *talk* or why, more recently, it has been pronounced variably in *all right*. A tendency to vocalize velar /l/ has been generalized in popular London accents, so that all words of the type *hill*, *table*, *milk*, or *bottle* now have it. Though stigmatized, the feature is spreading into educated usage.

In addition to the salient changes discussed above, Wells has noted further innovations currently spreading in RP. One of them, the tensing of final or pre-vocalic weak /ɪ/ to /iː/ (e.g., in *happy* or *happier*) has a firm base in popular London speech and in a wide variety of English dialects, so that, as with *t*-glottalling or /l/-vocalization, its spread in RP can be explained as the result of contact between the relevant varieties. Other changes noted by Wells are best seen as twentieth-century instances in RP of widespread or universal phonetic trends. For example, Wells notes some instances of plosive epenthesis, for example a move from /ɪnst/ to /ɪntst/ in *instance*, or from /nʃ/ to /ntʃ/ in *conscience*. The particular pronunciations may be new, but the phenomenon itself is not. Similar cases have sporadically been attested in previous stages of the history of English, for example in *against* or *whilst*, where the final "t" cannot be traced to the Old English roots of the words. Similarly natural changes are involved in what Wells calls "yod coalescence" (e.g.,

Table 5.1. *Variably pronounced words in contemporary RP (John Wells, Longman Pronunciation Survey)*

Item (with preferences in percentages)					Comment
absorb	/z/ 83	/s/ 17			drift to /z/
absurd	/s/ 77	/z/ 23			no change; /z/ high in Scotland, low in Wales
alto	/æ/ 71	/ɒ/ 14	/ɔː/ 8	/ɑː/ 7	
applicable	stress on second 84			on first 16	
Asia	/ʒ/ 51	/ʃ/ 49			
associate vs.	/s/ 69	/ʃ/ 31			
association	/s/ 78	/ʃ/ 22			

Source: http://www.phon.ucl.ac.uk/home/wells/concise-results.pdf

/tjʊəl > tʃʊəl/ in the final syllable of words such as *aspectual* or *perpetual*). He argues for the following staggered development in twentieth-century RP. From mid-century yod-coalescence established itself before unstressed vowels (as in *perpetual* or *graduate*), and from there it started spreading to stressed syllables (*endure*, *attitude*) and monosyllables (*tune*) from the late twentieth century. Twentieth-century instances of yod-coalescence build on previous such changes in the earlier history of English. Yod-coalescence accounts for the current pronunciations of many Middle English loans from French, such as *nature* or *virtue*, and for one such word, namely *literature*, even the first edition of Jones' *Pronouncing dictionary* still gives /lɪtrətjʊə/as one possible variant.

In addition to these changes, which are either fairly systematic shifts or at least instantiate natural phonetic tendencies known from the previous history of English or from other languages, any closer look at successive editions of the *Pronouncing dictionary* or at the results of John Wells' 1998 Pronunciation Preference Survey will reveal numerous shifts in preference for the pronunciation of individual words. Table 5.1 presents all items starting in the letter A from Wells' survey.

This short list is representative, containing as it does many of the usual suspects: variable stress in *applicable*, assimilation (*associate/association*), and possible influence from American English (with the voiced sibilant now replacing a traditionally voiceless British pronunciation in *Asia*). For some changes, however, it is difficult to generalize or even to propose an explanation after the fact. As John Wells himself puts it in a discussion of the conflicting trends in the voicing of /s/ in *absurd* and *absorb*, in the study of ongoing changes in RP "mysteries remain."

5.2.3 "A certain type of English speech at the beginning of the twentieth century:" RP in its social context[6]

It is difficult to see why the social status of RP should have been the subject of intense debate in Britain throughout the twentieth century. After all, Daniel Jones was careful to emphasize even in 1917 that his aim was descriptive rather than prescriptive. His claims for the utility of his *Dictionary* were rather modest, spelling out limited and uncontroversial goals for various types of users – native- and non-native speaking alike. However, as Jones' successor Gimson recognized in his Preface to a subsequent edition of the work (1967: vii): "A dictionary of this kind is largely descriptive in intent, but it also fulfils for a majority of readers a prescriptive function."

From the start, RP had a double role. On the one hand, it was a neutral accent providing a convenient target for foreign learners and serving as a functional standard in formal situations. By the time nationwide broadcasting arrived as a mass medium in the 1920s, a national standard pronunciation would have had to be developed if it had not existed. Where its role as functional standard is at stake, RP is an unmarked choice and generally inoffensive. On the other hand, RP has always been more than a functional standard of this kind. Shedding its local association with London and the southeast, it became a supra-regional accent, but it never entirely lost its class connotations, remaining a typical prestige accent in sociolinguistic terms – attractive to social climbers, but viewed with some antipathy by large segments of the population. In this regard, there was no noticeable change between the positions presented in the following extract from Charlotte Brontë's *Jane Eyre*, a mid-nineteenth-century novel, and post-World War II London as described in Doris Lessing's autobiography *Walking in the shade*. In *Jane Eyre*, the wandering and desperate protagonist has fallen unconscious in the winter night. Saved from certain death, she reveals herself as "one of us" rather than "them" to her genteel rescuers as much by her accent as by her fine clothes:

> "It is very well we took her in."
>
> "Yes; she would certainly have been found dead at the door in the morning had she been left out all night. I wonder what she has gone through?"
>
> "Strange hardships, I imagine – poor, emaciated, pallid wanderer!"
>
> "She is not an uneducated person, I should think, by her manner of speaking; her accent was quite pure; and the clothes she took off, though splashed and wet, were little worn and fine."
>
> (*Jane Eyre*, Chapter 29 [1847])

---

[6] The phrase is quoted from Walter Ripman's characterization of the norm described by Daniel Jones in the Preface to the *Pronouncing dictionary* (Jones 1917: v).

The same politics of accent operates in mid-twentieth-century London, although the writer now emphasizes the limits of the social universe in which RP carries prestige when she describes the doings of her two companions:

> The two young men took themselves around and about Earls Court, Notting Hill Gate, Soho, anywhere something was happening – crimes, scandals, protests, "demos" – and sat in pubs, cafés, bus shelters . . . . They were both outsiders, both outside by that unwritten law that says that the two great divisions of British society should be impenetrable to each other. Clancy's American accent and Alex's working-class voice, which he exaggerated when on these adventures, made them acceptable to what are known as ordinary people. They could go where people like me could not. It was all right for me when I still had my Rhodesian accent, which put me outside the system, but that had gone, and now, as is the way in these islands, I was judged by how I spoke.
>
> (*Walking in the shade: volume two of my autobiography, 1949–1962*
> 1997: 159f.)

When its role as class accent is at stake, it is not difficult to find expressions of the most violent antipathy against RP (or even localized variants of the "posh" accent),[7] such as, for example, the encounter represented in the following poem by Glasgow poet Tom Leonard:

> "i've not got a light,"
>   hi sayz, dead posh
>   so a looksit wullie
> an wullie looksit jimmy
>   an jimmy looksit me
>   n wi aw starts laffn.
> jistiz his face almost
>   hit thi grun a liftid
>   ma boot right back n
> smashdit rightniz mouth n
>   hi howlz. so jimmy
>   yanks im up n
> geez im wan wi thi knee
>   then thi nut. a didny no
>   wullie hid a blade but
> nix thing is oot n
>   right in there . . .
>
> (from "Unrelated incidents," in *Intimate voices* [1984])

---

[7] Note that in the first line of the following poem the use of the "Northern" form "I've not got" rather than the "I haven't got" more common in Southern speech opens up the possibility that the "posh" voice might be middle-class Glaswegian rather than RP – Peter Trudgill and Lynda Mugglestone, personal communication.

There is reason to believe that the class connotations of RP have lessened in the course of the twentieth century, because the defining community of speakers has changed – from the graduates of the country's elite and expensive public schools to broadcasters' voices heard on nationwide networks, at first in the public BBC and then in the mass media in general. Evidence for this claim is provided by the very development of the terminology of Jones' *Dictionary* itself. As will be remembered, Jones' first choice to name the accent he described was Public School Pronunciation (PSP), which he later replaced with RP, without, however, showing a strong positive commitment to either term. To A. S. C. Gimson, his successor as editor, the term "RP" had one advantage. It did not directly connote social class. If it was fuzzy, it at least had the potential of expressing the purely functional dimension of the standardization of pronunciation which Gimson felt was an increasingly important twentieth-century development. In his own words, "since the turn of the century, RP has become less and less the property of an exclusive social class. Its extension throughout a wider section of the population has doubtless led to some dilution of the earlier form" (1967: vii).

Peter Roach and James Hartman, the editors of the latest (1997) edition of the *Dictionary*, have taken the argument one step further by eliminating the term "RP" altogether: "The time has come to abandon the archaic name *Received Pronunciation*" (1997: v). Instead, they aim to describe "a more broadly-based and accessible model accent for British English" (1997: v), which they define as "BBC-English:" "the pronunciation of professional speakers employed by the BBC as newsreaders and announcers on BBC 1 and BBC 2 television, the World Service and BBC Radio 3 and 4, as well as many commercial broadcasting organizations such as ITN" (1997: v).

If one compares this to Jones' definition, which referred to spontaneous private communication ("everyday speech in the families of Southern English persons whose men-folk have been educated at the great public boarding-schools"), an obvious conclusion suggests itself. RP was standardized as a class accent and functioned as such on a national scale for the first half of the twentieth century. Subsequently, however, it was transformed into a functional standard which is less and less of a norm for individuals to orientate toward in their own casual speech but remains important in the public domain. This transition was eased by the fact that in the recent past, owing to an egalitarian and permissive social climate, many speakers opted out of the RP speaking community because they preferred the covert "solidarity" prestige of regional accents to the overt "power" prestige of the supra-regional standard. Pressures encouraging such a decision are satirized in the following personalized column from the *Sunday Times*:

> Many years ago my then future (now ex) husband used to reduce me to near-hysterics whenever we took a taxi back to his house. As soon as we neared home, he'd lean forward, slide open the glass partition, and tell

the cab driver: "There's a li'el slip road just dahn on the right, mate, alrigh? Cheers." Then he'd shut the partition, lean back, adjust the collar on his Prada coat, and, in his normal voice, say something like: "That claret at supper was utterly divine."

This happened most nights. He'd laugh, too, but he still continued addressing cabbies in his pretend accent. The husband wasn't – isn't – a braying Hooray of the incurable kind (I know someone who goes to "marse" every Sunday) and, with time, his of-the-people accent became pretty convincing, to the point where he now marches around Hackney, east London, speaking like a native whenever the mood takes him. It works beautifully until some enterprising market stallholder asks him if went to school local.

I used to think this was terribly funny until I started doing it myself. Put me on Radio 4 and I speak normally. Stick me in a taxi and my natural accent completely disappears. Take me to a smart restaurant and I'm Lady Bracknell; take me down the market and naturally, without thinking twice, I'll ask the stallholder: "Are you avin' a laugh?" when he tries to overcharge.

Like some schizoid chameleon, I alter my accent to match that of my interlocutor – but only if said interlocutor speaks, for want of a better phrase, like a Kevin. And there's an expression you don't hear very often any more, because political correctness has sprung to the rescue of every single kind of accent. Except mine.

The only accent it is now actively all right to pillory is the so-called "posh" – the clear enunciation that comes from being privately educated or having upper-middle-class parents. Mention the amazing ugliness of the Birmingham accent, for instance, and some bien pensant type will reproachfully inform you that it's a wonderful accent, actually, and that it's terribly important to maintain this kind of regional linguistic diversity (which it is). Make a joke about speaking like Tim Nice-but-Dim, on the other hand, and everybody will laugh like drains at the absurdity of public school voices. Why? Why is received pronunciation invalid and every other accent imaginable not so?

Speaking properly – because no matter how unfashionable it is to say it, I speak properly and many of the people I meet do not – has become comical.

(India Knight, "Speak proper? Not likely,"
Sunday Times, 11 November 2001: 5, 4)

While the internal linguistic history of RP in the twentieth century must be written on the basis of data provided by those who speak it, the social status of RP is to a large part decided by the attitudes of the vast majority of Britain's inhabitants who do not. Do they defer to it in public and formal communication by attempting to conform to its norms, or will they further challenge its authority by bringing their own nonstandard accents into the public spotlight? Seen from this perspective, the fact that RP is spoken natively by a small and probably diminishing minority is not really the important thing. What is important is its hold on spoken communication in the public domain – in the media, in education, in politics and the law. And, even if fewer people may speak it, it will remain as an important accent to listen to in Britain. For foreign learners of English all over the world, it will continue to be one of the major norms to approximate to.

5.3   "General American": myth or reality?

In comparison to the rich and coherent tradition of documentation that has grown up around British RP, the literature on the pronunciation of standard American English is scant. One explanation for this might be that a nationwide standard of pronunciation does not exist in the United States. As I will argue below, this is not true, although it has to be admitted that the American pronunciation standard is not defined as rigidly and exclusively as the British one. Its internal variability is much greater, and so is the proportion of the population that can be said to speak it. Nevertheless, the twentieth century saw a massive homogenization of pronunciation preferences in the public domain also in the United States, and this development is difficult to account for unless one assumes that speakers are conscious of some kind of national prestige norm.

The scarcity of scholarly literature on a standard pronunciation in the US is thus due to the fact that the emergence of a nationwide prestige accent is a recent phenomenon. The delay between political independence (which was achieved in 1776/1783) and the emergence of a national pronunciation norm in the second half of the twentieth century requires some explanation. If, as was clearly the case, identifiably American accents had arisen by the late eighteenth century, why wasn't one of them selected as a national norm during the nineteenth?

Turn-of-the-century (c. 1900) sources on educated pronunciation in America show that the subject was debated intensively and not uncontroversially, and go some way toward elucidating the conflicting pressures of possible norms which prevented the early breakthrough of a national standard accent. Unbelievably, in view of the American cultural nationalism and patriotic self-assurance of President Theodore Roosevelt's "Progressive Era," there were still some voices which advocated continuing deference to an external British norm. For example, the novelist Henry James, admittedly not a completely reliable witness in view of his subsequent emigration to England, deplored the absence of an educated American norm of speech in a lecture published in 1905:

> the last of American idiosyncrasies, the last by which we can be con-
> ceived as "represented" in the international concert of culture, would be
> the pretension to a tone-standard, to our wooing comparison with that
> of other nations. The French, the Germans, the Italians, the English

perhaps in particular, and many other people, Occidental and Oriental, I surmise, not excluding the Turks and the Chinese, have for the symbol of education, of civility, a tone-standard; we alone flourish in undisturbed and – as in the sense of so many other of our connections – in something like sublime unconsciousness of any such possibility.

(James 1905: 12)

In the subsequent illustration of his argument, Henry James is extremely critical of American speechways in general and of individual features of American accents in particular:

Our national use of vocal sound, in men and women alike, *is* slovenly – an absolutely inexpert daub of unapplied tone. (p. 25)

There are, you see, sounds of a mysterious and intrinsic meanness, and there are sounds of a mysterious intrinsic frankness and sweetness; and I think the recurrent note I have indicated – fatherr and motherr and otherr, waterr and matterr and scatterr, harrd and barrd, parrt, starrt, and (dreadful to say) arrt (the repetition it is that drives home the ugliness), are signal specimens of what becomes of a custom of utterance out of which the principle of taste has dropped. (p. 29)

Let me linger only long enough to add a mention of the deplorable effect of the almost total loss, among innumerable speakers, of any approach to purity in the sound of the *e*. It is converted, under this particularly ugly blight, into a *u* which is itself unaccompanied with any dignity of intention, which makes for mere ignoble thickness and turbidity. For choice, perhaps, "vurry," "Amurrica," "Philadulphia," "tullegram," "twuddy" (what becomes of "twenty" here is an ineptitude truly beyond any alliteration), and the like, descend deepest into the abyss. (p. 31)

If we are willing to trust the disgusted novelist as a faithful recorder of contemporary speechways, we can take this passage as early evidence for developments which were subsequently to culminate in the "Northern Cities Chain Shift" described by William Labov (see below). But, even though the last plea for Americans to accept British norms of educated pronunciation was published in 1925,[8] Henry James' call for Americans to model their pronunciation on Britain was hopelessly out of touch with contemporary linguistic reality even in 1905.

The majority view among educators and linguists at the time seems to have been that educated norms of speech should be encouraged in the United States

---

[8] *Euphon English in America*, by one E. M. DeWitt. See McMahon (1998: 402f.) for a discussion of an apparent resurgence at the time "of interest in the idea of English English (i.e., RP) being accorded the status of the standard accent of American English." Expert opinion at the time – represented by Hans Kurath in McMahon's discussion – of course recognized such recommendations for what they were – the probably well-intentioned efforts of "enthusiasts" (1998: 402).

but that they should be developed from local accents and, more importantly, that there should be a plurality of them, at least one each for the major traditional dialect regions of New England, the South and the "rest." This point of view is defended by George Hempl in his presidential address to the Modern Language Association, who mocks views of the type defended by Henry James:

> Still, – and here is another somewhat contradictory phase of the teacher's attitude toward the mother tongue – we are taught that, while *we* speak a careless and generally reprehensible English, the language is not so spoken elsewhere, at least not by educated and cultivated people. There even are places where it is quite generally spoken to perfection. When we ask for specific localities, our champion of the pure article linguistic generally makes a hesitating suggestion of Boston, or the first families of Virginia – only to add that most Bostonians whom he has met talked affectedly, and Virginians had such a funny way of speaking almost like darkies. Sometimes he crosses the sea and designates England as the blessed isle of English pure and undefiled. (Hempl 1904: xxxiii–xxxiv)

Viewed from the vantage point of the present, this assessment encapsulates the major revaluation which has taken place in the sociolinguistic stratification of American accents in the course of the twentieth century. Both the traditional New England accent (incidentally, a strong indirect link to RP through shared features such as *r*-lessness and the "broad" *a* [ɑ:]) and an educated Southern pronunciation are now marginal on the national scene and far from serving as models for speakers from other regions to orientate towards. In his own illustrative discussion, Hempl generally promotes pronunciations which were to become part of the national standard, such as the "flat" *a* [æ]:

> No teacher is warranted in trying to get his pupils to speak the English of another part of the English-speaking world. Because the vowel in *past, after, path,* etc., has come to be like that in *father* in Southern England and a small part of our Atlantic seaboard, that is no reason why the rest of the English-speaking world should be taught to be ashamed of its usage and try to change it. (1904: xlvii)

The implication of this passage is that while Hempl would be happy for New Englanders to continue with a broad *a*, Midwesterners should cultivate their own /æ/. Such pluralism continued well into the first half of the twentieth century. By c. 1930, the consensus was that the United States had a plural pronunciation norm, and that any of a variety of cultivated accents should not be described with regard to how it differed from another, but how it contrasted with local vulgar or vernacular usage. Thus, educated New England ("Boston") pronunciation was defined against rural New England, educated Southern against various vernacular speech styles, and educated Midwestern/inland speech against the local nonstandards.

This is largely the point of view adopted in the most important linguistic study of educated American pronunciation produced in the first half of the twentieth century, George Philip Krapp's *The pronunciation of standard English in America* (1919). Note that the very title implies a plurality of ways of pronouncing standard American English rather than one national norm. The author notes that educated pronunciation is not very closely tied to speaker's regional origin in the US but that this does not necessarily make it homogeneous.

> The universal negative is the last form of dogmatism upon which the careful student of American speech will insist. It is safer to indulge in a universal affirmative, to say that any pronunciation which may occur in cultivated speech, may occur in any region of America. For several large divisions, especially in the speech of the more obviously typical local representatives, we have a fairly defined feeling. We can distinguish with some certainty Eastern and Western and Southern speech, but beyond this the author has little confidence in those confident experts who think they can tell infallibly, by the test of speech, a native of Hartford from a native of Providence, or a native of Philadelphia from a native of Atlanta, or even, if one insist on infallibility, a native of Chicago from a native of Boston. This means of course that geographical distinctions are not of prime importance in the discussion of standard American speech.
>
> ...
>
> What the author has called standard may perhaps be best defined negatively, as the speech which is least likely to attract attention to itself as being peculiar to any class or locality.   (1969 [1919]: viii–ix)

Unlike British RP, which has positively definable and codified characteristics and has been actively promoted as a norm, the educated pronunciation of the United States reveals itself to be the result of dialect leveling and koinéization on the part of a geographically and socially mobile middle class. As for its historical development in the twentieth century, we note that the extent of the leveling thought to be required has increased considerably.

This is well illustrated by rhoticity, the most salient feature of American English in comparison to British RP and one of the most important sociolinguistic markers inside the country itself. Non-rhotic accents were much more common in radio broadcasts of the 1920s and 1930s than they are now, as can be shown in archival material.[9] Best known among later public figures cultivating a pronounced New England accent was, of course, President John F. Kennedy (1960–1963). But even he was unable to stop the relegation of the cultivated New England accent from the position of serious contender for

---

[9] For an easily accessible example, compare Orson Welles' famous *War of the worlds*, broadcast in 1938, available as a Hodder Headline Audiobook (HH598).

a national norm to a quaint archaic provincialism – a development which could not be foreseen at the beginning of the twentieth century.

If it is a fact that it was not necessary to adopt a rhotic pronunciation in order not to draw attention to one's speech on formal or public occasions in the early part of the twentieth century but it is necessary to do so now, the following question arises: What accounts for the homogenization of American educated and public speech around a bundle of inland (i.e. "non-Southern" and "non-New England") accents which share crucial features such as rhoticity, the flat a, or the flapping of /t/? Given the recentness of the development, a desire to assert political and cultural independence from Britain cannot have been the main motivation. More likely, one crucial factor was that the Northern inland region and the Northern Midwest became a demographic and economic center of gravity after the end of the Civil War (whose outcome clearly did not help the prestige of Southern speech) and that its accents were promoted by the national broadcasting networks from the 1920s onwards.

More recently, the focus of the debate on the rise of general American has shifted from the discussion of such rather mundane technicalities to more sinister ideological motivations. Bonfiglio (2002), for example, has argued that non-rhotic Southern and East Coast pronunciations lost prestige and attractiveness to others because in the eyes of both the language planners in early broadcasting and the populace they were tainted by association with race and ethnicity. Rather than signify a Boston Brahmin background, r-lessness, for example, was associated with African Americans and recent immigrants of southern and eastern European descent. The jocular reference to the best Virginia families sounding like blacks ("darkies" in the racist or at least condescending diction of the time) in George Hempl's address could be adduced as circumstantial evidence for the influence of these factors.

At the end of the twentieth century, there can thus be little doubt that a general American accent, or rather general American ways of pronunciation,[10] enjoy nationwide prestige. Among other things, this is shown by the fact that they are spreading rapidly "from above" into New England, where they have largely replaced the traditional accents, and the South, where local forms hold out more strongly even among elite speakers. In sociolinguistic city surveys – for example, William Labov's classic studies of New York City – the prestige of this national norm is also obvious, with rhoticity correlating consistently with middle-class rather than working-class background and, within the various social classes, with formal rather than informal discourse contexts.

Standardization of pronunciation in the United States in the twentieth century has thus yielded the same result as in Britain – a fairly homogeneous functional standard mainly propagated in the public sphere and exerting little

---

[10] This is the appropriate formulation as, unlike RP, General American is not *one* coherent accent because of its great internal variability.

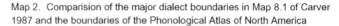

Map 2. Comparision of the major dialect boundaries in Map 8.1 of Carver
1987 and the boundaries of the Phonological Atlas of North America

Figure 5.2 Major dialect areas in the US based on the *Dictionary of American
regional English* (DARE, Carver 1987) and the *Phonological atlas of
North America* (Labov et al. 2006) (source: http://www.ling.upenn.
edu/phono_atlas/NationalMap/NationalMap.html)

influence on individuals' private pronunciation. But, while in Britain the
present situation is the result of a dilution of a class-based national prestige
accent, Americans have arrived at the present state without taking this detour.

If one looks at American vernacular usage, one will find that regional
diversity of pronunciation shows few signs of diminishing or disappearing.
Figure 5.2 shows that, in a comparison of the results of traditional dialectolo-
gical and recent sociolinguistic research, "the South" has even expanded.

What has changed in the course of the twentieth century is not so much the
linguistic geography of the United States itself as the power of the Southern
and New England regions to promote nationally acceptable educated accents
based on their own dialectal substrates. As Upton et al. have noted:

> Since the mid twentieth Century, however, there has been a trend among
> educated speakers, especially those of the younger generation, towards
> limitation of the use of marked regional features while speaking in formal
> settings. It is common for college students, for example, to speak without

much influence of regional pronunciation in the classroom, but to use regionally marked pronunciations among friends in the hallway. . . . This model is quite similar to what one hears in the national broadcast media, since broadcasters have long participated in the more general trend of younger educated speakers.   (2001: xiii–xiv)

Without undue simplification one can thus say that the twentieth century in the United States saw both a homogenization of speech, leading to a national standard promoted by professional elites in the public domain, and continuing and possibly even increasing heterogeneity, at vernacular level:

> This paradox – the strong continued existence of regional dialects when most Americans think that dialect variation is fading – is the topic for another essay . . ., but it is possible to say here that American English has developed a national dialect for the usually well-educated participants in a national marketplace for goods, services, and jobs. The well-educated share a national speech pattern within their own social stratum, unlike earlier periods in the history of American English when they shared regional dialects with working-class and lower-middle-class speakers.
>
> (Kretzschmar 2004: 55)

As the advent of this national prestige norm is so recent, it is impossible to write its history for the past century, as was done for RP in section 5.2. The past century has seen many phonetic changes in the accents that were to provide the basis of this norm, but it is more difficult to identify them than in RP because the synchronic variability found at any one time is greater. To understand the important trends in the contemporary pronunciation of American English it is necessary to consult the broad-based sociolinguistic surveys and to extrapolate from them. Innovations which have ceased to be geographically restricted, and have never had (or have lost) the social stigma attached to them, can be assumed to be standardizing. From the raw material thus offered in works like Labov's *Principles of linguistic change* (1994, 2001) or his *Atlas of North American English* (Labov et al. 2006), the following likely candidates for changes in progress in standard American English emerge:

1 Merger of /ɔ/ and /ɑ/
    This merger of two vowels which phonetically are long in American English leads to new pairs of homophones such as *cot* and *caught*, or *knotty* and *naughty*. It has been documented in early dialect records and seems to be spreading rapidly. Figure 5.3, from Labov's *Atlas*, gives the situation at the end of the twentieth century.
2 "Northern Cities Chain Shift"
    This development affects the short vowels /ɛ/, /æ/ and /ʌ/, and also /ɔ/ and /ɑ/, in a coordinated set of movements in vowel space. For example, /æ/ is raised and in extreme cases even diphthongized ([ɛ/ɛə/ ɪə]); /ɑ/ moves towards the position vacated, and /ɛ/ is centralized,

updated: Oct 4, 1996

Map 1. The Merger of /o/ and /oh/:
Contrast in production of /o/ and /oh/ before /t/ in COT vs. CAUGHT.

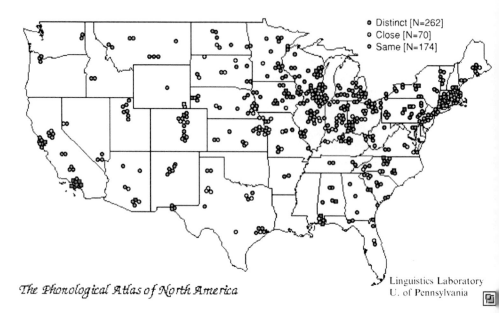

Distinct [N=262]
Close [N=70]
Same [N=174]

The Phonological Atlas of North America

Linguistics Laboratory
U. of Pennsylvania

Figure 5.3 Merger of the vowels in *cot* and *caught* (source: William Labov, http://
www.ling.upenn.edu/phono_atlas/ICSLP4.html#Heading2)

possibly to avoid confusion with raising /æ/. Thus, *Ann* comes to sound like the British pronunciation of *Ian*, or – to give one form illustrating the whole chain movement – *pack* like *peck* [pɛ(ə)k], *peck* like *puck*, *puck* like *pock*, and *pock* like *pack*.

3   Long /u/ (as in *boot*)

This vowel tends to be fronted and unrounded.

It will be noted that, with the exception of the fronting and unrounding of /u/, the ongoing changes will take the British and American standards further apart.

6   Language change in context: changing communicative and discourse norms in twentieth-century English

6.1   Introduction

In Chapters 3 to 5 we have surveyed twentieth-century changes in the structural inventory of standard English. We have noted statistical shifts in speakers' and writers' preferences in those cases in which the system provides options, and in a number of cases – of course, more so in the lexicon than in grammar or pronunciation – we have observed the emergence of new options altogether. We have approached change through contextualized corpus data, but the aim of the description was the reconstruction of changes in the decontextualized underlying system. For example, changing trends in the use of the progressive form were described without systematic reference to contexts of use for fairly abstract constructs such as "American English," "spoken English," or "spoken British English," and not with regard to specific groups of speakers operating in specific communicative contexts, for example, young people trying to formulate polite requests.

The abstract, decontextualized perspective on change is fully justified theoretically and also very useful presentationally, because it has allowed us to present the phenomena in an orderly fashion, moving from the lexicon through the grammar to pronunciation. It is, however, incomplete for at least two reasons. First, the orderly sequence of the presentation has obscured an important fact; namely, that in actual discourse the levels of structural organization constantly interact. Second, it is in discourse, in actual language use, that the experiments leading to structural innovation first take shape. A focus on discourse is thus particularly important in the present study, which deals with linguistic change at close historical range.

The first signs of structural or "system" change are often to be found in changes in stylistic conventions, sociolinguistic norms of propriety or in speakers' and writers' ideas of what constitutes a particular textual genre. Of course, such changing communicative fashions do not inevitably lead to structural change, but in a good many instances they are decisive, for example, because they speed up the spread of a structural innovation which, though theoretically available, was not much used before. Alternatively, a change in stylistic norms may remove the protected textual environments in which archaic and obsolescent forms were allowed to persist. What is most fascinating for the observer of changing discourse norms, however, is their role as interface mediating between structural-linguistic change on the one hand, and sociocultural changes on the other – a field of inquiry in which more is speculated about than is properly understood.

In a study of modals in American English, Myhill has posited a direct link between change towards a democratic individualism in nineteenth-century US society and certain developments in the field of modal verbs:

> Around the time of the [American] Civil War, the modals *must, should, may* and *shall* dropped drastically in frequency, and at the same time other modals, *got to, have to, ought, better, can* and *gonna*, sharply increased in frequency. The "old" and "new" modals overlap in some functions. . . . However, within these general functions . . . the "old" modals had general uses associated with hierarchical social relationships, with people control-ling the actions of other people, and with absolute judgments based on social decorum. . . . The "new" modals, on the other hand, are more personal, being used to, for example, give advice to an equal, make an emotional request, offer help, or criticize one's interlocutor.
>
> (Myhill 1995: 157)

Most of the changes referred to here are still going on, not only in American English, and they have figured prominently in the discussion of grammatical change in present-day English in Chapter 4. The link between language (as a structural system) and society posited by Myhill is suggestive, but probably too direct. As has been said, it is in contextualized discourse, in *parole*, that the social context most directly shapes language. Therefore, we need the analytical categories of textlinguistics and discourse analysis in order to describe how context shapes usage and, through conventionalization of usage, ultimately also the underlying system. What we shall attempt in the present chapter is to apply analytical categories which can be used to describe both linguistic and socio-cultural phenomena and see whether they can help us to model the relation between linguistic and social change in the twentieth century.

In this way it becomes possible to pull together isolated observations on individual changes, because they reveal themselves to be manifestations of a common underlying motivating factor. For example, apparently disparate phenomena such as the increasing frequency in written English of contractions, of the progressive, of some modal idioms and the *going to*-future, all point in one and the same direction: written English has become more informal and, possibly, also more oral.[1] Note that in this way we are not obliged to claim that

---

[1] While generally there is considerable overlap between formal and written language on the one hand and informal and spoken language on the other, the overlap is not perfect.

certain changes observed, say, in the system of modal verbs are caused by, or due to, specific social changes. More realistically, we can identify a prevailing social climate (in this case a tendency to prefer informal over formal modes of behavior), establish the current structural linguistic exponents of informality, and demonstrate certain correlations. Studying the precise ways in which structural changes in the system are mediated through such changes in communicative culture reveals that even the apparently autonomous "internal" linguistic changes in phonology and grammar are ultimately socially embedded.

Building on the work of sociologists of culture, historians (in particular, Norbert Elias and Eric Hobsbawm), critical discourse analysts (e.g., Norman Fairclough 1995), and previous work in historical corpus-linguistics (e.g., Biber 1988, 2003), the present chapter will show that the social history of the past century has been characterized by a trend towards informality. This trend has had a clear linguistic correlate, a narrowing of the stylistic gap between speech and writing, which will here be referred to as colloquialization (see section 6.2). It will also be useful to discuss the issue of Americanization anew in this light. In the preceding chapters, Americanization has been understood narrowly, as the spread of specific phonetic or lexico-grammatical features from American English into other regional varieties. The most pervasive Americanization of English, however, has probably taken place on another level – that of genre, style, and the discourse conventions now prevalent throughout the English-speaking world (and beyond) (see section 6.3).

6.2   The colloquialization of written English in the twentieth century

The most basic manifestation of language is informal face-to-face conversation among intimates and equals. Compared to this "natural" linguistic baseline, other modes of communication require some degree of elaboration. To a certain extent, this elaboration is motivated functionally. For example, the fact that writing usually involves communication across space and time will make it necessary to spell out references to the context of situation which may be left implicit in speech. However, the structural elaboration of polite, formal, or written language is far in excess of what is strictly necessary; it contains an element of arbitrariness, artifice, ritual, and fashion.

In an influential paper, Chafe (1982) defines spoken and written language as two extremes on a continuum. Spoken language is described as fragmented and involved; written language, as integrated and detached. Sentence-initial

---

Noun-phrase name appositions of the type *disgraced former Tory MP Jeffrey Archer*, for example, which are a fast-spreading feature in the language of the British press (see Jucker 1992), are informal in style but hardly used in the spoken language.

conjunctions, first and second person reference, and emphatic particles like *really* and *just* are found to be typical of the fragmented, involved style. Characteristic features of the detached style, among others, are nominalizations and the frequent use of the passive voice. Chafe's description is convincing but impressionistic. A more rigorous and systematic version of the approach was developed for the purposes of corpus analysis by Douglas Biber. His multi-feature, multi-dimensional approach consists of a statistically complex analysis of a large number of structural features in a given corpus, whose frequencies are shown to correlate systematically along a number of interpretive dimensions. The obvious advantage of the procedure is that it makes it possible to identify markers whose contribution to an overall stylistic effect was not suspected by the analyst. In a study of a range of present-day English corpora, Biber (1988) presents three empirically defined dimensions which distinguish speech from writing – namely, "Informational versus Involved Production," "Elaborated versus Situation-Dependent Reference," and "Abstract versus Nonabstract Style." Using parts of what was to become the ARCHER corpus, Biber and Finegan (1989) add a diachronic dimension by showing that, at their own differential rates, three genres – namely essays, letters, and fiction – have all moved closer to the "oral" mode over the past two centuries. They conclude that the "drift described here is similar to Sapir's in that it is long-term, consistent, and cumulative in a particular direction" (1989: 516). They suggest that the observed drift was motivated by a number of conscious and subconscious causes, including an aesthetic preference for colloquial or plain styles shared by such unlikely allies as the seventeenth-century experimental scientists who founded the Royal Society, the late eighteenth-century Romantic poets, and the American nationalist Noah Webster (1989: 512–514). Another factor which is argued to have played an important role is a changing demography, in which schooling became available to wider sections of the population and writing ceased to be the elite pursuit that it had been.

A rare example of change in the opposite direction, away from the spoken mode, is presented by the history of medical writing, described in Biber et al. (1993: 8–9). This development signals a reconceptualization of medicine as a scholarly discipline – from a speculative-philosophical pursuit appropriately carried out in the essayistic genre to a branch of the natural sciences.

Summarizing his research of the past two decades, Biber has outlined the history of English style since around 1600 in a sketch which serves well as a backdrop to an investigation of short-term developments in the twentieth century:

> Written registers in English have undergone extensive stylistic change over the past four centuries. Written prose registers in the seventeenth century were already quite different from conversational registers, and those registers evolved to become even more distinct from speech over the course of the eighteenth century . . ..

However, over the course of the nineteenth and twentieth centuries, popular written registers like letters, fiction, and essays have reversed their direction of change and evolved to become more similar to spoken registers, often becoming even more oral in the modern period than in the seventeenth century. These shifts result in a dispreference for certain stereotypically literate features, such as passive verbs, relative clause constructions and elaborated noun phrases generally.   (Biber 2003: 169)

There is every sign of a turbulent acceleration of the drift described by Biber in the course of the latter half of the twentieth century, probably reflecting an unprecedented mobilization of formerly relatively stable class-based hierarchies in large parts of the English-speaking world. In particular, there is a small but growing body of research to suggest that the trend toward colloquialization, evident for so long in "popular written registers," has begun to affect formal writing, as well (cf., e.g., Westin [2002] on the changing language of newspaper editorials in the twentieth century).

It is interesting to note that, when it comes to the modern preference for colloquial over elaborated style, for informal over formal conduct, and for spontaneity of expression over ritual and custom, the findings of linguists converge with the assessments of cultural historians, social theorists and critical discourse analysts. "Informalization," for example, is a central term in Nobert Elias' 1939 classic *Über den Prozeß der Zivilisation* (*The civilising process*), which deals with the emergence of European secular elites from the fifteenth to the nineteenth century. This is not the place to do full justice to the author's intricate analysis, but put in the simplest possible terms the argument is that archaic and feudal cultures require strong rituals to contain emotion and aggression, whereas "modern" individuals can be allowed some informality and relaxation because they are the products of an extended process of civilization and domestication. Elias' grand historical *tour d'horizon* would not be relevant for the present study if he had not followed it up with analyses of a contemporary European society, twentieth-century Germany, in his *Studien über die Deutschen* (*Studies on the Germans*), which traces the spread of informal conduct, including informality in linguistic codes of address, in great detail (1989: 329–360).

There is nothing, either in Elias' analysis or in fact, which suggests that his findings should be restricted to twentieth-century Germany. English-speaking societies have developed along broadly similar lines. In his history of the twentieth century, Eric Hobsbawm singles out a "demotic turn in the tastes of the middle- and upper-class young" (1994: 331) as one of the most significant cultural trends in the post-World War II industrialized world. What he seems to have in mind as corroborative evidence is fashions in dress and popular music, but the argument can easily be extended to language, as it is precisely the same type of "demotic" taste which, for example, provides the ultimate motivation for the late twentieth-century changes in British RP discussed in Chapter 5 above.

The history of communication in contemporary Britain is a central concern of the school of critical discourse analysis which has grown up around the work of Norman Fairclough (e.g., 1992, 1995). In his view, the communicative history of the country's recent past has been characterized by the three interlocking developments of the "technologization," "democratization," and "informalization" of public discourse. Thereby, the term "technologization" refers to a tendency for complex communicative processes to be broken up into several modules, ideally well-defined, easily teachable, and, above all, marketable. Thus, what used to be the provision of spiritual guidance, a "deep" relationship between adviser and advised, becomes counseling, available by several recipes in several terminologies, from standardly trained experts. What used to be the process of higher education, the disinterested pursuit of intellectual goals by students and teachers, is redefined as an array of readily available course packages supplied to customers by providers.[2]

The technologization of discourse is, of course, a mixed blessing but it may sometimes have an unexpected empowering effect. By eroding the power of traditional elites it may contribute to a "democratization" of discourse conventions. In the present, technological advances (for example, in the media) and an outwardly egalitarian social climate help to give a public forum to sections of the community that would have been silenced in previous periods of the history of English.[3] Easy proof of this assertion is provided by the Internet, which has not only been a powerful agent entrenching the globally dominant position of (standard) American English, the "default" language of the new medium, but, above and beyond that, has provided unprecedented opportunities for the spread of lesser-known standard varieties and even stigmatized nonstandards. Thus, searches for terms such as *bakkle* (a conventional orthographic rendering of the Jamaican Creole for *bottle*) will refer the user to a rich Web-based subculture of discussion groups linking Jamaicans in the Caribbean with members of the community in the British, US, or Canadian "diaspora." Similarly, documentation is available in this way for lexical Indianisms such as *speed money* ("bribe") or *to chargesheet* (verb).

While the twin notions of technologization and democratization of discourse focus on the participants of the communicative process and the context of situation, the third concept, "informalization," refers to the language itself. Fairclough illustrates this as follows:

---

[2] Lack of space forces me to present these examples in a more pointed fashion than they appear in Fairclough's differentiated analysis.

[3] For Fairclough, who derives much of his inspiration from the neo-Marxist tradition of "new left" social theory, this democratization of discourse is not the undiluted blessing it appears to be at first sight. Rather, it "turns out to be ambivalent, either part of a genuine relaxation or used strategically as a technology" (1992: 221).

Conversational discourse has been, and is being projected from its primary domain in the personal interactions of the private sphere, into the public sphere.   (Fairclough 1992: 98)

One dimension of this manifestation of informality is a shift in the relationship between spoken and written discourse. We had examples of this from newspapers. . . . The expression "talking like a book" reflects a popular perception of how written language has influenced more formal speech, and one finds the shift towards conversation not only throughout the printed media and advertising, but also in new designs for official forms, such as claim forms for social welfare payments. . . . The shifts of speech towards writing may have had their heyday; contemporary cultural values place a high valuation on informality, and the predominant shift is toward speech-like forms in writing.   (Fairclough 1992: 204)

Despite their common concerns, historical corpus-linguists, cultural historians, and critical discourse analysts have not, on the whole, taken much note of each other's work. This is a pity, because these different approaches to a common problem complement each other almost ideally. Historians and critical discourse analysts are very good at identifying possible motivations for linguistic developments but will not usually be bothered with linguistic analysis beyond the anecdotal demonstration of a point. Corpus-linguists, on the other hand, usually lay out the facts fairly completely, but deal rather speculatively and superficially with possible extralinguistic causes of linguistic developments.

The term "colloquialization" – first introduced in Mair (1997a: 203–205) – is intended to provide precisely the type of analytical concept which is needed to integrate the two approaches. As a linguistic term, it covers a significant stylistic shift in twentieth-century English:

- away from a written norm which is elaborated to maximal distance from speech and towards a written norm that is closer to spoken usage, and
- away from a written norm which cultivates formality towards a norm which is tolerant of informality and even allows for anti-formality as a rhetorical strategy.

Obviously, the colloquialization of the written language is a development which is in evidence to a greater or lesser extent in different communities synchronically, and at different times diachronically. One thing, however, is certain, too: it will never work itself out to the limit, as a written norm which is identical to colloquial speech would be highly dysfunctional.

A first idea of the extent to which the colloquialization of written English progressed in the course of the twentieth century could be gleaned from Westin's (2002) study of newspaper editorials mentioned above. Using Biber's methodology, Westin investigates a corpus of editorials in three "up-market" British newspapers spanning the years from 1900 to 1993, with instructive results: the language of these editorials has become more informal, and this tendency is shown to have accelerated in the latter half of the twentieth century. As Westin and Geisler put it in a follow-up to the original study:

> The results of the dimension score analyses show that, during the 20th century the language of British up-market editorials became less narrative . . . but more persuasive and argumentative . . . . It also became less abstract . . . and less dependent on referential elaboration . . ., which resulted in more informal language. . . .
>
> The analyses also indicate that it was mainly during the latter part of the 20th century that these changes took place, since on three of the dimensions, the last time period (representing the years 1960 through 1993) stands out as different from the preceding two periods.   (Westin and Geisler 2002: 150)

As the second half of the twentieth century seems to be a crucial period in the development, the "Brown quartet" of corpora is ideally suited for a study of such developments in a broader variety of written genres, and from a comparative British-American perspective (which is important, as American English is often assumed to lead in the change towards more informal modes of expression in writing). Among the fifteen genre categories provided for in the original "Brown" design, it is the "press" (A–C) and "science" (J) sections which are most homogeneous and therefore suitable for a comparative evaluation in the four corpora.

Neither press style nor the conventions of academic writing remain entirely stable over the thirty-year period covered by the four corpora. Not surprisingly, the speed of response to social and cultural pressures is greater in the press than in the science texts. In the press, colloquialization manifests itself on two different levels, in textual macro-structure as well as on the microstructural level of choice between formal and informal grammatical constructions or lexical items. Press texts of the 1990s (F-LOB and Frown) contain far more quotations and – real or fabricated – passages of direct speech than those of the 1960s (LOB and Brown). The intended stylistic effect is to make the texts appear more dramatic, interesting, and accessible and, presumably, also to involve the reader emotionally. Table 6.1 gives the frequencies for the morphological forms of the most common quotation-introducing verb, *say*, in the relevant sections of the four corpora.

The situation is clear. The frequency of the quotation-introducing verb has not increased in the science texts. Therefore, no "oralization" of the textual macro-structure needs to be assumed for this genre. On the other hand, direct quotations have increased significantly both in British and American journalistic writing, which is a strong indication of change towards a more oral/conversational textual macro-structure in the press.

Let us now move on to the micro-structural aspect of colloquialization, which manifests itself in growing preferences for informal over formal options

Table 6.1. *Frequencies of* say *in selected genre categories of four corpora*

	LOB	Brown	F-LOB	Frown
Press (A–C)	617	624	775	1,147
Science (J)	138	113	147	96

A–C: BrE-AmE 1961 n.s.; BrE diachr. $p < 0.001$; AmE diachr. $p < 0.001$; BrE-AmE 1991/92 $p < 0.001$
J: BrE-AmE 1991/92 $p < 0.01$; all others not significant

Table 6.2. *Verb and negative contractions in the four corpora (from Leech and Smith 2005)*

		1961	1991/1992	Log likelihood[4]	Difference (percent)
BrE (LOB/F-LOB)	Verb contractions	3,143	3,898	79.1	+23.7
	Negative contractions	1,950	2,482	62.6	+26.9
AmE (Brown/Frown)	Verb contractions	2,822	5,073	644.6	+79.3
	Negative contractions	2,098	2,983	152.5	+41.8

where both are available. Among grammatical constructions currently spreading in writing because writers wish to strike a more accessible, informal, or colloquial note in their work are the progressive, the *get*-passive (both dealt with in Chapter 4), zero-relative clauses, verb contractions (e.g., *it's*), and negative contractions (*-n't*). The frequencies for contractions of both types in the four corpora as a whole are presented in Table 6.2.

The shift towards contracted forms is strongest in American English (AmE), which may in part be due to the fact that written American English has gone more "oral" at the level of textual macro-structure, and spellings such as *it is not* do not sit easily in passages of direct speech. Table 6.3, which gives the

---

[4] Leech and Smith (2005) use log likelihood to assess the statistical significance of their findings. A log-likelihood value of 6.6 or more is equivalent to $p < 0.01$ in the standard chi-square test.

Table 6.3. *Contraction ratios (*not-*contractions) in journalistic and academic prose*[5]

	Contracted forms	Uncontracted strings	Contraction ratio
LOBpress	162	637	20.3
FLOBpress	266	529	33.5
Brownpress	210	480	30.4
Frownpress	543	392	58.1
LOB-J	16	624	2.5
FLOB-J	31	655	4.5
Brown-J	15	627	2.3
Frown-J	33	515	6.0

Table 6.4. *Decline in frequency of use of the* be-*passive in the four reference corpora (from Leech and Smith 2005)*

	1961	1991/1992	Log likelihood	Difference (percent)
British English (LOB/F-LOB)	13,331	11,708	109.8	−12.4
American English (Brown/Frown)	11,650	9,329	263.7	−20.1

frequencies for the press and science texts separately, reveals that, as expected, the general drift has affected the press texts more profoundly.

It could be argued that writers are not entirely free in their choice of form but influenced by prescriptive recommendations or, in the case of journalists, by even stricter conventions of house style. But even a change in house style in this case would just be a belated reflection of actual change in community preferences, and support the argument for a growing tendency towards the colloquialization of written English.

The colloquialization of the norms of written usage in the recent past has caused increases in the use of some grammatical structures, but decreases in the frequency of others. An example is the *be*-passive, which has been declining in frequency according to the evidence of the four written corpora, shown in Table 6.4.

These raw frequencies were computed on the basis of the part-of-speech-tagged versions of the corpora, and no attempt has been made to differentiate between central and peripheral passives. Such a qualitative follow-up was undertaken for sub-samples of the academic-writing texts (category J) by Hundt

---

[5] Included were only those forms where variation between contracted and uncontracted strings is possible (i.e., *ain't* was excluded).

and Mair (1999: 231), who were able to show a statistically significant decline of the passive in the text type in which it is most common by far. The percentage of passives dropped from 24.8 in LOB to 20.2 in F-LOB, and from 20.8 in Brown to 14.8 in Frown.

Many style guides, particularly in the United States, are now advising against the use of the passive voice in academic writing, and the issue has become a subject of public debate in the scientific community. In response to a survey conducted by the Teacher Science Network, no less an authority than Sir Robert May, President of the Royal Society, came out strongly in favor of the direct, "active" style. The Teacher Science Network had originally advocated this style in popular and pedagogical science writing in schools, but Sir Robert wanted to see it extended to all texts:

> Thank you for sending me a copy of *TSNews*. I enjoyed the opportunity to see it. The column, on page 3[,] about whether one should use the active or passive voice in "scientific" writing really caught my attention. I was particularly horrified to discover that "most TSN scientists say" that the passive style is more appropriate for scientists writing research papers, and that "most TSN primary and Secondary Teachers say" that they are not sure which style they think scientists should use. Admittedly, both groups agree that school children should adopt the direct, "I did", style, although even here we have the looney view that the passive style might be more appropriate for older children. At the risk of going over-the-top, I would put my own view so strongly as to say that, these days, use of the passive voice in a research paper is, more often than not, the hallmark of second rate work.

> The two major general scientific journals, *Nature* and *Science*, have an interesting history in this regard. For at least the past thirty years, *Nature* has edited articles that are presented in the passive voice, to transform them into the "I did" style. To the contrary, until relatively recently, *Science* remained under the antique delusion that work was more scientific if performed by the impersonal forces of history rather than by real people, and it was in the habit of editing manuscripts to transform them from the active into the passive voice; I had several bitter arguments over this point, over the years. But *Science* has made great strides in the past decade, becoming (in my view) more fully competitive with *Nature* in many ways, particularly in its front material. Not surprisingly, a major change has been the switch to editing manuscripts presented in the passive voice to transform them into the active voice. The notion that it is somehow more "scientific" to suggest that some impersonal, dispassionate actor or whatever did the work – thus conferring more authority upon it – rather than the person writing the report did it him or herself, belongs to a[n] older generation. Anyone who writes in this style today simply is not likely to be at the cutting edge.

Table 6.5. *Frequency of noun+common-noun combinations in four corpora*

	LOB	Brown	F-LOB	Increase (percent)	Frown	Increase (percent)
Totals	22,696	25,706	25,775	+13.6	29,585	+15.1
Press (A–C)	5,769	6,655	6,172	+7.0	6,910	+3.8
Learned (J)	4,640	5,046	5,046	+8.8	5,703	+13.0
General prose (D–H)	8,756	10,441	11,562	+32.0	12,885	+23.4
Fiction (K–R)	2,448	3,564	3,366	+37.5	3,724	+4.5

> In short, I believe that Primary and Secondary teachers should, without any reservation, be encouraging all their students – younger or older – to be writing in the active voice. That actually reflects the reality – the students are doing the work – and at the heart of science must be the recognition that it is work being done by people! In the long run, more authority is conferred by this direct approach than by the pedantic pretence that some impersonal force is performing the research![6]

In all the cases of variation between formal and informal options presented so far, the informal one was shown to have spread in English writing in the recent past. In the grammar of the verb, there are very few counter-examples, for instance, the recent spread of the subjunctive, a formal variant, in British writing, but they do not change the general picture.

Has the trend towards more colloquial writing thus progressed almost unhindered in the recent past? The answer to this question is in the negative, as there seems to be one group of constructions which has proved impervious to the development, namely those noun phrase structures which help the compression of information, such as for example, noun compounds of various types. In a comparison of the tagged versions of LOB and F-LOB Mair et al. (2002: 250) were able to show that the number of nominal tags had increased moderately (+ 5.3 percent), whereas the verbal tags had remained stable (−0.9 percent). By comparison, the frequency of selected types of nominal compounds increased dramatically. Table 6.5 gives the relevant findings for noun + common-noun combinations (chosen because they were least likely to represent proper names).[7]

---

[6] This letter, with accompanying introduction from *TSNews* (Newsletter of the Teacher Science Network), first appeared in *TSNews* 15 (Spring 2002). It is here reproduced from *Osmosis* 24 (Spring 2003), the newsletter of the "Science and Plants for Schools" website (http://www.saps.plantsci.cam.ac.uk/ osmos/os24.htm#8).

[7] The figures support a trend already apparent in the comparison of the tagged LOB and F-LOB; see Mair et al. (2002: 252–254). Detailed comparison of the present figures for LOB and F-LOB with the older publication is not recommended, as different search

Note that the sharpest increases are not found where they might be expected, namely in the information-centered genres of press and academic writing, but in general prose and fiction. A possible explanation is that press and science were already close to saturation level with regard to information density in the 1960s, whereas the trend towards compression of information was allowed freer rein in the reshaping of general prose and fiction. Put in simple terms, the ideal implicit in present-day English writing style in all genres is to maximize information density, but to avoid additional stylistic ornament or formality in order to give the impression that the resulting texts remain easy to read and accessible. Present-day writing conventions thus emerge as a compromise between "the competing demands of popularization vs. economy" (Biber 2003: 169).

6.3   Americanization?

There is a long tradition of complaint outside the United States that American English has been a dominant influence on the development of other varieties, and that world English is being homogenized on American norms. That this scenario of Americanization is incompatible with another popular one – namely that, like Latin before it, the English language might break up into a range of independent daughters which are only partly intelligible mutually – does not seem to allay the fears of those who are worried about American influence.

Indeed, instances of American influence on other varieties of English in the twentieth century are not hard to find. Given the global presence of the United States in what may well be referred to as the "American Century" in future historiography, they are not surprising, at all. Twentieth-century American neologisms have routinely been adopted into other varieties of English (and other languages, for that matter), and American influence is the factor responsible for the unexpected revival of a near-defunct grammatical category, the mandative subjunctive.

However, a dispassionate look at contemporary linguistic developments shows that popular discussions hopelessly overemphasize the influence of American English on the development of the language as a whole. In a familiar process of psychological transfer, a fear of political, economic, and cultural domination by the United States seems to have been projected on to the language. Having acknowledged the importance of the American variety in the development of the English language in the twentieth century, what are the exaggerations which need to be corrected?

First, we need to realize that many instances in which British (or Australian, or Irish, etc.) usage seems to follow American practice do not necessarily

routines were employed and the corresponding figures from the tagged versions of Brown and Frown were not yet available at the time.

represent direct American influence. Rather, they show all varieties of English developing along the same lines and toward the same putative end-point, but at slightly different speeds. Consider, for example, well-known processes of morphological regularization in the verbal paradigm, such as the gradual ascendancy of regular past and participle forms for verbs such as *learn* (*learnt* → *learned*) or *dream* (*dreamt* → *dreamed*). Such processes have advanced further in American English, probably because in the course of colonial dialect leveling and subsequent acquisition of English by generations of non-English-speaking immigrants the regular forms got an extra boost, but the tendency towards regularization has been independently present in all other varieties. Similarly, the recent spread of the bare infinitive with *help*, or of *do* in the negation and question forms of *need* in British English, do not represent straight takeovers from America. As has been shown in Chapter 4, the regional usage contrast that could be observed between British and American English in the first half of the twentieth century was a temporary one, because relevant shifts in usage preferences in individual varieties are embedded in a long-term process of grammaticalization which is transforming the core grammar of English, and thus the language as a whole. Also, it needs to be emphasized that, in addition to straightforward Americanization and parallel developments, standard varieties of English outside the US are still capable of independent lexical and structural innovation – a truth which is so obvious that it merely needs to be repeated because of an occasional irrational fear of American linguistic dominance in other parts of the English-speaking world. As a case in point discussed in the present study, we might refer to the use of gerundial constructions without *from* after the *prevent*-class of verbs in British English.

Second, American influence operates selectively. As has been shown, it is pervasive in the lexicon, modest in the grammar, and almost nonexistent in pronunciation. Also, it tends to be restricted to communicative domains with a global reach – from international science and research to entertainment and mass culture. It is less in evidence in local communicative domains (for example, ordinary face-to-face conversation) or domains with a strong local tradition (for example, literary writing, where works written by British writers would be unlikely to be mistaken for the work of Americans).

At least in the popular perception, the American influence on the changing and future structure of English tends to be exaggerated. American influence on changing discourse conventions, on the other hand, is generally underestimated. From simple discourse routines, such as *you're welcome* uttered in acknowledgment of *thank you*, through politeness conventions, as evident, for instance, in the spread of first-name address to institutional domains such as doctor–patient interaction, to the definition of what constitutes a proper example of a text type such as a curriculum vitae or a resume, American norms of usage have presented important and attractive models to users of English outside the United States.

In all, American English will not become the standardizing and homo-genizing factor it is commonly feared to be as long as the models presented to other speakers of the language and the world at large remain as heteroge-neous as they are today. Corporate America as represented by globally active media giants such as CNN is, after all, not the only agent in the spread of American English. Even Hollywood movies are linguistically quite heteroge-neous, giving exposure both to mainstream American English and a wide variety of regional and ethnic varieties. Rap and hip-hop musicians have cultivated a highly controversial idiom incorporating aspects of America's most stigmatized dialects since the late 1970s, and this idiom has by now become so attractive to rebellious youth and marginalized communities all over the world as to lead one commentator to declare that "the world is a ghetto and rap is its music" (Dorsey 2000: 405). Particularly when it is nonstandard forms of American English which are spreading in other commu-nities, closer analysis shows that we are rarely dealing with simple processes of linguistic Americanization but with a more complex phenomenon: the negotiation of vernacular norms in a globalized communicative habitat – as was demonstrated, for example, in a recent study of the causes which make more and more New Zealanders opt for the supposedly American emphatic negative "no way" (Meyerhoff and Niedzielski 2003).

6.4   Analysis of selected sample texts

In the year 2003, *Granta*, the literary magazine, published an extract from a novel in progress by Sarah Waters in which the author, born in 1966, recreates the atmosphere of 1940s Britain.[8] As very few referential clues are given to the intended setting, the text is a perfect illustration of the importance of a discourse-stylistic "feel" in placing a text regionally or dating it to a specific period in the recent past. In the short historical term, it is rare to find incontrovertible phonetic or lexico-grammatical diagnostics which would uniquely identify a given text or utterance as either "now" or "sixty years ago." But the cumulative effect from choices taken consistently in one direction usually builds up fairly reliable regional or period profiles. The extract opens as follows:

> "Helen, why don't we put some food together and take it as a picnic to the park?"
>
> "All right," said Helen.
>
> They packed bread, cheese, apples and lettuce in a check tea towel; Julia fished out an old madras tablecloth they had used as a dust sheet when painting the flat; they put it all in a canvas bag. In one of the streets

[8] Sarah Waters, "Helen and Julia," *Granta* 81 (2003): 17–32.

which ran from their square was a Polish delicatessen: there they bought slices of sausage, more cheese, and two bottles of wheat beer.

"I feel like the leader of a Brownie troop," said Helen, shouldering the canvas bag.

"You look more glorious than that," said Julia. "Like a girl in a Soviet mural."

Helen imagined herself: square-faced, large-limbed, rather hairy; but she said nothing. They began the walk across Marylebone. The bottles of beer rocked together in the bag. The streets had a bleached, exhausted feel, not unpleasant; they were dusty as a cat's coat is dusty, when it has lain all day in the sun. The cars were so few, one could hear the cries of individual children, the slap and bounce of balls, the sound of wirelesses and gramophones from open windows, the ringing of telephones.

(p. 17)

The mention of *gramophones* and *wirelesses* in the last few lines of the extract is a first definite cultural-linguistic clue that the setting evoked here is not the Britain of today. However, before that a linguistic atmosphere has been built up which makes the appearance of such clear hints not entirely unexpected. It may not always be easy to decide whether it is a word, or an expression, or even the situation referred to, which is dated. Madras cloth, for example, is not much in use today; the word *madras* happens to be entirely absent from the BNC and does not have an entry in the 2002 edition of the *Longman dictionary of contemporary English*.[9] The reference to Soviet murals in this particular context is a complicated linguistic gesture which at the same time dates the fictional text and drops a possible hint that the women might belong to the leftist intellectual scene of the 1930s, the "Red Decade." The general-purpose positive evaluator *glorious* (instead of *great, cool,* or *fab*) is also useful in establishing period and class "feel" in a fictional text because this class of adjective has a high rate of turnover and is notoriously subject to rapid lexical change.

As the text moves on, the density of the hints is reduced considerably, but passages such as the following serve to maintain the atmosphere:

"That was a favourite of my father's. . . . And Yorkshire pudding is jolly tasty with syrup on it. It's only another form of pancake, after all. Isn't it? She waited. "Julia?"

"What?"

"Must you look away like that, when we are talking?"   (p. 20)

---

[9] In a competitive market, dictionary publishers tend to promote their product by pointing to the large number of neologisms included in each new edition. The present example shows that this is not an entirely unproblematical sales strategy – all the more so as many of the neologisms included early on in their life will not catch on and will therefore have to be removed from subsequent editions.

Here the use of *must* – instead of one of its late twentieth-century equivalents such as *do you have to* or *do you need to* – points to the early twentieth century, while the presence of the adverbial modifier *jolly* introduces additional, more specific information on period and on the speakers' social class.

Sarah Waters' literary experiment in reconstructing the language of the past inspires us to ask two questions which have been implicit in much of the discussion in the present book. Has the English language changed in the course of the twentieth century? The answer is: 'Yes, but only slightly.' In her story, as in the corpora surveyed in the present study, we will find few words which are genuinely new, and even fewer grammatical constructions, phrases, or collocations. The second question is: 'Have the ways changed in which people make use of the structural and stylistic options the English language makes available to them?' And here the answer is: 'Yes, very much so.' The period "feel" of a text emerges in the unique combination of features, none of which need be a clear diagnostic in its own right.

An analysis of Sarah Waters' experiment, recreating the linguistic atmosphere of more than half a century ago, has enabled us to see how a period "feel" emerges in a text. Similar insights result from a direct comparison of specimens of specific textual genres written at different points of time. Consider, for example, the following sports report, written in 1901, which will be compared to a similar text produced ninety years later:

Sport and Play

Football

The League table was left in a somewhat incomplete state last Saturday by the abandonment of the Notts Forest–Bury match. The game was abandoned through the rain, which came down in such extraordinary quantities that it was almost impossible to see the flight of the ball. The Preston North End–Bolton Wanderers fixture was stopped through the same cause.

The clubs at the head of the table which now stand the best chance of winning the competition are Notts Forest, 23 matches played, 31 points; Sunderland, 23 matches played, 29 points; Newcastle United, 21 games played, 27 points; and Bury 22 games, 27 points. He would be a bold prophet who should definitely name the winner out of these four.

Our "famous football team" this week is a southern club, but one of the most famous of these, namely, Woolwich Arsenal. With only twenty-three points to their credit for twenty-one matches played in the Second Division of the League, their aspirations of elevation to the First League next season are doomed. They hope, however, to make a better fight in the English Cup competition, and this they are quite likely to do, notwithstanding the strong opponents they will have to tackle.

The present unsatisfactory position of West Bromwich Albion in the League table has led the directors of the club to put the players into special training. Brine baths and long walks are the principal features of their new preparation for matches.

The Bury officials have resolved to take no further action with regard to the attack which was made on the players and directors after their match with Sheffield Wednesday on Saturday week. It will be remembered that the assault took place after the Bury team had driven from the Wednesday's ground in their brake. The Sheffield Wednesday directors have expressed their regret to the Bury club, and have posted placards throughout the city, offering a reward of £10 for information which will lead to the conviction of the offenders.

Even if we did not know the source of this text (as it happens, *Illustrated Mail*, 26 January 1901: 16), we would be able to date it to the beginning rather than the end of the twentieth century without any expert knowledge of the history of British football or the current status of brine baths as remedy for under-performing players. As in the literary text, the telltale signs would not be any individual words or grammatical constructions, but the level of formality and important features of textual macro-structure. It is safe to say that formal turns of phrase such as "it will be remembered that . . .," "the present unsatisfactory position," or "aspirations of elevation to the First League" would not occur at the same level of concentration in a modern equivalent of this report. Also, any putative modern equivalent would be extremely unlikely to do without passages of direct speech or similar characteristics of "oralized" discourse. Compare, for example, the following report, which is from the *Evening Standard* (4 September 1991: 49):

A rugby challenge for Wales

Collins takes a break from riots

by Chris Jones

CARDIFF flanker Richie Collins has warmed up for Wales's match with France tonight – by facing rioting mobs.

Collins, a police officer, has been on duty in the Ely area of Cardiff which has seen repeated outbreaks of violence. Collins made it to the final training session yesterday after two nights on the front line and said: "I am a policeman and I had to be on duty.

"But I am glad to have got away for this game. There is a great spirit in the squad and I am pleased to be relieved of those police duties to be part of what I believe will be a big night for Welsh rugby."

The Welsh team has been radically changed since the 60-point hammering by Australia in Brisbane in July. There is a new manager, coach and captain and – according to pre-match build up – a new self belief.

Captain Ieuan Evans, of Llanelli, said: "There is a confidence in this team which may surprise a lot of people. That doesn't mean we'll beat France but we may achieve a result that not many are expecting.

"Our coach Alan Davis has given us something which has been lacking, self belief."

All Welsh supporters want to see this team play with the pride that was lacking in Brisbane. A solid performance, particularly up front, will give Wales hope and open the way for a better World Cup challenge next month.

Alan Davies, the ex-England B coach, is masterminding the Welsh recovery and he said: "When I first came to Wales I expected to find good players – and they are here. I am more than happy with the progress we have made although, realistically, no-one should expect us to win against a well organised side like France."

This match has been arranged to mark the arrival of floodlights at the National Stadium, needed for World Cup matches. They will also be used for the Welsh soccer team's internationals.

The further shortening of paragraphs which were not overly long even in 1901, the liberal use of direct speech, and the generally informal choices of vocabulary all prove that colloquialization has profoundly transformed the genre of sports reportage since the early 1900s.

Conclusion

A book on language change in progress cannot have a neat ending. Many of the developments described in the preceding chapters are still in flux, and the end-points remain uncertain in many cases. A number of trends, however, have emerged that, while certainly not exceptionless, are pervasive enough to deserve pointing out in a conclusion to a book on changes in standard English in the past century.

In phonology, the major development of the past century has been the emergence of an array of educated standard accents, broadly along national lines. Where there was no single national pronunciation standard in 1900, as in the United States, there is one now. By contrast, the sphere of influence of RP has contracted geographically. Where educated speakers outside the British Isles deferred to RP – that is, an external or "exonormative" standard – in the first half of the twentieth century, as many of them tended to do in the dominions and colonies of the British Empire, this deference has usually not persisted, and new "endonormative" national educated accents have arisen in the wake of decolonization. A difficult remaining issue is, in fact, the present status of RP, because its role has strengthened and diminished at the same time. As has been pointed out, it ceased to function as the prestige accent of an empire when that empire dissolved as a political agent. If it ever was the national pronunciation standard of the United Kingdom, it certainly does not play this role any longer. Regional autonomy in Scotland, Northern Ireland, and probably even Wales, has seen to that. On the other hand, RP today is much more than the prestige accent of England. It is still the most important norm for foreign learners of English in Europe and many other parts of the world and, alongside American English, it continues to be one of the two reference accents of standard English with a truly global reach.

However, the fact that English has now become a pluricentric language does not mean that all the national standards are equal. Some new standards, such as, for example, (natively spoken educated) South African English, are autonomous norms with a purely national reach.[1] Some, such as Australian English, or – to mention more controversial examples of post-colonial second-language standards – Nigerian English and Indian English, have some supra-national significance, which, however, clearly does not put them on a par with the globally recognized British and American norms.

What has changed is not only individual pronunciation features or the number of standard accents, but also attitudes towards them. Processes of linguistic standardization have a functional and an ideological dimension. Linguistic standardization is functional, inevitable and necessary in large and technologically advanced communities of speakers because it ensures easy communication across large geographical distances, across social classes and different ethnic groups, and across national boundaries. Beyond what is neces-sary in these purely functional terms, standardization is also ideologically driven. It is not just practical and useful dialect leveling on a larger scale, but involves an element of "suppression of optional variability" (Milroy and Milroy 1991: 17) for its own sake. Certain pronunciation variants are enforced or stigmatized by dominant elites as social markers, symbolic correlates of mem-bership (or lack thereof) in a dominant group, so that a proper pronunciation becomes an element of proper social conduct and, ultimately, even of the speaker's perceived moral integrity. At the risk of oversimplifying, one could summarize twentieth-century developments by saying that the functional pressures for standardization have strengthened further as a result of the rise of the audiovisual media, whereas the ideological pressures have weakened as a result of the egalitarian, democratic, and to an extent anti-authoritarian, ethos that has come to characterize public discourse in the industrialized Western world in the second half of the twentieth century.

As for lexical innovation in standard English, the past century has seen an explosive growth in vocabulary, and considerable advances in lexicography and documentation methods, which make an investigation of this growth possible. As Chapter 3 has shown, it is a vain undertaking merely to catalog individual new words or new meanings. Our investigation has shown that there have also been noticeable changes in the underlying patterns of lexical enrichment. It seems that after a prolonged period (from 1066 to around 1850) in which borrowing from other languages was a major source of new words in English, we have now returned to a situation in which most new words are created from the language's own resources, through productive processes of word formation. Some word-formation patterns have dramatically increased their productivity in this process. For example, acronyms, a category of new words not even regularly attested before the twentieth century, made their way into late

---

[1] In fact, this local educated norm is under threat on two fronts. Some culturally conserva-tive white South Africans may not yet fully embrace it and still defer to RP, while its future as the national pronunciation norm for a new multiracial state remains uncertain.

twentieth-century everyday English in massive quantities from specialized domains such as government and science.

While in the case of the new standard accents it makes sense to speak of the emergence of several Englishes in the twentieth century, words travel fast – so fast, in fact, that most variety-specific lexical peculiarities remain transient and the underlying global unity of the language at the lexical level is not in doubt. A search for all entries labeled as "orig[inally] U.S." in the OED and first attested in the year 1930 will reveal eleven items: *to boff* (on the head), *dinette*, *drive-in*, *foodism*, *freeway*, *gangbuster*, *gobo*, *Mickey Mouse*, *snozzle*, *strip-teaser*, *to zipper*. A look at the quotations shows that all these words are known outside the US by now, and that most of them soon lost any "American" associations and are now unselfconsciously used for local contexts outside the United States.

The list of the 1930 entries labeled "chiefly U.S." contains ten items: *ass-backwards*, *to boff*, *dong*, *to holster*, *kinescope*, *lubritorium*, *mixmaster*, *enophile* (as a spelling variant for *oenophile*), *over easy* and *paesano*. As can be seen, the list has some overlap with the previous one, mostly due to different meanings of a word being differently labeled. The general tendency, though, is clear enough: what has remained American is outdated or marginal vocabulary (e.g., *kine-scope*), vocabulary tied to mundane home activities such as cooking (*over easy*), and in several cases the OED label may simply be wrong (*dong*). The 1930 first attestations which have remained exclusively American are *tetched*, a conventional nonstandard spelling for *touched*, *bunker buster* (in the sense of *golfer*[2]) and the pseudo-Yiddish slang term *schnozzle* ("nose"). It might be argued that the almost instant adoption of American vocabulary in other varieties of English reflects the political, economic, and cultural dominance of the United States in the twentieth century, and that the reverse traffic is less common. Indeed, it is unlikely that a New Zealand coinage such as *chillybin* (for *cold box* or *cold bag*) will make it into most other varieties of English, but the persistence of lexical regionalisms in informal styles must not blind us to the fact that at the level of vocabulary there is one English standard, and the minor and usually temporary contrasts between different English-speaking communities are due to slightly different ways in which these communities make use of a common resource.

As for its grammatical structure, formal and written standard English was very homogeneous at the beginning of the twentieth century. Further homogenization took place in the course of the century partly because developments in the major varieties which had been set in motion two or three centuries ago continued unfolding and are now approaching their end-point (cf., e.g., the

---

[2] The usual current military senses of the term are not attested until 1944 ("member of a military unit with a mission to destroy or capture enemy bunkers") and 1953 ("missile or weapon designed . . . to destroy a military bunker").

"overdue" elimination of auxiliary syntax for possessive *have* in British English), and partly also because of the increasing prestige of formal American usage outside the United States (e.g., the spread of the mandative subjunctive to other national varieties). Both trends were expected. Among the more surprising findings of the present study is the fact that in more local areas of the grammar – for example, complementation preferences with specific verbs (cf., e.g., the cases of *prevent, stop, save*) – the past century has been marked by increasing divergence.

Also, much evidence has been provided in the preceding analysis that divergence is tolerated in speech even in areas where there is almost complete conformity in writing. A simple but striking illustration of this tendency was provided by the corpus evidence on prepositional usage with the adjective *different*, where the written data showed overwhelming dominance of *different from* in all varieties, whereas there were strong regional preferences for either *different to* or *different than* in speech. The interaction of contrasting forces was demonstrated in the study of modals of obligation and necessity. All varieties and all genres are losing *must* and showing increases for *have to*. It takes a look at spoken data, however, to realize that *have got to* has developed into a stable grammatical Briticism.

As was pointed out repeatedly in the present study, shifting frequencies of grammatical constructions in corpus data need not necessarily point to changes in the underlying systems of grammatical choices, but may be symptoms of changes in genre conventions or communicative styles. In other words, even when the underlying grammatical system is stable, historically evolving traditions of speaking and writing may lead speakers to make certain choices more often, or to make them in new and unusual environments.

Among these discourse changes treated in Chapter 6, two stand out as similarly pervasive but occasionally conflicting with each other – namely, a tendency to increase information density in most written genres and a counter-trend promoting informality and colloquialism. The former trend shapes the grammar of the noun phrase; for example, by encouraging the use of nominal sequences with little explicit marking of syntactic structure. Arguably, noun phrases of the type

> Black Country car sales group West Midland Motors (F-LOB A38)
>
> San Francisco Redevelopment Agency Executive Director Edward Helfeld (Frown A2)
>
> New York State pension investment task force (Frown J39)
>
> a modified sodium dodecyl sulphate polyacrylamide gel electrophoresis method for visualization of factor VIII heavy chain polypeptides
> (F-LOB J)

were possible in the eighteenth and nineteenth centuries, but it was only in the course of the twentieth century that they became frequent. Traditionally, they were associated with the under-specified block syntax of headline style, but now they have spread from journalistic and academic prose to all written genres, presumably because they help achieve higher values of information density than alternatives such as *West Midland Motors, the car sales group from the Black Country* or *the task force appointed to monitor investment in pension funds in the State of New York/ the task force appointed by the State of New York to monitor investment in pension funds.*

Tempting though crystal-ball gazing may be, I will not venture more than a few concluding speculations on the future shape of English. Extrapolating from present trends in pronunciation, we are unlikely to see convergence in the British and American norms in the coming decades. If anything, American and British speakers will sound even more different in the year 2100 than they do today. In grammar, the terrain is rather unclear. It is unlikely that long-term trends attested in all major varieties, such as the decrease in the frequency of *must*, will be reversed. Whether they will proceed further, or whether current usage preferences will stabilize, is another matter. With regard to the minor trends noted toward an increasing grammatical divergence among national standards of English, the coming decades should show whether current trends in the complementation of verbs of preventing will run their course and add another full-blown categorical contrast of the *got/gotten* type to the small inventory of such items or whether current changes in British usage will peter out and leave British English with an optional local variant in addition to a common international one (roughly the situation which we find today). Both courses of development are possible, but there is nothing in the current evidence which would make either outcome more likely.

One trend which will be particularly important to follow in the near future is the colloquialization of the norms of written usage. If current developments proceed unchecked, they will inevitably lead to some destandardization – simply because regionally and socially specific usages are more common in informal speech than in the more highly regulated domains of formal speech and writing. English will obviously not break up into mutually unintelligible daughter languages, but the ease with which written texts from any specific national community are currently read and understood in other parts of the English-speaking world may suffer somewhat in the process.

Attacking an allegedly outmoded traditional emphasis on formality, routine, and ritual in communication and social conduct may have another potentially negative outcome, as has been pointed out in a recent sociological study of late twentieth-century informality (Misztal 2000). The removal of formal constraints on behavior may leave members of a community confused rather than liberated because they lose a sense of orientation – an argument which applies as much to social conduct in general as to choice of linguistic register in particular. For example, in verbal conflicts carried out in public forums, a standardized and formalized procedure for voicing criticism, anger, and complaint may be superior to the spontaneous and supposedly authentic expression of such sentiments in informal language. A highly emotional public rhetoric is subject to inflationary pressure. For example, public expression relying on the shock value of informal, slang, or taboo vocabulary to achieve an air of authenticity and spontaneity will be effective for a short period of time only; after that, stylistic leveling will be the inevitable result of the over-use of highly restricted and specialized lexical resources. Also, informality is not necessarily the removal of pressure or oppressive constraints which it may appear to be at first sight. On the contrary, it may itself develop into a subtle strategy of coercion once it has become a new norm. We have to take care so as not to end up in the worst, rather than the best, of both worlds – informal decision-making in backrooms rather than formal democratic processes in politics, and mock-egalitarian communicative norms in rigidly hierarchical organizations. As Barbara Misztal has put it, "now the 'tyranny of informality' is also an element of a new corporate culture" (2000: 63).

Such are the speculations which may be prompted by investigating language change in progress, but they have led too far away from an investigation of linguistic issues. The present book on language change in English in the course of the twentieth century started off with a quotation by Ludwig Wittgenstein, in which language was likened to a city. Its last word shall go to the great linguist Dwight Bolinger (1907–1992), who, as part of his much wider-ranging interests, also wrote on change in progress in contemporary English. He has found a striking image for the dual nature – fast and slow, abrupt and gradual – of linguistic change. To describe it, he offers a geographical metaphor of another type and takes up an example which has been discussed in this book:

> Viewed close up, language changes by fits and starts. A linguistic regu-
> larity does not suddenly dissolve and reorganize itself into some new and
> different regularity, but fights on from the outposts even after it has lost
> the citadel. The seascape of our language is dotted with islands of little
> idioms that once upon a time embraced whole kingdoms of usage, but
> have shrunk to the point where all we can do is catalog them as quaint
> exceptions. The present passive participle vanished long ago from an
> expression such as *The oats are threshing*. It disappeared only yesterday
> from *The houses are building*, and is still part of the tricky style in *Time*
> magazine. It remains with us in *The coffee is making*, thanks in part to
> automatic percolators that have assimilated this construction to other
> kinds of activity that do not require the uninterrupted attention of the
> cook: *The water is boiling, The eggs are frying, The cereal is cooking*. The
> reinterpreted regularity is "self-propelled activity," but it was not
> achieved overnight. (Bolinger 1968: 130f.)

Appendix 1 Brief survey of the corpora used for the present study

The following table is loosely based on a comparable list in Meyer (2002: 142–149), with additions and deletions as necessary. Corpora are given in alphabetical order, based on the names most commonly used in the corpus-linguistic community (which is also usually the name by which they are introduced in the present study). The list does not include digitized text databases, such as newspaper archives and electronic dictionaries, which have also been used.

Name of corpus	Size and composition	Access and reference
ARCHER (= A Representative Corpus of Historical English Registers)	1.7 million words documenting speech-based/popular and specialist/academic written registers in British and American English from 1650 to 1990	Limited access
Bank of English Corpus	415 million words of orthographically transcribed speech and writing (as of October 2002); texts are continually added	Collins-Cobuild website: http://titania.cobuild. collins.co.uk/boe_info. html
British National Corpus (BNC)	C. 100 million words of samples of varying length containing spoken (c. 10 million words) and written (c. 90 million words) British English	BNC website: http://info.ox. ac.uk/bnc/index.html
Brown Corpus	1 million words of edited written American English; divided into 2,000-word samples from various genres (e.g. press reportage, fiction, government documents)	Available on ICAME CD-ROM ICAME website: http:// nora.hd.uib. no/corpora.html
CREA (= Corpus de Referencia del Español Actual)	Online reference corpus compiled under the direction of the Real Academia Española documenting present-day Spanish usage in Spain and Latin America	Website at: http://corpus.rae. es/creanet.html
Corpus of Spoken Professional American English (CSPAE)	Approximately 2 million words taken from spoken transcripts of academic meetings and White House press conferences	Athelstan website: http://www.athel.com/ cpsa.html
F-LOB (Freiburg-Lancaster-Oslo/Bergen) Corpus	1 million words of edited written British English published in 1991; divided into 2,000-word samples in varying genres; intended to replicate the LOB Corpus	Available on ICAME CD-ROM

Table (*cont.*)

Name of corpus	Size and composition	Access and reference
Frown (= Freiburg-Brown) Corpus	1 million words of edited written American English published in 1992; divided into 2,000-word samples in varying genres; intended to replicate the Brown Corpus	Available on ICAME CD-ROM
Helsinki Corpus	Approximately 1.5 million words of Old, Middle, and Early Modern English divided into samples of varying length	Available on ICAME CD-ROM
International Corpus of English (ICE)	A range of 1 million-word corpora (600,000 words of speech, 400,000 words of writing) representing native- and official-language national varieties of English (e.g. American, British, Irish, Indian, etc.); six corpora complete so far (Great Britain, New Zealand, East Africa, India, Singapore, Philippines)	Project homepage at: http://www.ucl.ac.uk/english-usage/ice
LOB (= Lancaster-Oslo/Bergen Corpus)	1 million words of edited written British English published in 1961 and divided into 2,000-word samples; modeled after the Brown Corpus	Available on ICAME CD-ROM
London-Lund Corpus	Approximately 500,000 words of spoken British English from various genres (e.g. spontaneous dialogues, radio broadcasts); orthographic transcription with extensive prosodic marking	Available on ICAME CD-ROM
Longman Corpus of Spoken American English (LCSAE)	5 million words of orthographically transcribed everyday conversations by more than 1,000 Americans	Not publicly accessible

MICASE (= Michigan Corpus of Academic Spoken English)	C. 1.7 million words of spoken English recorded in US academic settings	Project website at: http://www.hti. umich.edu/m/micase/
OED Baseline 1700, 1800, 1900	Corpora compiled from the OED quotation base for the present study (see Appendix 2 below for procedures)	Not publicly accessible
Santa Barbara Corpus of Spoken American English (CSAE)	Samples of varying length of different kinds of spoken American English: spontaneous dialogues, monologues, speeches, radio broadcasts, etc.; "first release" (c. 70,000 words) publicly available	Project website at: http://www.linguistics. ucsb.edu/research/ sborpus/default.htm; "first release" distributed through Linguistic Data Consortium (LDC) (see http://www.ldc.upenn. edu/Catalog/ LDC2000S85.html)

Appendix 2 The OED Baseline Corpora

Creation and structure of the Baseline Corpora

The present study makes frequent reference to the three "OED Baseline" corpora which were created from the quotations contained in the 2nd (1989 [1994]) edition of the OED on CD-ROM to represent the state of the language at around 1900, 1800, and 1700 respectively. Baseline1900 includes all quotations dated between 1896 and 1905; Baseline1800, those between 1796 and 1805; and Baseline1700, those from 1696 to 1705. The quotations were retrieved in ten annual files each, and the makeup of the Baseline corpora is as described in Table A2.1.

As some quotations are assigned to more than one specific year, there may be minimal differences between the actual totals and the figures retrieved through a global search for citations from a complete ten-year period.

Table A2.1. *Composition of the OED Baseline Corpora*

Baseline1900	Number of quotations	Baseline1800	Number of quotations	Baseline1700	Number of quotations
1896	7,044	1796	6,277	1696	1,694
1897	9,328	1797	4,052	1697	6,406
1898	7,866	1798	2,988	1698	2,377
1899	7,897	1799	3,348	1699	2,164
1900	6,002	1800	4,428	1700	5,395
1901	5,834	1801	3,129	1701	1,674
1902	6,628	1802	4,278	1702	2,109
1903	5,436	1803	2,624	1703	2,811
1904	5,570	1804	2,417	1704	4,194
1905	5,021	1805	3,875	1705	2,187
Total (actual)	66,626		37,416		31,011
Total (OED)	66,619		37,415		31,011

Estimating the size of the Baseline Corpora

The main reason why it is difficult to give the exact size of a Baseline Corpus is the information on textual sources which is prefixed to each individual quotation. While it would have been possible to suppress this information automatically, this was not desirable, as it would have made the interpretation of the results more difficult or uncertain in many cases.

It is possible to estimate the size of the corpora on the basis of the average lengths of the quotations for the periods in question as given in Hoffmann (2004: 25); that is, 13 words for the period from 1500 to 1800 and 14 words for the period around 1900. Taking his values as a starting point, the size of the Baseline Corpora can be estimated at c. 933,000 words for Baseline1900, c. 486,000 words for Baseline1800, and c. 403,000 words for Baseline1700.

As in the present study results from the Baseline Corpora are systematically compared to those obtained from the four one-million-word reference corpora (Brown, LOB, Frown, F-LOB), it is useful to also consider the following correspondences. Table A2.2 compares the frequencies of the five most common words in Baseline1900 and the corpora of the "Brown family." The figures are Wordsmith counts based on the versions of the corpora distributed by ICAME, which may minimally diverge from those in the published literature.

Note that frequencies in the four "Brown family" corpora diverge but that the rank order of the five most common words is identical, which is evidence that they are indeed well-matching databases. But there is a good match also between the four corpora and the Baseline1900 Corpus. The preposition *in*, which is among the top five in Baseline, occupies rank six in the four other corpora, and *to*, rank four in the four corpora, occupies position six in Baseline.

Note that these frequencies do not allow easy extrapolation of the size of the Baseline Corpus, as the values for *the*, *of*, and *a* on the one hand, and *and*, on the other, point in incompatible directions. This may be due to the fact that these four function words tend to occur both in the source references and in the quotations. Table A2.3 therefore gives the frequencies for items which typically do not occur in source references but in quotation texts only.

Table A2.2. *The five most common words in Baseline, Brown, LOB, Frown, and F-LOB*

	Baseline	Brown	LOB	Frown	F-LOB
Rank 1	*the* 82,266	*the* 69,460	*the* 66,697	*the* 62,368	*the* 64,815
Rank 2	*of* 45,486	*of* 36,214	*of* 35,355	*of* 32,276	*of* 34,147
Rank 3	*a* 33,146	*and* 28,792	*and* 27,341	*and* 28,004	*and* 27,293
Rank 4	*in* 24,453	*to* 26,069	*to* 26,653	*to* 26,200	*to* 27,058
Rank 5	*and* 21,249	*a* 23,385	*a* 22,518	*a* 23,335	*a* 23,249

Table A2.3. *"Absolute frequencies (rank)" for selected function words in five corpora*

	Baseline	Brown	LOB	Frown	F-LOB
been	2,352 (59)	2,467 (43)	3,116 (37)	2,107 (49)	2,845 (39)
their	2,221 (61)	2,653 (40)	2,792 (41)	2,735 (37)	2,929 (38)
there	2,213 (63)	2,710 (39)	3,093 (38)	2,030 (52)	2,773 (40)
if	1,577 (98)	2,170 (50)	2,438 (45)	2,179 (47)	2,340 (44)
would	1,314 (112)	2,711 (38)	2,673 (43)	2,418 (40)	2,308 (45)

These figures again show a very good match among the four one-million-word corpora and further suggest that the textual material contained in the Baseline Corpus is somewhat less than one million words – in fact not too far from the estimate of 933,000 words arrived at on the basis of Hoffmann's (2004) calculation of average quotation lengths. (The surprisingly low figures in Baseline for *if* and *would* are possibly due to the fact that the OED's volunteer readers were biased against complex sentences with conditional clauses as illustrative examples.) In sum, Baseline1900 is thus a fairly good match for Brown, LOB, Frown, and F-LOB in size and a tolerably good match in composition.

The estimates for the other two Baseline Corpora can be considered reliable to a similar degree, so that, if due caution is exercised in interpreting the results, comparisons of results obtained in the "Brown family" and the Baseline Corpora can be expected to yield instructive results.

Appendix 3 Estimating text size in the newspaper archives and the World Wide Web

To estimate the amount of text analyzed in searches of digital newspaper archives or the Web, it is possible to extrapolate from frequencies in large corpora whose size is known. After some experimentation it was decided to extrapolate not from the frequencies of individual lexical items but from selected medium-frequency collocations which could with good reason be assumed to

- not vary across regional varieties of English,
- be diachronically stable (i.e. not involved in ongoing processes of diachronic change), and
- be relatively independent of register, topic, and textual genre.

Table A3.1 gives the frequencies for ten such diagnostic collocations in the BNC (c. 100 million words), the publicly accessible portions of the Bank of English corpus (> 200 million), and in seven annual compact discs of *The Guardian on CD-ROM*, which – since 1994 – has also included the *Observer*.

This table shows several things. First, as expected, the frequencies for the Cobuild Corpus are consistently higher than for the BNC, which proves that the ten collocations are indeed fairly good diagnostics. Second, the amount of text available on each compact disc has grown steadily over the years, and not only because from 1994 the discs have included the *Observer*. Third, and somewhat unfortunately, however, trends for individual collocations vary considerably. Thus, estimates arrived at on the basis of *deep breath* diverge from those arrived at on the basis of *heavy rain* or *coming year*. For the 1990 *Guardian*, the range of relevant estimates extrapolated from BNC frequencies would be from an unreasonably low 2.45 million words (*deep breath*) through 24 (*heavy rain*) or 27.68 (*coming year*) million to a high of 41.07 million (*biggest problem*). These fluctuations are not a problem if, as is done in the present study, the newspaper archives are consulted merely to check whether a particular form is used, and, if so, whether its discourse frequency is rising in absolute terms or in proportion to an alternative. If, however, normalized frequencies (e.g. per million words) were calculated for purposes of comparison

Table A3.1. *Frequency of selected collocations in two corpora and eight newspaper archival discs**

	BNC	Collins Cobuild	1990	1992	1994	1996	1998	2000	2002	2004
deep breath	571	768	14	26	34	56	54	64	88	85
early age	369	878	57	79	106	114	145	170	144	179
biggest problem	112	632	46	64	94	105	119	123	157	143
coming year	271	782	75	63	83	70	86	102	105	106
bad luck	266	700	56	87	107	117	142	170	188	166
heavy rain	225	628	54	103	95	76	122	137	108	117
greatly exaggerated	36	83	12	10	16	13	36	19	27	21
wildly exaggerated	10	22	4	6	11	3	8	6	11	4
badly damaged	193	461	43	57	60	64	69	87	54	83
severely damaged	94	241	27	31	22	28	27	33	49	22

*Figures refer to number of stories containing the search item in question. It is possible, though not very common, that one story contains several occurrences.

of the digital archives with each other or with other corpora, more sophisticated estimates would have to be provided, for example, by averaging extrapolations or by going straight to the discs in order to check the size of the information stored in gigabytes.

To represent the tendencies of textual growth in the newspaper archives, the annual averages were computed for the ten collocations. These are 38.8 for 1990; 54.6 for 1992; 62.8 for 1994; 64.6 for 1996; 75.4 for 1998; 91.1 for 2000; 91.3 for 2002; and 92.6 for 2004. As is shown in Figure A3.1, the inclusion of the *Observer* from 1994 does not seem to have had much of an impact. There was continuous growth in the amount of text throughout the 1990s, followed by a period of stability in the years since 2000.

Similar considerations hold for the interpretation of frequencies obtained from Web searches. Table A3.2 below compares the frequencies for the ten diagnostic collocations in the BNC with those obtained in searches of selected top-level national Web domains.

Figure A3.2 represents the frequencies obtained for *deep breath* over a period of several months, to give an idea not only of the synchronic composition of the English-language Web at any one time, but also of Web growth through time.

The figures in Table A3.2 and Figure A3.2 give a fairly good idea of the proportion of the various domains relative to each other, and they allow a very rough estimate of the amount of material looked at. Thus, the .edu and .uk domains are clearly the biggest (and roughly equal in size to each other). Next in size are the .us, .au, and .ca ones, which each seem to contain roughly a third of the material found in the two bigger ones. With regard to diachronic

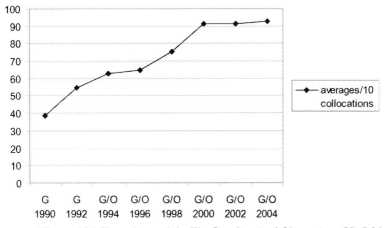

Figure A3.1 Textual growth in *The Guardian (and Observer) on CD-ROM*

Table A3.2. *Frequencies of ten collocations in the BNC and selected top-level Web domains**

	BNC	.uk	.au	.nz	.ie	.za	.edu	.us	.ca
deep breath	571	28,400	7,650	3,920	699	744	19,700	8,900	8,340
early age	369	55,300	20,300	3,690	4,180	3,850	60,800	11,900	19,300
biggest problem	112	30,600	11,300	2,930	1,850	2,950	30,300	6,400	9,940
coming year	271	95,400	28,500	7,500	12,000	5,130	151,000	32,500	39,700
bad luck	266	32,500	16,500	2,440	1,780	2,220	20,300	6,010	8,620
heavy rain	225	32,600	17,000	6,340	3,740	1,970	20,700	6,410	6,460
greatly exaggerated	36	3,480	1,520	199	304	142	5,370	444	1,710
wildly exaggerated	10	541	167	22	20	20	408	34	174
badly damaged	193	18,100	5,020	699	1,600	711	6,870	1,690	2,840
severely damaged	94	11,100	4,840	570	643	703	12,300	4,250	3,380

*Accessed 11 March 2004

tendencies, the comparison between Figure A3.2 (documenting late 2002/early 2003) and Table A3.2 (March 2004) reveals spectacular growth – for example, from c. 15,000 and 16,000 instances of *deep breath* in .uk and .edu material to 28,400 and 19,700 a year later. What is mysterious are some temporary drops in frequency apparent from the longitudinal study represented in Figure A3.2, especially in the .uk and .ca domains.

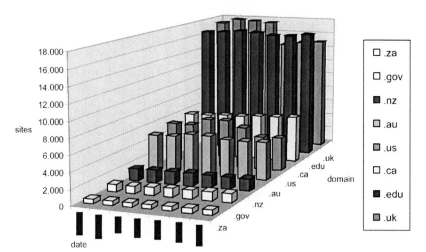

Figure A3.2 *Deep breath* in top-level Web domains, December 2002 to March
        2003

The preceding estimates were concerned with proportions of various Web
domains to one another. It is probably more risky to estimate absolute amounts
of text by extrapolation from collocation frequencies in the BNC. Using this
method, the 7,650 instances of *deep breath* in the Australian (.au) Web material
would indicate a size of around 1.34 billion words. Performing the same
calculation on *early age*, on the other hand, we would arrive at the rather
different estimate of 5.5 billion words. In view of such fluctuation, estimates
should never be based on individual collocations but on aggregate frequencies,
if undertaken at all.

Appendix 4 A quarterly update of the OED Online (New Edition) – 13 March 2003: *Motswana* to *mussy*

13 March 2003 saw the publication of the range of entries *Motswana–mussy* in the New Edition. In addition to revised versions of Second Edition entries, this range contains the following completely new entries:

Motswana, *n.* and *a.*

Mott, *n.*

motty, *n.*[2]

motu, *n.*[1]

motus peculiaris, *n.*

motyhole, *n.*

motza, *n.*

mouclade, *n.*

mouffle, *n.*

moufful, *n.*

mould-breaking, *a.*

moulding board, *n.*[2]

mouldly, *a.*

mouldy chops, *n.*

mouli-légumes, *n.*

moulin à legumes, *n.*

moundsman, *n.*

mountain, *v.*

mountain bike, *n.*

mountain bike, *v.*

mountain biker, *n.*

mountain biking, *n.*

Mountainboard, *n.*

mountain lark, *n.*

mountain oak, *n.*

mountainscape, *n.*

Mountains of the Moon, *n.*

mountain wave, *n.*

mountain wind, *n.*

mountainy man, *n.*

mountebankwise, *n.*

Mount of Pity, *n.*

Mount Sinai manna, *n.*

mourner's bench, *n.*

mournful-like, *a.* (and *adv.*)

mourning black, *n.*

mours, *n.*

Mourvedre, *n.*

mouseburger, *n.*

mouth bow, *n.*

mouthfeel, *n.*

mouth-grenade, *n.*

mouth-organist, *n.*

movable festival, *n.*

move-up, *a.*

movida, *n.*

moving cluster, *n.*

mow, *v.*[5]

mowburning, *n.*

MOX, *n.*

Mozarabical, *a.*

Mozarabite, *n.*

Mozart, *n.*

MP3, *n.*

MPEG, *n.*

mpingo, *n.*

Mpongwe, *a.* and *n.*

Msgr., *n.*

Mt, *n.*

M-theory, *n.*

m'tutor, *n.*

Mu, *n.*[2]

mu, *n.*[3] and *int.*

mu, *n.*[4]

mu, *n.*[5]

muchee, *a.* (and *adv.*)

muci-, *comb. form*

mucigel, *n.*

mucigenic, *a.*

mucilage, *v.*

muckamuck, *v.*

Muckerism, *n.*[1]

mucket, *n.*

muckety-muck, *n.*

muckite, *n.*[1]

muckite, *n.*[2]

mucko-chummo, *a.* (and *adv.*)

mucoidy, *n.*

mucolipid, *n.*

mucolipidosis, *n.*

muconate, *n.*

muconic, *a.*

mucoperichondrial, *a.*

mucoperichondrium, *n.*

mucoperiosteal, *a.*

mucoperiostitis, *n.*

mucopolysaccharidosis, *n.*

mucormycotic, *a.*

mucosally, *adv.*

mucositis, *n.*

mucous acid, *n.*

MUD, *n.*[3]

mudball, *n.*

mudbug, *n.*

mudbugging, *n.*

mud-cart, *n.*

MUDder, *n.*[2]

MUDding, *n.*[2]

muddle-pated, *a.*

mudge, *n.*[1]

mudge, *n.*[2]

Mudgee, *n.*

mudguts, *n.*

mudhif, *n.*

Mudian, *n.* and *a.*

mud kicker, *n.*

mud-like, *a.*

mud-nester, *n.*

mud pike, *n.*[1]

mudscape, *n.*

mud-slogger, *n.*

mud sunfish, *n.*

Mudville, *n.*

mud-wrestle, *n.*

mud-wrestle, *v.*

mud-wrestler, *n.*

mud-wrestling, *n.*

muffuletta, *n.*

muffy, *n.*

mugged, *a.*[2]

Muggle, *n.*[4]

muggy, *a.*[2]

mughlai, *a.* (and *n.*)

mugilid, *n.* and *a.*

muhr ashrafi, *n.*

muid, *n.*[2]

Muisca, *n.* and *a.*

mujerado, *n.*

Mukhabarat, *n.*

mukhiya, *n.*

mulai, *n.*

mulched, *a.*

mulcher, *n.*

mule, *v.*

mules, *v.*

muley, *n.*[2]

mulgara, *n.*

mulgronnick, *n.*

mulierast, *n.*

mulled, *a.*[3]

Müller, *n.*[5]

muller, *v.*[1]

muller, $v.^4$
mullered, *a.*
Müllerian, $a.^2$
Muller's ratchet, *n.*
Müller-Thurgau, *n.*
mullet, $n.^8$
mullet, $n.^9$
mullocker, *n.*
Mullumbimby, *n.*
Mulready, *n.*
multi, $n.^5$
multi, $n.^6$
multi, $n.^7$
multi, $n.^8$
multi-address, *a.*
multi-addressing, *n.*
multi-angle, *a.*
multi-angled, *a.*
multibarrel, *n.* and *a.*
multibit, $a.^1$
multibit, $a.^2$
multibuy, *n.* and *a.*
multicalibre, *a.* and *n.*
multicast, *a.* and *n.*
multicast, *v.*
multicasting, *n.*
multicell, *a.*
multicentrically, *adv.*
multi-channelled, *a.*
multi-choke, *n.* and *a.*
multicoat, *v.*
multi-coat, *a.*
multi-coated, *a.*
multi-coating, *n.*
multicopy, *n.* and *a.*
multicopying, *n.*
multicult, *n.* and *a.*
multiculti, *a.* and *n.*
multiculturalist, *n.* and *a.*
multiculturism, *n.*
multicursal, *a.*
multi-cylindered, *a.*
multidrug, *a.*
multiexposure, *n.* and *a.*

multiflex, *a.*
multifocally, *adv.*
multifork, *a.*
multiforked, *a.*
multiformly, *adv.*
multifractal, *a.* and *n.*
multi-fuelled, *a.*
multifunctionality, *n.*
multigene, *n.* and *a.*
multigenic, *a.*
multigravid, *a.*
multi-gym, *n.*
multihole, *a.*
multilamellated, *a.*
multilayeredness, *n.*
multilayering, *n.*
multiline, *a.* and *n.*
multilocularity, *n.*
multi-male, *a.*
multi-member, *a.*
multi-membered, *a.*
multi-mike, *a.* and *n.*
multimiked, *a.*
multimiking, *n.*
multimineral, *a.* and *n.*
multimodally, *adv.*
multi-mode, *a.* and *n.*
multimorph, *n.* and *a.*
multinuclearity, *n.*
multipack, *n.*
multipass, *a.*
multipathing, *n.*
multi-pattern, *a.*
multipedal, *a.*
multiphonic, *a.*
multiphonics, *n.*
multiplatform, *a.*
multi-play, *a.*
multiplayer, *a.* and *n.*
multiplicate, *v.*
multiplicated, $a.^2$
multiplicating, *n.*
multiport, *n.* and $a.^2$
multi-port, $a.^1$

multipotency, *n.*
multipotentiality, *n.*
multiprogrammability, *n.*
multiprogrammable, *a.*
multiregional, *a.*
multiregionalism, *n.*
multiregionalist, *n.*
multiring, *a.*
multiroom, *a.*
multiroomed, *a.*
multiserver, *a.*
multiservice, *a.*
multisession, *a.*
multi-skill, *a.*
multi-skilled, *a.*
multi-skilling, *n.*
multi-speciality, *a.*
multi-specialty, *a.*
multistandard, *a.*
multistate, *a.*
multi-station, *a.*
multistrand, *a.* and *n.*
multistratal, *a.*
multistratified, *a.*
Multisync, *n.* and *a.*
multitask, *v.*
multitasker, *n.*
multithread, *v.*
multithreading, *n.*
multitone, *a.*
multitrack, *v.*
multitracked, *a.*
multitracker, *n.*
multitracking, *n.*
multi-utility, *a.* and *n.*
multivalver, *n.*
multivariable, *a.*
multivesicular, *a.*
multivocality, *n.*
multiwell, *a.*
multiwindow, *a.*
multiwindowed, *a.*
multi-year, *a.*
Multnomah, *n.*

multured, *a.*
mum and dad, *a.*
mumbo-jumbery, *n.*
mum-in-law, *n.*
mummer, *v.*[1]
mummers' play, *n.*
mumpery, *n.*
mumsiness, *n.*
munchy, *a.*
mundan, *n.*
Mundari, *n.* and *a.*
mundbreach, *n.*
mundbriche, *n.*
mundowie, *n.*
mundu, *n.*
Mundugumor, *n.* and *a.*
mu-neutrino, *n.*
mung, *v.*
munge, $v.^2$
munged, *a.*
mungite, *n.*
mungy, $a.^2$
muni, *a.*
munificence, $n.^2$
munite, *a.*
munjon, *n.*
Munro-bagger, *n.*
Munro-bagging, *n.*
Munroist, *n.*
Munsee, *n.* and *a.*
muntry, *n.*
muntu, *n.*
Muong, *n.* and *a.*
muonless, *a.*
muraenid, *n.* and *a.*
murder, $n.^2$
murderabilia, *n.*
murderation, *n.* (and *int.*)
murderball, *n.*
Murderers' Row, *n.*
murdering bird, *n.*
murdering pie, *n.*
murder-mongering, *a.*
murdersome, *a.*

Murdochian, $a.^1$
Murdochian, $a.^2$
murdrum, $n.$
murgh, $n.$
murgi, $n.$
muricacean, $a.$ and $n.$
muricidal, $a.$
muricide, $n.^1$
muricide, $n.^2$
murid, $a.$ and $n.^2$
muriel, $n.$
muriqui, $n.$
Murji'ah, $n.$
Murji'ite, $n.$ and $a.$
murken, $v.$
murlonga, $n.$
murmell, $v.$
Murmi, $n.$ and $a.$
Murngin, $n.$ and $a.$
Muromachi, $n.$
Murphy, $n.^3$
Murraya, $n.$
murri, $n.$
murry, $adv.$ (and $a.$)
murshid, $n.$
muru, $v.$
murunga, $n.$
Mus, $n.^2$
Musaf, $n.$
Mus. Bac., $n.$
Musca, $n.$
muscadel, $n.$
Muscadelle, $n.$
muscicapid, $n.$ and $a.$
muscimol, $n.$
muscle-box, $n.$
muscle boy, $n.$
muscledom, $n.$
musclehead, $n.$
muscoid, $a.^2$ and $n.^2$
muscone, $n.$
muscovitic, $a.$
musculo-glandular, $a.$
musculus, $n.$

Mus. Doc., $n.$
muse, $n.^5$
museful, $a.^1$
muselar, $n.$
museum, $v.$
museum-going, $n.$
museum-going, $a.$
museumification, $n.$
museumization, $n.$
museumize, $v.$
museumobile, $n.$
mush, $n.^6$
mush, $v.^5$
mushaira, $n.$
musher, $n.^1$
mushin, $n.$
mushmouth, $n.$ and $a.$
mushmouthed, $a.$
music drama, $n.$
music-dramatist, $n.$
musicking, $n.$
music theatre, $n.$
music volute, $n.$
musie, $n.$
Muskego, $n.$
muskimoot, $n.$
Muslimah, $n.$
Muslimization, $n.$
Muslimness, $n.$
muso, $n.$
musquashing, $n.$
Musqueam, $n.$ and $a.$
mussascus, $n.$
musseet, $n.$
mussing, $n.$
Mussorgskian, $a.$

In addition to these completely new entries, a number of new subordinate entries were added to existing entries. These included:
(Under **mottled**, $a.$)
  mottled maple
  mottled umber

(Under **motto**, *n.*)
  motto candy
(Under **moulting**, *n.*)
  moulting hormone
(Under **mound-building**, *a.*)
  mound-building bird
(Under **mount**, *n.*[1])
  mount foot
(Under **mountain**, *n.* and *a.*)
  mountain boy
  mountain breeze
  mountain Malaga
  mountain railroad
  Mountain State
  mountain bison
  mountain chicken
  mountain fowl
  mountain gazelle
  mountain gorilla
  mountain nyala
  mountain pygmy possum
  mountain reedbuck
  mountain shrimp
  mountain vole
  mountain zebra
  mountain-cedar
  mountain crowder
  mountain currant
  mountain heather
  mountain maize
  mountain male fern
  mountain sage
  mountain spignel
(Under **Mountainboard**, *n.*)
  mountainboarder
  mountainboarding
(Under **mountain pine**, *n.*)
  mountain pine beetle
(Under **mountebank**, *n.*)
  mountebank eagle
(Under **mounting**, *n.*)
  mounting paper
  mounting post
(Under **mourner**, *n.*[1])

mourner's line
mourner's seat
(Under **mourning**, *n.*[1])
  mourning ground
  mourning head
  mourning string
  mourning sword
(Under **mourning**, *a.*)
  mourning granite
  mourning ground warbler
  mourning iris
  mourning-vein
(Under **mouse**, *n.*)
  mouse-birth
  mouse's heart
  mouse opossum
  mouse spider
  mouse button
  mouse click
  mouse-click
  mousemat
  mouse pad
  mouse port
  mouse potato
(Under **mouse-eared**, *a.*)
  mouse-eared cress
  mouse-eared scorpion grass
(Under **mousehole**, *v.*)
  mouseholing
(Under **mousetrap**, *n.*)
  mousetrap word
(Under **mouseweb**, *n.*)
  mousewebbed
(Under **moustache**, *n.*)
  Moustache Pete
(Under **moustached**, *a.*)
  moustached bat
(Under **mouth**, *n.*)
  mouth-blown
  mouth brooder
  mouth hook
(Under **mouth-watering**, *a.*)
  mouth-wateringly
(Under **movable**, *a.* and *n.*)

movable doh
movable sign
(Under **movement**, *n.*)
movement detector
(Under **movie**, *n.*)
movie brat
movie mogul
(Under **moving**, *a.*)
moving image
moving-magnet
moving part
moving sidewalk
moving stairway
moving walkway
(Under **mowdie**, *n.*)
mowdie-hill
mowdie hillock
mowdie-man
(Under **mower**, *n.*[1])
mower-conditioner
(Under **Mr**, *n.*)
Mr Cool
Mr Nice Guy
Mr Universe
(Under **mucilage**, *n.*)
mucilage duct
(Under **mucin**, *n.*)
mucin cell
mucin-like
(Under **mucinous**, *a.*)
mucinous degeneration
(Under **muck**, *n.*[1])
muck-drag
muck-shifting
muck-silver
muck stick
(Under **mucked**, *a.*)
mucked-out
(Under **mucker**, *n.*[1])
mucker pose
mucker-up
(Under **mucking**, *n.*)
mucking-in
(Under **muck-up**, *n.*)

muck-up day
(Under **mucky**, *a.*)
mucky pup
(Under **muco-**, *comb. form*)
mucoepidermoid
mucogingival
mucosubstance
mucothermal
mucothermic
(Under **mucocutaneous**, *a.*)
mucocutaneous lymph node
    syndrome
(Under **muconic**, *a.*)
muconic acid
(Under **mucous**, *a.*)
mucous colitis
(Under **mud**, *n.*[1])
mud horse
mud map
mud-masked
mud-pipes
mud pit
mud pot
mud pup
mud-scraper
mud tank
mud wagon
mud-eye
mud goose
mud oyster
mudprawn
mud shark
mud shrimp
mud snake
(Under **muesli**, *n.*)
muesli-belt malnutrition
(Under **muff**, *n.*[1])
muff-dive
muff-diving
(Under **mug**, *n.*[1])
mug-hunting
mug tree
(Under **mug**, *n.*[6] and *a.*[2])
mug lair

(Under **mukluk**, *n.*)
  mukluk telegraph
  mukluk wireless
(Under **mulberry**, *n.* and *a.*)
  mulberry blight
(Under **mule**, *n.*[1])
  mule-picket
(Under **mulga**, *n.*)
  mulga snake
(Under **mulierast**, *n.*)
  mulierastic
(Under **mullock**, *n.*)
  mullock reef
(Under **multi-**, *comb. form*)
  multibacillary
  multicistronic
  multicystic
  multinodular
  multinucleolate
  multipennate
  multiporous
  multiresistant
  multi-stemmed
  multiterminal
  multitrunked
  multi-armed
  multicausal
  multi-denominational
  multi-figured
  multiflowered
  multijointed
  multi-orgasmic
  multipeaked
  multipronged
  multireligious
  multisectoral
  multisensory
  multitalented
  multi-timbral
  multibus
  multi-tester
  multi-activity
  multi-album
  multi-axis

multibeam
multibody
multicandidate
multichain
multi-chip
multi-choice
multichord
multi-city
multi-column
multiconductor
multi-country
multi-county
multi-course
multicrore
multi-currency
multi-daylight
multi-destination
multi-diameter
multi-digit
multi-disc
multi-drop
multielectron
multienzyme
multi-field
multifile
multi-frequency
multigrain
multihit
multilanguage
multi-length
multilocus
multimachine
multimegabit
multimegawatt
multi-metal
multi-microphone
multi-mirror
multi-mission
multimovement
multi-parameter
multipartisan
multiperiod
multiphoton
multi-pin

multiplate
multi-platinum
multiproblem
multi-product
multiprotocol
multi-range
multi-row
multi-site
multispecies
multi-spindle
multisport
multistep
multi-strike
multisubunit
multisystem
multi-ton
multi-turn
multivendor
multiwire
(Under **multifaceted**, *a.*)
  multifacetedness
(Under **multiflex**, *a.*)
  multiflex offense
(Under **multigene**, *n.* and *a.*)
  multigene family
(Under **multi-mode**, *a.* and *n.*)
  multimode fibre
(Under **multiple**, *n.* and *a.*)
  multiple superparticular
  multiple-drug
  multiple-mirror
  multiple bond
  multiple chemical
    sensitivity
  multiple gene
  multiple integral
  multiple listing
  multiple orgasm
  multiple point
  multiple scattering
  multiple tangent
(Under **multiplying**, *n.*)
  multiplying machine
(Under **multiplying**, *a.*)

multiplying eye
multiplying punch
(Under **multi-purpose**, *a.*)
  multi-purpose vehicle
(Under **multispectral**, *a.*)
  multispectral scanner
(Under **multistranded**, *a.*)
  multistrandedness
(Under **multi-user**, *a.*)
  multi-user dungeon
(Under **multi-year**, *a.*)
  multi-year ice
(Under **multure**, *n.*)
  multure-ward
(Under **multure**, *v.*)
  multuring
(Under **mumbling**, *a.*)
  mumbling word
(Under **mummy**, *n.*^{2})
  mummy track
(Under **mumps**, *n.*^{2})
  mumps virus
(Under **mund**, *n.*)
  mundbyrd
(Under **municipal**, *a.* and *n.*)
  municipal corporation
  municipal socialism
(Under **muon**, *n.*)
  muon neutrino
(Under **murder**, *n.*^{1} and *int.*)
  murder board
  murder house
  Murder, Inc.
  Murder, Incorporated
  murder two
(Under **mure**, *a.*^{1})
  mure-mouthed
(Under **murexide**, *n.*)
  murexide colour reaction
  murexide test
(Under **murgeon**, *v.*)
  murgeoning
(Under **murine**, *a.* and *n.*)
  murine opossum

(Under **Murphy**, *n.*²)
Murphy's face
(Under **muscle**, *n.*)
muscle banner
muscle dysmorphia
muscle magazine
muscle memory
muscle pull
muscle scar
muscle shirt
muscle toning
(Under **muscular**, *a.*)
muscular artery
(Under **museum**, *n.*)
museum beetle
(Under **mushroom**, *n.* and *a.*)
mushroom body
mushroom cap
mushroom compost
mushroom growing
mushroom management
mushroom sinker
mushroom worker's lung
(Under **mushy**, *a.*)
mushy peas
(Under **music**, *n.* and *a.*)
music appreciation
music cassette
music director
music festival
music historian
music-historical
music history
music-play
music power
music store
music theory
music therapist
music therapy
music video
(Under **music**, *v.*)
musicked
(Under **musical**, *a.*)
musical beds

musical bow
musical ear
musical sand
musical statues
musical theorist
musical theory
(Under **musk**, *n.*)
musk clover
musk orchid
musk stork's-bill
(Under **mussel**, *n.*)
mussel bake
mussel marble

Out-of-sequence new entries

13 March 2003 also saw the publication of the following new entries from across the alphabet:
apotemnophilia, *n.*
arsehole, *n.*
arseholed, *a.*
arse-lick, *v.*
arse-licker, *n.*
ass-backward, *adv.* and *a.*
ass-backwards, *adv.* and *a.*
bagsy, *v.*
bass-ackward, *a.*
bass-ackwards, *adv.* and *a.*
Batswana, *n.* and *a.*
bed-space, *n.*
bigorexia, *n.*
bigorexic, *a.* and *n.*
blog, *n.*
blog, *v.*
blogger, *n.*
blogging, *n.*
bruschetta, *n.*
chronon, *n.*
Claddagh, *n.*
clapometer, *n.*
clear water, *n.*
clientelism, *n.*
clientelistic, *a.*

clientism, *n.*
clocked, *a.*[2]
clocker, *n.*[3]
clocking, *n.*[2]
dead-leg, *v.*
dead leg, *n.*
deaf-blind, *a.* and *n.*
deaf-blindness, *a.* and *n.*
disappeared, *a.* and *n.*
dischuffed, *a.*
disintermediate, *v.*
disintermediated, *a.*
disintermediator, *n.*
dolee, *n.*
doley, *n.*
Down, *n.*[4]
dragon boat, *n.*
dragon lady, *n.*
Dungeons and Dragons, *n.*
dysmorphia, *n.*
dysmorphic, *a.*
dysmorphism, *n.*
dysmorphophobia, *n.*
dysmorphophobic, *a.* and *n.*
early doors, *n.* and *adv.*
emotional intelligence, *n.*
extranet, *n.*
First World, *n.* and *a.*
First Worlder, *n.*
flat-pack, *n.* and *a.*
fly-through, *n.* and *a.*
Fortean, *a.* and *n.*
Forteana, *n.*
frittata, *n.*
FX, *n.*
intranet, *n.*
leaderless resistance, *n.*
lone parent, *n.* and *a.*
lookism, *n.*
lookist, *a.* and *n.*
novela, *n.*
pear-shaped, *a.*
Polle syndrome, *n.*
rellie, *n.*

rello, *n.*
rent-a-quote, *a.* and *n.*
reoffender, *n.*
rugger bugger, *n.*
rumpo, *n.*
rumpy-pumpy, *n.*
schemie, *n.*
screenager, *n.*
SFX, *n.*[1]
SFX, *n.*[2]
sizeism, *n.*
sizeist, *a.* and *n.*
slaphead, *n.*
slap-headed, *a.*
spread bet, *n.*
spread betting, *n.*
stude, *n.*
studenty, *a.*
Sturgeon's Law, *n.*
sussed, *a.*
taqueria, *n.*
telenovela, *n.*
tobaccy, *n.*
transgender, *a.* and *n.*
transgendered, *a.* and *n.*
transgenderism, *n.*
transgenderist, *n.*
twelve-step, *v.*
twelve step, *n.*
twelve-stepper, *n.*
unplugged, *a.*
UNSCOM, *n.*
weblog, *n.*
weblogger, *n.*
weblogging, *n.*

In addition to these completely
new entries, the following
out-of-sequence subordinate
entries were added:
(Under **agenda**, *n.*)
  Agenda 21
(Under **air**, *n.*[1])
  air rage

(Under **alpha**, *n.*)
alpha geek
alpha male
(Under **applause**, *n.*)
applause meter
(Under **arc**, *n.*)
story arc
(Under **arse**, *n.*)
arse about face
my arse!
– my arse
to – one's arse off
to work (etc.) one's arse off
to – the arse off someone
arse bandit
(Under **as**, *adv.* [*conj.*, and *rel. pron.*])
as if!
(Under **B**)
BDD
(Under **beacon**, *n.*)
beacon school
(Under **bed**, *n.*)
bed of nails
to get into bed with
to be in bed with
bed-blocker
bed-blocking
bed check
bed-night
bedspring
bed tax
bed tea
bed wagon
(Under **body**, *n.*)
body dysmorphic disorder
(Under **C**)
CTC
(Under **chronic**, *a.*)
chronic factitious disorder
chronic factitious disorder with
  physical symptoms
(Under **church**, *n.*)
church planting
(Under **city**, *n.*)

city technology college
(Under **clean**, *a.*)
clean room
(Under **client**, *n.*)
client application
client program
client-server
(Under **club**, *n.*)
join the club
club kid
(Under **D**)
D and D
(Under **dead**, *a.* [*n.*[1], *adv.*])
dead cat bounce
to be dead meat
(Under **digital**, *a.* and *n.*)
digital divide
(Under **direct**, *a.* and *adv.*)
direct marketing
direct response
(Under **disco**, *n.*[1])
disco biscuit
(Under **dry**, *a.* [*adv.*])
dry-fried
dry-fry
dry-frying
dry hump
dry-hump
dry-humping
(Under **E**)
EQ
(Under **early**, *a.* and *n.*)
early adopter
to take an early bath
to send for an early bath
early bath
to take an early shower
to give a person an early shower
early shower
(Under **earth**, *n.*[1])
Earth Charter
(Under **educational**, *a.*)
educational age
educational quotient

(Under **emotional**, *a.*)
emotional quotient
(Under **encephalization**, *n.*)
encephalization quotient
(Under **fabricate**, *v.*)
fabricated or induced illness
fabricated or induced
illness in children by carers
(Under **fat**, *a.* and *n.*²)
fat client
fat camp
(Under **feel**, *n.*)
to get (also have, etc.) a feel for
(Under **floor**, *n.*¹)
floor-filler
(Under **flying**, *ppl. a.*)
flying bishop
(Under **food**, *n.*)
food coma
food desert
food mile
(Under **fork**, *n.*)
replication fork
(Under **friendship**, *n.*)
friendship bracelet
(Under **fuel**, *n.*)
fuel poverty
(Under **Gaelic**, *a.* and *n.*)
Gaelic football
(Under **granary**, *n.*)
granary bread
(Under **grandfather**, *n.*)
grandfather rights
(Under **granny**, *n.*)
granny dumping
granny-sit
granny-sitter
granny-sitting
(Under **hero**, *n.*)
hero-to-zero
to go (etc.) from hero to zero
(Under **history**, *n.*)
you're (also I'm, we're, etc.)
history

the rest is history
(Under **key**, *n.*¹)
to lock (a thing) up and throw away
the key
to (lock a person up and) throw
away the key
(lock-them-up-and-)throw-away-
the-key
(Under **L**)
LTP
(Under **long-term**, *a.*)
long-term potentiation
(Under **people**, *n.*)
people carrier
(Under **physical**, *a.*)
physical theatre
(Under **piece**, *n.*)
piece of piss
(Under **recreational**, *a.*)
recreational drug
(Under **reverse**, *a.* and *adv.*)
reverse anorexia
reverse anorexia nervosa
reverse mutation
(Under **S**)
SIG
SME
SPAD
(Under **sex**, *n.*)
sex and shopping
sex industry
sex tour
sex tourism
sex tourist
sex toy
sex work
sex worker
(Under **sexual**, *a.*)
sexual harassment
(Under **slapper**, *n.*¹)
old slapper
(Under **special**, *a.*, *adv.*, and *n.*)
special education
special school

special interest group
(Under **supply**, *n.*)
supply chain
(Under **tartan**, *n.*[1])
tartan tax
(Under **thin**, *a.* [*n.*] and *adv.*)
thin client
(Under **third**, *a.* [*adv.*, *n.*])
third rail
third wave
(Under **through-**, *comb. form*)
throughcare
throughfall
(Under **toast**, *n.*[1])
you're (also I'm, we're, etc.) toast
(Under **wacky**, *a.*)
wacky baccy
wacky tobaccy
wacky weed
(Under **zero**, *n.*)
to go (etc.) from zero to hero
zero-to-hero

Finally, new meanings were added to
the following entries:
alpha, *n.*
arse, *n.*

bald-head, *n.*
bounce, *v.*
clock, *v.*[1]
convergence, *n.*
curvy, *a.*
direct, *a.* and *adv.*
disappear, *v.*
disappearance, *n.*
draw, *n.*
effect, *n.*
factitious, *a.*
forever, *adv.*
graphic, *a.* and *n.*
lone, *a.*
raving, *n.*[1]
relax, *v.*
relaxed, *ppl. a.*
relaxer, *n.*
relaxing, *vbl. n.*
scag, *n.*
scheme, *n.*[1]
shark, *n.*[1]
shark, *v.*[1]
sharking, *vbl. n.*[1]
special, *a.*, *adv.*, and *n.*
walker, *n.*[1]
zap, *v.*

References

Aarts, Flor, and Bas Aarts. 2002. "Relative *whom*: 'a mischief-maker.'" In Andreas Fischer, Gunnel Tottie, and Hans-Martin Lehmann, eds. *Text types and corpora*. Tübingen: Narr. 123–130.

Aitchison, Jean. 1991. *Language change: progress or decay?* 2nd edition. Cambridge: Cambridge University Press.

2003. "From Armageddon to war: the vocabulary of terrorism." In Jean Aitchison and Diana M. Lewis, eds. *New media language*. London: Routledge. 193–203.

Algeo, John. 1988. "British and American grammatical differences." *International Journal of Lexicography* 1: 1–31.

ed. 1991. *Fifty years among the new words: a dictionary of neologisms, 1941–1991.* Cambridge: Cambridge University Press.

1998. "Vocabulary." In Suzanne Romaine, ed. *The Cambridge history of the English language*, vol. IV, *1776–1997*. Cambridge: Cambridge University Press. 57–91.

Amis, Kingsley. 1997. *The King's English: a guide to modern usage*. London: Harper-Collins.

Ammon, Ulrich. 1998a. *Ist Deutsch noch internationale Wissenschaftssprache? Englisch auch für die Lehre an den deutschsprachigen Hochschulen*. Berlin: de Gruyter.

ed. 1998b. *Variationslinguistik = Linguistics of variation = La linguistique variationelle*. Tübingen: Niemeyer.

Arnaud, René. 1983. "On the progress of the progressive in the private correspondence of famous British people (1800–1880)." In Sven Jacobson, ed. *Papers from the Second Scandinavian Symposium on Syntactic Variation*. Stockholm: Almqvist & Wiksell. 83–91.

Ayto, John. 1999. *Twentieth-century words*. Oxford: Oxford University Press.

Baayen, R. Harald, and Antoinette Renouf. 1996. "Chronicling *The Times*: productive lexical innovations in an English newspaper." *Language* 72: 69–96.

Bailey, Richard W. 1996. *Nineteenth century English*. Ann Arbor, MI: University of Michigan Press.

Barber, Charles. 1964. *Linguistic change in present-day English*. London and Edinburgh: Oliver and Boyd.

Barnhart, Robert K., Sol Steinmetz, and Clarence L. Barnhart. 1990. *Third Barnhart dictionary of new English*. New York: Wilson.

Baron, Naomi S. 2003. "Why email looks like speech: proofreading, pedagogy and public face." In Jean Aitchison and Diana M. Lewis, eds. *New media language*. London: Routledge. 85–94.

Barry, John A. 1991. *Technobabble*. Cambridge, MA: MIT Press.

Bauer, Laurie. 1994. *Watching English change: an introduction to the study of linguistic change in standard Englishes in the twentieth century*. London: Longman.

2002. "Inferring variation and change from public corpora." In Jack Chambers, Peter Trudgill, and Natalie Schilling-Estes, eds. *The handbook of language variation and change*. Oxford: Blackwell. 97–111.

Bell, Alan. 1988. "The British base and the American connection in New Zealand media English." *American Speech* 63: 326–344.

Berg, Thomas. 1999. "Stress variation in British and American English." *World Englishes* 18: 123–143.

Berglund, Ylva. 2000. "*Gonna* and *going to* in the spoken component of the British National Corpus." In Christian Mair and Marianne Hundt, eds. *Corpus linguistics and linguistic theory*. Amsterdam: Rodopi. 35–49.

Biber, Douglas. 1988. *Variation across speech and writing*. Cambridge: Cambridge University Press.

2003. "Compressed noun-phrase structures in newspaper discourse: the competing demands of popularization vs. economy." In Jean Aitchison and Diana M. Lewis, eds. *New media language*. London: Routledge. 169–181.

Biber, Douglas, and Edward Finegan. 1989. "Drift and evolution of English style: a history of three genres." *Language* 65: 487–517.

Biber, Douglas, Susan Conrad, and Randi Reppen. 1998. *Corpus linguistics: investigating language structure and use*. Cambridge: Cambridge University Press.

Biber, Douglas, Edward Finegan, and Dwight Atkinson. 1993. "ARCHER and its challenges: compiling and exploring a representative corpus of historical English registers." In Udo Fries, Gunnel Tottie, and Peter Schneider, eds. *Creating and using language corpora*. Amsterdam: Rodopi. 1–13.

Biber, Douglas, Stig Johansson, Geoffrey Leech, Susan Conrad, and Edward Finegan. 1999. *The Longman grammar of spoken and written English*. London: Longman.

Bloomfield, Leonard. 1933. *Language*. New York: Holt, Rinehart & Winston.

Bodine, Ann. 1975. "Androcentrism in prescriptive grammar: singular 'they', sex-indefinite 'he', and 'he or she'." *Language in Society* 4: 129–146.

Bolinger, Dwight. 1968. *Aspects of language*. New York: Harcourt Brace.

1980. *Language: the loaded weapon*. London: Longman.

Bonfiglio, Thomas Paul. 2002. *Race and the rise of standard American*. Berlin: Mouton de Gruyter.

Brinton, Laurel. 1988. *The development of English aspectual systems: aspectualizers and postverbal particles*. Cambridge: Cambridge University Press.

Burchfield, Robert. 1989. *Unlocking the English language*. London: Faber & Faber.

rev. 1996. *The new Fowler's modern English usage*. First edited by Henry Watson Fowler. Revised edition. Oxford: Clarendon Press.

Bynon, Theodora. 1977. *Historical linguistics*. Cambridge: Cambridge University Press.

Carver, Craig M. 1987. *American regional dialects: a word geography*. Ann Arbor, MI: University of Michigan Press.

Chafe, Wallace. 1982. *Integration and involvement in speaking, writing, and oral literature.* Norwood, NJ: Ablex.

Claudius, R. Howard. 1925/1926. "Different – to, from, or than?" *American Speech* 1: 446.

Coates, Jennifer. 1983. *The semantics of the modal auxiliaries.* London: Croom Helm.

Compes, Isabel, Silvia Kutscher, and Carmen Rudorf. 1993. *Pfade der Grammatikalisierung: ein systematischer Überblick.* Working paper 17. Köln: Institut für Sprachwissenschaft der Universität.

Comrie, Bernard. 1976. *Aspect.* Cambridge: Cambridge University Press.

Crystal, David. 2001. *Language and the Internet.* Cambridge: Cambridge University Press.

Danchev, Andrei, and Merja Kytö. 1994. "The construction *be going to* + infinitive in Early Modern English." In Dieter Kastovsky, ed. *Studies in Early Modern English.* Berlin: Mouton de Gruyter. 59–77.

2001. "The *go*-futures in English and French viewed as an areal feature." *NOWELE: Studies in North-Western European Language Evolution* 40: 29–60.

Dekeyser, Xavier. 1975. *Number and case relations in 19th century British English: a comparative study of grammar and usage.* Antwerp: De Nederlandsche Boekhandel.

Denison, David. 1998. "Syntax." In Suzanne Romaine, ed. *The Cambridge history of the English language*, vol. IV, *1776–1997.* Cambridge: Cambridge University Press. 92–329.

Dennis, Leah. 1940. "The progressive tense: frequency of its use in English." *Publications of the Modern Language Association of America* 55: 855–865.

Depraetere, Ilse. 2003. "On verbal concord with collective nouns in British English." *English Language and Linguistics* 7: 1–43.

Depraetere, Ilse, and An Verhulst. Forthcoming. "*Must* and *have to* in ICE-GB; a survey of its meanings."

Dorsey, Brian. 2000. *Spirituality, sensuality, literality: blues, jazz, and rap as music and poetry.* Wien: Braumüller.

Eagleson, Robert D. 1989. "Popular and professional attitudes to prestige dialects." In Peter Collins and David Blair, eds. *Australian English: the language of a new society.* St. Lucia, Queensland: University of Queensland Press. 150–157.

Elias, Norbert. 1976 [1939]. *Über den Prozeß der Zivilisation: soziogenetische und psychogenetische Untersuchungen.* 2 vols. Frankfurt: Suhrkamp. (English translation *The civilizing process: sociogenetic and psychogenetic investigations.* [Oxford: Blackwell, 2000.]

1989. *Studien über die Deutschen: Machtkämpfe und Habitusentwicklung im 19. und 20. Jahrhundert*, ed. Michael Schröter. Frankfurt: Suhrkamp.

Ellis, Alexander J. 1869–1889. *On early English pronunciation: with especial reference to Shakspere and Chaucer.* London: Trübner.

Elsness, Johan. 1997. *The perfect and the preterite in contemporary and earlier English.* Berlin: Mouton de Gruyter.

forthcoming. "Colonial lead? On the development of the present perfect/preterite opposition in American and British English." In Günter Rohdenburg and Julia Schlüter, eds. *Grammatical differences between British and American English.*

Erdmann, Peter. 1997. *The for . . . to construction in English.* Frankfurt: Lang.

Fabricius, Anne. 2002. "Ongoing change in modern RP: evidence for the disappearing stigma of t-glottalling." *English World-Wide* 23: 115–136.

Fairclough, Norman. 1992. *Discourse and social change*. Cambridge: Polity Press.

1995. *Critical discourse analysis: the critical study of language*. London: Longman.

Fanego, Teresa. 1996a. "The development of gerunds as objects of subject-control verbs in English (1400–1760)." *Diachronica* 13: 29–62.

1996b. "On the historical developments of English retrospective verbs." *Neuphilologische Mitteilungen* 97: 71–79.

Fischer, Olga. 1988. "The rise of the *for NP to V* construction: an explanation." In Graham Nixon and John Honey, eds. *An historic tongue: studies in English in memory of Barbara Strang*. London: Routledge. 67–88.

Foster, Brian. 1968. *The changing English language*. London: Macmillan.

Fowler, Joy. 1986. "The social stratification of (r) in New York City department stores, 24 years after Labov." Ms., New York University.

Frank, Roberta. 1988. "'Interdisciplinary': the first half century." In Eric G. Stanley and T. F. Hoad, eds. *Words: for Robert Burchfield's sixty-fifth birthday*. Cambridge: Cambridge University Press. 91–101.

Gimson, Albert C. 1967. "Preface." In Daniel Jones. *Everyman's English pronouncing dictionary: containing over 58,000 words in international phonetic transcription*. 13th edition. London: Dent.

Givón, Talmy, and Lynne Yang. 1994. "The rise of the English *get*-passive." In Barbara Fox and Paul J. Hopper, eds. *Voice: form and function*. Amsterdam: Benjamins. 119–149.

Görlach, Manfred. 1999. *English in nineteenth century England: an introduction*. Cambridge: Cambridge University Press.

2001. *A dictionary of European anglicisms: a usage dictionary of anglicisms in sixteen European languages*. Oxford: Oxford University Press.

Greenbaum, Sidney. 1986. "The *Grammar of contemporary English* and *A comprehensive grammar of the English language*." In Gerhard Leitner, ed. *The English reference grammar*. Tübingen: Niemeyer. 6–14.

Greenbaum, Sidney, and Janet Whitcut. 1988. *Longman guide to English usage*. London: Longman.

Habermas, Jürgen. 1988. *Theorie des kommunikativen Handelns*. 2 vols. Frankfurt: Suhrkamp. (English translation *Theory of communicative action*. Boston, MA: Beacon Press, 2000, 2001.)

Halliday, M. A. K. 1994. *An introduction to functional grammar*. 2nd edition. London: Arnold.

Harrington, Jonathan, Sallyanne Palethorpe, and Catherine Watson. 2000. "Monophthongal vowel changes in Received Pronunciation: an acoustic analysis of the Queen's Christmas Broadcasts." *Journal of the International Phonetic Association* 30: 63–78.

Hatcher, Anna. 1943. "Mr. Howard amuses easy." *Modern Language Notes*, 1 (January): 8–17.

Hawkins, John. 1986. *A comparative typology of English and German: unifying the contrasts*. London: Croom Helm.

Heacock, Paul, and Carol-June Cassidy. 1998. "Translating a dictionary from British to American." In Hans Lindquist, Staffan Klintborg, Magnus Levin, and Maria Estling, eds. *The major varieties of English: papers from MAVEN 97, Växjö, 20–22 November 1997*. Växjö: University of Växjö Press. 93–99.

Hempl, George. 1904. "President's address." *PMLA* 19: xxxi–liii.

Himmelfarb, Gertrude. 1995. *The de-moralization of society: from Victorian virtues to modern values.* London: IEA Health and Welfare Unit.

Hobsbawm, Eric. 1994. *Age of extremes: a history of the short twentieth century.* London: Joseph.

2003. *Interesting times: a twentieth-century life.* London: Abacus.

Hoffmann, Sebastian. 2004. "Using the OED quotations database as a corpus – a linguistic appraisal." *ICAME Journal* 28: 17–30.

Hopper, Paul, and Elizabeth Closs Traugott. 2003. *Grammaticalization.* 2nd edition. Cambridge: Cambridge University Press.

Howard, Philip. 1984. *The state of the language: English observed.* London: Hamilton.

Huddleston, Rodney, and Geoffrey K. Pullum. 2002. *The Cambridge grammar of the English language.* Cambridge: Cambridge University Press.

Hughes, Geoffrey. 1988. *Words in time: a social history of the English vocabulary.* Oxford: Blackwell.

1991. *Swearing: a social history of foul language, oaths and profanity in English.* Oxford: Blackwell.

2000. *A history of English words.* Oxford: Blackwell.

Hundt, Marianne. 1998a. *New Zealand English grammar – fact or fiction? A corpus-based study in morphosyntactic variation.* Amsterdam: Benjamins.

1998b. "*It is important that this study (should) be based on the analysis of parallel corpora:* on the use of the mandative subjunctive in four major varieties of English." In Hans Lindquist, Staffan Klintborg, Magnus Levin, and Maria Estling, eds. *The major varieties of English: papers from MAVEN 97, Växjö, 20–22 November 1997.* Växjö: Växjö University Press. 159–173.

2001. "What corpora tell us about the grammaticalisation of voice in *get*-constructions." *Studies in Language* 25: 49–87.

2004. "Animacy, agentivity, and the spread of the progressive in Modern English." *English Language and Linguistics* 8: 47–69.

2006. *English mediopassive constructions: a cognitive, corpus-based study of their origin, spread and current status.* Amsterdam: Rodopi.

Hundt, Marianne, and Christian Mair. 1999. "'Agile' and 'uptight' genres: the corpus-based approach to language change in progress." *International Journal of Corpus Linguistics* 4: 221–242.

Iyeiri, Yoko, Michiko Yaguchi, and Hiroko Okabe. 2004. "*To be different from* or *to be different than* in present-day American English." *English Today* 20(3): 29–33.

Jagger, J. Hubert. 1940. *English in the future.* London: Thomas Nelson and Sons.

James, Henry. 1905. "The question of our speech," *The question of our speech/the lesson of Balzac: two lectures.* Boston and New York: Houghton Mifflin.

Jay, Martin. 1998. *Cultural semantics: keywords of our time.* Amherst, MA: University of Massachusetts Press.

Jenkins, Jennifer. 2003. *World Englishes: a resource book for students.* London: Routledge.

Jespersen, Otto. 1909–1949. *A modern English grammar on historical principles.* 7 vols. Copenhagen: Munksgaard.

Johansson, Stig, and Knut Hofland. 1989. *Frequency analysis of English vocabulary and grammar: based on the LOB corpus.* Oxford: Clarendon.

Jones, Daniel. 1924 [1917]. "Preface." In Daniel Jones. *Everyman's English pronouncing dictionary*. London: Dent.
Josey, Meredith Pugh. 2004. "A sociolinguistic study of variation and change on the Island of Martha's Vineyard." PhD, New York University.
Jucker, Andreas H. 1992. *Social stylistics: syntactic variation in British newspapers*. Berlin/New York: Mouton de Gruyter.
Kennedy, Graeme D. 1998. *An introduction to corpus linguistics*. London: Longman.
Kjellmer, Göran. 1985. "*Help to/help θ* revisited." *English Studies* 66: 156–161.
Krapp, George Philip. 1969 [1919]. *The pronunciation of standard English in America*. New York: AMS Reprints.
Kretzschmar, William A. 2004. "Regional dialects." In Edward A. Finegan and John R. Rickford, eds. *Language in the USA: Themes for the 21st century*. Cambridge: Cambridge University Press. 39–57.
Krug, Manfred. 2000. *Emerging English modals: a corpus-based study of grammaticalization*. Berlin/New York: Mouton de Gruyter.
Kytö, Merja, and Suzanne Romaine. 1997. "Competing forms of adjective comparison in Modern English: What could be more quicker and easier and more effective?" In Terttu Nevalainen and Leena Kahlas-Tarkka, eds. *To explain the present: studies in the changing English language in honour of Matti Rissanen*. Helsinki: Société Néophilologique. 329–352.
Kytö, Merja, and Suzanne Romaine. 2000. "Adjective comparison and standardization processes in American and British English from 1620 to the present." In Laura Wright, ed. *The development of standard English 1300–1800: theories, descriptions, conflicts*. Cambridge: Cambridge University Press. 171–194.
Labov, William. 1966. *The social stratification of English in New York City*. Washington, DC: Center of Applied Linguistics.
    1981. "What can be learned about change in progress from synchronic description?" In David Sankoff and Henrietta Cedergren, eds. *Variation omnibus*. Edmonton, Alberta: Linguistic Research. 177–201.
    1994. *Principles of linguistic change*, vol. I, *Internal factors*. Oxford: Blackwell.
    2001. *Principles of linguistic change*, vol. II, *Social factors*. Oxford: Blackwell.
Labov, William, Sharon Ash, and Charles Boberg. 2006. *The atlas of North American English: phonetics, phonology and sound change*. Berlin: Mouton de Gruyter.
Leech, Geoffrey. 2003. "Modality on the move: the English modal auxiliaries 1961–1992." In Roberta Facchinetti, Manfred Krug, and Frank R. Palmer, eds. *Modality in contemporary English*. Berlin: Mouton de Gruyter. 223–240.
    2004. "Recent grammatical change in English: data, description, theory." In Karin Aijmer and Bengt Altenberg, eds. *Advances in corpus linguistics: papers from the 23rd International Conference on English Language Research on Computerized Corpora (ICAME 23)*. Amsterdam: Rodopi. 61–81.
Leech, Geoffrey, and Jonathan Culpeper. 1997. "The comparison of adjectives in recent British English." In Terttu Nevalainen and Leena Kahlas-Tarkka, eds. *To explain the present: studies in the changing English language in honour of Matti Rissanen*. Helsinki: Société Néophilologique. 353–374.
Leech, Geoffrey, and Nicholas Smith. 2005. "Recent grammatical change in written English: some preliminary findings of a comparison of American and British English." In Antoinette Renouf, ed. *The changing face of corpus linguistics: papers*

from the 24th International Conference on English Language Research on Computerized Corpora (ICAME 24). Amsterdam: Rodopi. 185–204.

Lehmann, Christian. 1991. "Grammaticalisation and related changes in contemporary German." In Elizabeth Closs Traugott and Bernd Heine, eds. *Approaches to grammaticalisation*, vol II. Amsterdam: Benjamins. 493–535.

Levin, Magnus. 2001. *Agreement with collective nouns in English*. Lund: Lund University Press.

Levinson, Stephen C. 1987. *Pragmatics*. Cambridge: Cambridge University Press.

Lewis, Clive Staples. 1960 [1932]. *Studies in words*. Cambridge: Cambridge University Press.

Liedtke, Ernst. 1910. *Die numerale Auffassung der Kollektiva im Laufe der englischen Sprachgeschichte*. Königsberg: Karg & Manneck.

Lightfoot, David. 1979. *Principles of diachronic syntax*. Cambridge: Cambridge University Press.

1999. *The development of language: acquisition, change, and evolution*. Malden, MA: Blackwell.

McMahon, Michael K. C. 1998. "Phonology." In Suzanne Romaine, ed. *The Cambridge history of the English language*, vol. IV, *1776–1997*. Cambridge: Cambridge University Press. 373–535.

Mair, Christian. 1994. "Crosslinguistic semantic motivation for the use of a grammatical construction in English and German: *X is impossible to do/X ist unmöglich zu schaffen.*" *Papers and Studies in Contrastive Linguistics* 29: 5–15.

1995. "Changing patterns of complementation, and concomitant grammaticalisation, of the verb *help* in present-day British English." In Bas Aarts and Charles F. Meyer, eds. *The verb in contemporary English: theory and description*. Cambridge: Cambridge University Press. 258–272.

1997a. "Parallel corpora: a real-time approach to the study of language change in progress." In Magnus Ljung, ed. *Corpus-based studies in English*. Amsterdam: Rodopi. 195–209.

1997b. "The spread of the *going-to*-future in written English: a corpus-based investigation into language change in progress." In Raymond Hickey and Stanislaw Puppel, eds. *Language history and linguistic modelling: a festschrift for Jacek Fisiak on his 60th birthday*. Berlin: Mouton de Gruyter. 1537–1543.

2001. "Early or late origin for *begin + V-ing*? Using the OED on CD-Rom to settle a dispute between Visser and Jespersen." *Anglia: Zeitschrift für Englische Philologie* 119: 606–610.

2002. "Three changing patterns of verb complementation in Late Modern English: a real-time study based on matching text corpora." *English Language and Linguistics* 6: 105–131.

Mair, Christian, and Marianne Hundt. 1995. "Why is the progressive becoming more frequent in English? A corpus-based investigation of language change in progress." *Zeitschrift für Anglistik und Amerikanistik* 43: 111–122.

Mair, Christian, and Geoffrey Leech. 2006. "Current Changes." In Bas Aarts and April McMahon, eds. *The handbook of English linguistics*. Oxford: Blackwell.

Mair, Christian, Marianne Hundt, Nicholas Smith, and Geoffrey Leech. 2002. "Short-term diachronic shifts in part-of-speech frequencies: a comparison of the tagged LOB and F-LOB corpora." *International Journal of Corpus Linguistics* 7: 245–264.

Matthews, Brander. 1921. *Essays on English.* New York: Scribners.

Matthews, Richard. 1993. "'Copping it' or 'bloody asking for it': the *get*-passive and related constructions." In Richard Matthews, *Papers on semantics and grammar.* Frankfurt: Lang. 11–54.

Mencken, H. L. 1963. *The American language.* 4th edition. Revised by Raven I. McDavid. New York: Knopf.

Meyer, Charles F. 2002. *English corpus linguistics: an introduction.* Cambridge: Cambridge University Press.

2003. "The Lexis/Nexis database as historical corpus." Presentation at the 24th International Conference on English Language Research on Computerized Corpora, Guernsey (Channel Islands), 24 April 2003, handout.

Meyerhoff, Miriam, and Nancy Niedzielski. 2003. "The globalization of vernacular variation." *Journal of Sociolinguistics* 7: 524–555.

Michaels, Leonard, and Christopher Ricks, eds. 1980. *The state of the language.* Berkeley: University of California Press.

Milroy, James, and Lesley Milroy. 1991. *Authority in language: investigating language prescription and standardisation.* 2nd edition. London: Routledge.

Mish, Frederick C., ed. 1986. *12,000 words: a supplement to Webster's Third New International Dictionary.* Springfield, MA: Merriam-Webster.

Misztal, Barbara A. 2000. *Informality: social theory and contemporary practice.* London: Routledge.

Mondorf, Britta. 2003. "Support for *more*-support." In Günter Rohdenburg and Britta Mondorf, eds. *Determinants of grammatical variation in English.* Berlin: Mouton de Gruyter. 251–304.

Mossé, Fernand. 1947. *Esquisse d'une histoire de la langue anglaise.* Lyon: éditions IAC.

Mugglestone, Lynda. 2003. *"Talking proper": the rise of accent as social symbol.* 2nd edition. Oxford: Clarendon.

Mühleisen, Susanne. 2003. "Towards global diglossia? English in the sciences and the humanities." In Christian Mair, ed. *The politics of English as a world language: new horizons in postcolonial cultural studies.* ASNEL Papers 7. Amsterdam: Rodopi. 107–118.

Myhill, John. 1995. "Change and continuity in the functions of the American English modals." *Linguistics: An Interdisciplinary Journal of the Language Sciences* 33: 157–211.

Nehls, Dietrich. 1988. "On the development of the grammatical category of verbal aspect in English." In Josef Klegraf and Dietrich Nehls, eds. *Essays on the English language and applied linguistics on the occasion of Gerhard Nickel's 60th birthday.* Heidelberg: Groos. 173–198.

Nevalainen, Terttu, and Helena Raumolin-Brunberg. 2003. *Historical sociolinguistics: language change in Tudor and Stuart England.* London: Longman.

Olofsson, Arne. 1990. "A participle caught in the act: on the prepositional use of *following*." *Studia Neophilologica* 62: 23–35, 129–149.

Övergaard, Gerd. 1995. *The mandative subjunctive in American and British English in the twentieth century.* Stockholm: Almqvist and Wiksell International.

Palmer, Frank Robert. 1990. *Modality and the English modals.* 2nd edition. London: Longman.

Plag, Ingo. 1999. *Morphological productivity: structural constraints in English derivation.* Berlin: Mouton de Gruyter.

Plag, Ingo, Christiane Dalton-Puffer, and Harald Baayen. 1999. "Morphological productivity across speech and writing." *English Language and Linguistics* 3: 209–228.

Potter, Simeon 1975. [1969]. *Changing English*. London: Deutsch. 2nd edition.

Price, Jenny. 2003. "The recording of vocabulary from the major varieties of English in the *Oxford English Dictionary*." In Christian Mair, ed. *The politics of English as a world language: new horizons in postcolonial cultural studies*. Amsterdam: Rodopi. 121–136.

Quirk, Randolph, Sidney Greenbaum, Geoffrey Leech, and Jan Svartvik. 1985. *A comprehensive grammar of the English language*. London: Longman.

Raab-Fischer, Roswitha. 1995. "Löst der Genitiv die *of*-Phrase ab? Eine korpusgestützte Studie zum Sprachwandel im heutigen Englisch." *Zeitschrift für Anglistik und Amerikanistik* 43: 123–132.

Rayson, Paul, Geoffrey Leech, and Mary Hodges. 1997. "Social differentiation in the use of English vocabulary: some analyses of the conversational component of the British National Corpus." *International Journal of Corpus Linguistics* 2: 133–152.

Rickford, John R., Thomas A. Wasow, Norma Mendoza-Denton, and Juli Espinoza. 1995. "Syntactic variation and change in progress: loss of the verbal coda in topic restricting *as far as* constructions." *Language* 71: 102–131.

Ricks, Christopher, ed. 1991. *The state of the language: 1990s edition*. London: Faber and Faber.

Ripman, Walter. 1924. "Preface." In Daniel Jones. *Everyman's English pronouncing dictionary*. London: Dent.

Roach, Peter, and James Hartman. 1997. "Preface." In Daniel Jones. *English pronouncing dictionary*. 15th ed. Cambridge: Cambridge University Press.

Romaine, Suzanne, ed. 1998. *The Cambridge history of the English language*, vol. IV, 1776–1997. Cambridge: Cambridge University Press.

Romaine, Suzanne, and Deborah Lange. 1991. "The use of *like* as a marker of reported speech and thought: a case of grammaticalization in progress." *American Speech* 66: 227–279.

Rosenbach, Anette. 2002. *Genitive variation in English: conceptual factors in synchronic and diachronic studies*. Berlin: Mouton de Gruyter.

Sapir, Edward. 1921. *Language: an introduction to the study of speech*. New York: Harcourt, Brace and Co.

Scheible, Silke. 2005. "*Upgrading, downsizing* & Co: revitalising a moribund word formation pattern in twentieth century English." *Arbeiten aus Anglistik und Amerikanistik* 30: 177–200.

Serpollet, Noëlle. 2001. "The mandative subjunctive in British English seems to be alive and kicking . . . Is this due to the influence of American English?" In Paul Rayson, Andrew Wilson, Tony McEnery, Andrew Hardie, and Shereen Khoja, eds. *Proceedings of the Corpus Linguistics 2001 Conference*. Lancaster University: UCREL Technical Papers 13: 531–542.

Siemund, Rainer. 1995. "'For who the bell tolls': Or, why corpus linguistics should carry the bell in the study of language change in present-day English." *Arbeiten aus Anglistik und Amerikanistik* 20: 351–377.

Smith, Nicholas. 2002. "Ever moving on? The progressive in recent British English." In Pam Peters, Peter Collins, and Adam Smith, eds. *New frontiers of corpus research:*

papers from the twenty-first International Conference on English Language Research on Computerized Corpora, Sydney 2002. Amsterdam: Rodopi. 317–330.

2003. "Changes in the modals and semi-modals of strong obligation and epistemic necessity in recent British English." In Roberta Facchinetti, Manfred Krug, and Frank R. Palmer, eds. *Modality in contemporary English.* Berlin: Mouton de Gruyter. 241–266.

Spears, Richard A., ed. 1993. *NTC's dictionary of acronyms and abbreviations: the most useful and up-to-date guide to American English.* Lincolnwood, IL: National Textbook Company.

Stark, Andrew. 1999. "Now feel the pain." Review of Andrew Burstein, *Sentimental democracy. Times Literary Supplement,* 20 August: 6.

Strang, Barbara. 1970. *A history of English.* London: Routledge.

1982. "Some aspects of the history of the being construction." In John Anderson, ed. *Language form and linguistic variation: papers dedicated to Angus McIntosh.* Amsterdam: Benjamins. 427–474.

Szmrecsanyi, Benedikt. 2003. "*Be going to* vs. *will/shall*: does syntax matter?" *Journal of English Linguistics* 31: 295–323.

Taeymans, Martine. 2004. "An investigation into the marginal modals *dare* and *need* in British present-day English." In Olga Fischer, Muriel Norde, and Harry Perridon, eds. *Up and down the cline – the nature of grammaticalization.* Amsterdam: Benjamins. 97–114.

Trudgill, Peter. 1974. *The social differentiation of English in Norwich.* Cambridge: Cambridge University Press.

1988. "Norwich revisited: recent linguistic changes in an English urban dialect." *English World-Wide* 9: 33–49.

1990. *The dialects of England.* Oxford: Blackwell.

1999. *Dialects.* London: Routledge.

Trudgill, Peter, and Jean Hannah. 2002. *International English: a guide to varieties of standard English.* 4th edition. London: Arnold.

Tsunoda, Minoru. 1983. "Les Langues internationales dans les publications scientifiques et techniques." *Sophia Linguistica* 13: 144–155.

Tulloch, Sara. 1991. *The Oxford dictionary of new words.* Oxford: Oxford University Press.

Upton, Clive, William A. Kretzschmar, and Rafal Konopka. 2001. *The Oxford dictionary of pronunciation for current English.* Oxford: Oxford University Press.

Visser, Frederikus Th. 1970–1978. *An historical syntax of the English language.* 3 vols. Leiden: Brill.

Vosberg, Uwe. 2004. "Cognitive complexity and the establishment of *-ing* constructions with retrospective verbs in Modern English." In Marina Dossena and Charles Jones, eds. *Insights into Late Modern English.* Frankfurt: Lang. 197–220.

Wald, Benji, and Lawrence Besserman. 2002. "The emergence of the verb–verb compound in twentieth century English and twentieth century linguistics." In Donka Minkova and Robert Stockwell, eds. *Studies in the history of the English language: a millennial perspective.* Berlin: Mouton de Gruyter. 417–447.

Webster's Dictionary of English Usage. Springfield, MA: Merriam-Webster, 1989.

Weiner, E. Judith, and William Labov. 1983. "Constraints on the agentless passive." *Journal of Linguistics* 19: 29–58.

Wells, J. C. 2000. *Longman pronunciation dictionary*. Harlow: Longman.

Wells, John. 1997. "What's happening to Received Pronunciation." *English Phonetics* (English Phonetic Society of Japan) 1: 13–23.

Westin, Ingrid. 2002. *Language change in English newspaper editorials*. Amsterdam: Rodopi.

Westin, Ingrid, and Christer Geisler. 2002. "A multi-dimensional study of diachronic variation in British newspaper editiorials." *ICAME Journal* 26: 133–152.

Wignell, Edel. 2002. "*Get to go*: this (prepositional) life." *Ozwords: newsletter of the Australian National Dictionary Centre* (November): 7. Also available at www.anu. edu.au/andc/pubs/ozwords.php.

Williams, Raymond. [1976] 1983. *Keywords: a vocabulary of culture and society*. London: Fontana.

[1961] 1981. *The long revolution*. London: Chatto & Windus.

Wilson, Kenneth G. 1987. *Van Winkle's return: changes in American English, 1966–1986*. Hanover, CT: University Press of New England.

Wood, Frederick T. 1962. *Current English usage*. London: Macmillan.

Zandvoort, Reinhard W. 1957. *Wartime English: materials for a linguistic history of World War II*. Groningen: Wolters.

Index